UNIX Performance Tuning

Sys Admin
Essential Reference Series

R&D Books
Lawrence, KS 66046

R&D Books
1601 West 23rd Street, Suite 200
Lawrence, Kansas 66046
USA

Distributed in the U.S. and Canada by:
Publishers Group West
P.O. Box 8843
Emeryville, CA 94662
ISBN: 0-87930-470-7

Miller Freeman
A United News & Media company

Table of Contents

## Chapter 1

Scheduled Rebooting

Larry Reznick

UNIX runs 24 hours a day every day of the year, and it does a pretty good job. But I've found that, after a long time of continuous running, it can sometimes get confused. Without scheduled rebooting, various UNIX systems lose track of certain processes, some internal tables appear to get out of whack, and zombie processes seem to take over the system. No manufacturer's UNIX seems better than any other in this respect. After seeing these problems occur on SunOS, HP-UX, SCO, and ESIX, I can't blame it on any manufacturer's variances. UNIX just needs rebooting every so often.

Rebooting every UNIX workstation and server about once a month is sufficient. Leave any workstation or server alone for longer and the system may work just fine until you need it the most. Can you afford to have your system act bizarrely in the midst of important operations? I couldn't. I've seen systems run for months without serious troubles, but then strange anomalies would start showing up when running an application on one station that nobody noticed when running the same application on other stations. Occasionally, unusual error messages popped up. People lost time waiting for the reboot that corrected everything. Rebooting regularly when the system is comparatively idle works more smoothly than waiting until the system demands fixing.

You can set a cron job to wake up once a month — more or less often as needed — and see whether the system is running a critical application. If the system is not running any critical programs, advise everybody that the system is going down and reboot. The simplest way to do this appears in the rebootsys script (Listing 1.1). rebootsys checks the process list for any critical programs. If any are currently running, it won't reboot. If all critical programs are absent, it reboots.

Listing 1.1   rebootsys *script.*

```
:
#    rebootsys
#
#    Check for a set of programs that might be running. If
#    they aren't running, reboot the system.
#
#    Copyright, 1993 by Lawrence S Reznick

PROGS="menum|menuo|closeday|nightrun|uucico|ctar"
BOOTPROG="/etc/reboot"
SYSNAME=`/bin/uname`

/bin/ps -e | /usr/bin/egrep "$PROGS" > /dev/null

if [ $? = 0 ]
then
    mail -s "Can't reboot $SYSNAME" siteadmin << alldone
Attempted to reboot $SYSNAME but found one of
"$PROGS"
was still running.

Notice the date & time of this mail message. Will try again.
alldone

    exit 1
fi

$BOOTPROG

exit 0
```

rebootsys **Script**

Listing 1.1 uses the PROGS variable to hold a list of critical program names, separated by vertical bars. egrep(1) uses the bar (|) to separate multiple regular expressions for simultaneous searching. If egrep finds any of those strings, it shows the line containing the match. When egrep succeeds, it sets the $? exit status variable to a nonzero. Finding a 0 exit code means at least one critical program matched. Strictly, egrep returns one nonzero value indicating an operation error even though it may have found a match, but I didn't think this would happen frequently enough to worry about.

PROGS holds a limited number of program names. egrep handles a limited number of parallel searches. If you have more than the half-dozen critical programs demonstrated in Listing 1.1, put the program names in a file named noreboot.progs, with each program listed on a separate line. Then change the PROGS line to:

```
PROGS="-f /usr/local/data/noreboot.progs"
```

Be sure to set read-only permissions for noreboot.progs to prevent editing. This PROGS= line runs without changing the script's egrep command line. egrep applies every string in the match file against the process list that ps(1) pipes into it. However, egrep still takes only a limited number of expressions in this file. If you have many more critical processes to check for, you may need to set up multiple files and insert a loop in the script to deliver each file to egrep's search through the process list.

Using egrep's -f option, $PROGS looks a little strange in the warning mail message. This message tells the users aliased to siteadmin that rebootsys couldn't run. When the critical program names appear more directly in the PROGS variable, those names are included in this mail message. But with the -f option, you'd see the filename containing the matches preceded by -f. Seeing the filename might act as a beneficial reminder of where to find the critical program names, but seeing the program names spelled out might be more helpful. If so, change the line reading

```
"$PROGS"
```

to use

```
'echo \'cat \\\'echo $PROGS | cut -d" " -f2\\\'\''
```

This messy-looking command line embeds an echo command inside the mail message's here script. echo starts cat as another shell substitution to output the contents of the file named in the PROGS variable. However, PROGS has egrep's -f argument, which cat doesn't like. So, I embed yet another shell substitution to isolate the filename in the $PROGS second argument. I send $PROGS to cut(1), which splits the string into fields separated by a space and selects the filename in the second field.

Extra backslashes escape either the back-apostrophe or the backslash itself. I submit the extracted filename to cat, which submits the file's contents to echo, which outputs each critical program's name on one long line.

BOOTPROG holds the command line for rebooting the system. Listing 1.1 shows /etc/reboot, a special program that SCO provides for a quick reboot. You may also find /usr/ucb/reboot(1M) on some systems. These programs are equivalent to using init 6 (see init(1M)). Don't use reboot or init 6 on anything but a test system, because neither gives any warning to users. Both programs just reboot — now! Not very nice, but great for testing. When you're ready to install rebootsys, change BOOTPROG to use shutdown(1M):

```
BOOTPROG="/usr/sbin/shutdown -y -g120 -i6"
```

This allows users working on the system — if anyone is working at the time you set cron to run this script — a two-minute grace period before rebooting. Anyone depending on the system over the network will have to wait for the system to return, but they'll get a warning message, too. Change the -g option's number of seconds if you prefer a different grace period.

Rebooting Using cron

Once you've set your system's critical programs, and you've tested to be sure that rebootsys reboots only when the critical programs aren't running, install the following line in your root crontab.

```
1 5 1 * * /usr/local/bin/rebootsys
```

This simple version runs rebootsys at 5:01 a.m. on the first of every month. It may be too simple. If any critical program is running, rebootsys won't try to reboot the system again until the first of next month. Should your system be quieter at a different time, set that time instead.

Assume you want to reboot no more frequently than once a month, but each time rebootsys looks at the process status those pesky critical programs are running. You may find your system not rebooting for months at a time. Adjusting the crontab time may not help much if you have shifts working round the clock on the system. Specifying several hours in the crontab won't work much better. For instance, if you try

```
1 1,3,5,7,9,11,13,15,17,19,21,23 1 * * /usr/local/bin/rebootsys
```

one of those two-hour periods may reboot. The problem occurs when you get another reboot two hours later. Rather than turn the first of every month into hell day, consider using an empty file to signal a reboot. So long as the file exists, rebootsys hasn't run yet, and you can let rebootsys run again. If the file doesn't exist, don't let rebootsys run. Try these crontab entries:

```
0 0 1 * * touch /tmp/try.reboot
1 * 1 * * test -f /tmp/try.reboot && /usr/local/bin/rebootsys
```

At exactly midnight on the first of every month, cron creates try.reboot in the /tmp directory. One minute later, and every hour thereafter, cron checks the existence of /tmp/try.reboot. If the file still exists, cron runs rebootsys. Some critical applications run so frequently that you may find checking only once an hour insufficient to catch when the application stops running. Change the minute setting to every half-hour, every quarter-hour, or as often as you think appropriate.

Every reboot should clean out files in the /tmp directory, so try.reboot will not exist, thus preventing rebootsys from running again for the rest of that day. If you'd rather the cron job clean up the file after rebootsys runs successfully, add

```
&& rm -f /tmp/try.reboot
```

after rebootsys's invocation on the crontab line. If rebootsys fails, its exit 1 prevents the rm. Only when $BOOTPROG runs does rebootsys quit successfully, triggering the rm.

## Chapter 2

The System Performance Monitor

William Genosa

Cars equipped with gauges often provide some indication of problems before they become serious. Cars equipped with idiot lights often alert the driver after the problem has already become severe. The System Performance Monitor is designed as a set of gauges for a computer. The program provides a visual indication of system activity as well as a means of alerting the system administrator before potential problems cause poor performance and unscheduled downtime.

The program was written on a 3B2 1000-80 running AT&T System V Rel 3.2.2 and used for database applications. As the number of concurrent users steadily increased, the performance of the machine degraded. The purpose of the program is to notify the system administrator when system tunable parameters may need to be adjusted.

Program Overview

The program is designed around the `sar` utility supplied with the operating system. `sar` collects performance statistics at time intervals determined by a `cron` entry for `sys`. The System Performance Monitor can also be started by a `cron` entry and should be adjusted to run at the same frequency as `sar`. The program redirects output to `/dev/tty22` where the information is displayed on a terminal. Warnings are sent to the system console when vital thresholds are exceeded. The thresholds are determined by examination of the current system tunable parameters. AT&T provides the command `/etc/sysdef` to display the current settings.

Listing 2.1

```
##############################################################
###                The System Performance Monitor          ###
###                          by,                            ###
###                      Bill Genosa                        ###
##############################################################
### The number of concurrent users.
###---------------------------------------------------------------

USERS=`who | wc -l`                      ### Total number of users both
                                         ### direct and network sessions

NUSERS=`who | grep tty[a-z] | wc -l`     ### Count pseudo ttys in use

### The runqueue or number of processes in memory waiting execution.
###---------------------------------------------------------------

RUNQ=`sar -q | grep -v Aver | tail -2 | awk '{print $2}'`

### The percentage of time that the runqueue is occupied.
###---------------------------------------------------------------

RUNOCC=`sar -q | grep -v Aver | tail -2 | awk '{print $3}'`

### Process table utilization.
###---------------------------------------------------------------

PROC=`sar -v | grep -v Aver | tail -2 | awk '{print $2}'` ### Gives ratio.
PROCALA=`echo $PROC | awk '-F/' '{print $1}'`             ### Entries used.
```

How It Works

The program starts by finding the number of users currently logged into the system. It counts TCP/IP rlogin and telnet sessions by looking for pseudo ttys, which are designated by a letter following the tty description. This example is configured for 64 pseudo ttys, the maximum allowed on this machine. The program next examines the runqueue to determine the number of processes in memory waiting execution (jobs scheduled for I/O are not part of this figure). If the runqueue is high (above five), expect the runqueue to be occupied for a high percentage of time. If it is not, the system may be I/O bound or swapping. Check the read and write cache hits and the available free memory.

Listing 2.1 (continued)

```
### File table utilization.
###------------------------------------------------------------

FILE=`sar -v | grep -v Aver | tail -2 | awk '{print $6}'`  ### Gives ratio.

FILEALA=`echo $FILE | awk '-F/' '{print $1|}'`             ### Entries used.

### Memory utilization.
###------------------------------------------------------------

MEM=`sar -r | grep -v Aver | tail -2 | awk '{print $2}'`  ### Free pages.

SWAP=`sar -w | grep -v Aver | tail -2 | awk '{print $4}'`  ### Swaps/sec.

SWCH=`sar -w | grep -v Aver | tail -2 | awk'{print $6}'`  ### Processes
                                                          ### switched.

FLT=`sar -p | grep -v Aver | tail -2 | awk '{print $2}'`  ### Address page
                                                          ### faults.

### Disk cache buffer utilization.
###------------------------------------------------------------

RCACHE=`sar -b | grep -v Aver | tail -2 | awk '{print $4}'`    ### Read
                                                              ### hits.

WCACHE=`sar -b | grep -v Aver | tail -2 | awk '{print $7}'`    ### Write
                                                              ### hits.
```

The program goes on to check the process and file table entries. Each running process occupies a slot in the process table. The size of the process table is a tunable parameter. The program compares the number of entries to a threshold, so as to warn the administrator before a process table overflow occurs. Similarly, each open file occupies a slot in the file table. The file table size is also a tunable parameter. The number of file table entries is also compared to a threshold, so that an alarm can be sounded before a file table overflow occurs.

When a system runs low on memory, it swaps processes from memory to disk. The System Performance Monitor checks available memory and triggers an alarm on the basis of a threshold set to the tunable parameter GPGSLO, which determines when the system will start swapping to free memory. The program also checks the number of pages per second being swapped from memory to disk, as well as the number of processes switching per second and the number of address translation page faults (an address translation page fault occurs when the system attempts to access a valid page of memory which has been swapped to disk).

Listing 2.1 (continued)

```
### Terminal and printer activity.
###---------------------------------------------------------------

REC=`sar -y | grep -v Aver | tail -2 | awk '{print $2}'`    ### Raw char's
                                                             ### received.
XMT=`sar -y | grep -v Aver | tail -2 | awk '{print $4}'`    ### Raw char's
                                                             ### transmitted.
### Network interface statistics.
###---------------------------------------------------------------

NETXMT=`nistat -b 0 | grep "Packets transmitted" | awk '{print $5}'`

NETCOL=`nistat -b 0 | grep "Transmit collisions" | awk '{print $3}'`

NETROC=`echo "$NETCOL*100/$NETXMT" | bc`        ### Collisions multiplied by
                                                ### 100 and divided by the
                                                ### number of packets that
                                                ### were xmitted equals the
                                                ### rate of collision.
nistat -c > /dev/null                           ### Clear all ni statistics.
```

Disk access is slow and can hurt performance, but can be reduced when transfers are completed from cache buffers. A tunable parameter called BDFLUSHR sets the frequency at which buffers are flushed to disk. The program checks successful cache hits on both read and write operations. Changing BDFLUSHR is not recommended, but if your cache hits are poor and there's enough available free memory, you may be able to improve performance by increasing the disk buffers.

Terminal and network activity are the last areas the program monitors. A high number of raw characters being input can indicate a bad modem or terminal. A high number of characters being output may be caused by reports printing on high-speed printers. The netstat command is used to check the health of the network. The number of collisions multiplied by 100 is then divided by the number of packets transmitted to provide a collision rate. A rate above 10 percent is high and may degrade the network performance. Possible causes include faulty hardware, misconfigured hardware, and poorly scheduled network-intensive tasks.

Listing 2.1 (continued)

```
#### Clear the screen and output the information to a terminal.
####-------------------------------------------------------------------

tput clear > /dev/tty22                           #### Clear the screen

echo "\n"
echo " T H E    S Y S T E M P E R F O R M A N C E   M O N I T O R"
echo "\n"
echo This report was generated at `date`.
echo There is a total of $USERS logged into the system.
echo There are $NUSERS logged in across the network.
echo There are $RUNQ runnable jobs in memory waiting for the CPU.
echo The runqueue is occupied $RUNOCC percent of the time.
echo The process table utilization is $PROC.
echo The file table utilization is $FILE.
echo The number of free memory pages is $MEM.
echo There are $SWAP pages\/sec of memory being swapped to disk.
echo There are $SWCH processes being switched.
echo There are $FLT address translation faults.
echo The disks are hitting cache $RCACHE percent on read operations.
echo The disks are hitting cache $WCACHE percent on write operations.
echo There are $REC raw characters\/sec being received from terminals.
echo There are $XMT characters\/sec being xmitted to terminals and printers.
echo The network has a $NETROC percent rate of collision.
```

Tuning Parameters: How-to and Cautions

The tunable parameters for this machine are kept in object files under the directory /etc/master.d. After a parameter is changed in one of the object files, the mkboot command must be executed to make the object file bootable. Bootable objects on this machine are stored in the /boot directory. When making the KERNEL bootable, always use the -k option with the mkboot command. Use the command touch /etc/system to force the machine to generate a new /unix. Since there is always a chance that your system may not boot after you've made changes, be sure to copy your current /unix to /0unix before you make the changes.

Always consult your documentation before making changes to bootable parameters. An excellent third-party source on this topic is the book *System Performance Tuning*, published by O'Reilly & Associates. Be aware that many tunable parameters have dependencies on other tunable parameters. For example, if you increase the size of the process table, you must also increase the number of active regions because each process will have three active regions — text, data, and stack. The number of active regions should therefore be three times the size of the process table. Always obey the boundaries of the tunable parameter. For example, to increase the number of disk buffers from 64 to 128 would be more desirable than to change from 64 to 135. Good luck and happy tuning.

Listing 2.1 (continued)

```
###  Alert the System Administrator if thresholds are exceeded.
### ---------------------------------------------------------------------

if [ $PROCALA -ge 800 ]                 ### Process table configured
                                        ### for 850.
then
echo Message from the System Performance Monitor at `date`. > /dev/console
echo The process table utilization is $PROC.            > /dev/console
echo ^G^G^G^G^G                                         > /dev/console
                                        ### ^G = bell.
fi


if [ $FILEALA -ge 1600 ]                ### File table configured
                                        ### for 1600.
then
echo Message from the System Performance Monitor at `date`. > /dev/console
echo The file table utilization is $FILE.               > /dev/console
echo ^G^G^G^G^G                                         > /dev/console
                                        ### ^G = bell.
fi
```

Listing 2.1 (continued)

```
if [ $MEM -le 50 ] ### GPGSLO is configured for 25.
then
echo Message from the System Performance Monitor at `date`. > /dev/console
echo The number of free memory pages is $MEM.              > /dev/console
echo ^G^G^G^G^G                                            > /dev/console
                                                           ### ^G = bell.
fi


if [ $NUSERS -ge 54 ] ### Maximum TCP sessions is 64.
then
echo Message from the System Performance Monitor at `date`. > /dev/console
echo There are $NUSERS logged in across the network.       > /dev/console
echo ^G^G^G^G^G                                            > /dev/console
                                                           ### ^G = bell
fi


### Sar is set to run every 10 minutes on this machine. Set the
### Performance Monitor to sleep 10 minutes between executions.
###-------------------------------------------------------------------------

sleep 600

exec /usr/admin/progs/sysperfmon > /dev/tty22

###-----------------------------E N D -------------------------------------
```

## Chapter 3

A System Load
Monitoring Trilogy

Leor Zolman

One of my big concerns as system administrator has been to seek out new and useful ways to smooth out the CPU system load on a single-CPU Xenix installation.

Overnight and background job spooling utilities allow our users a great degree of direct control over their use of system resources. From time to time, the users must make decisions such as whether to launch a long series of reports in the background or to run them overnight, instead. Some users, however, are not technical enough to comfortably use the standard UNIX/Xenix diagnostic utilities to get a handle on the system load. Without a tool to translate the load figures spewed by programs such as uptime into plain English, those users would lack the information with which to make job scheduling decisions.

To address this problem, and to assist me in gauging the effects of various efficiency-related system policies and tools, I have developed the set of shell scripts described in this chapter. The first script, load, provides a single number and English-language analysis of the current system load for nontechnical users. The second script, a, generates some useful instantaneous statistics for the system administrator's perusal, including the system load, the total number of system jobs, and the average number of jobs per user. The final script, `sysload.sh`, is a long-term system load tracking facility with automatic periodic averaging. All information processed by these scripts is internally generated using the standard UNIX utilities `ps`, `who`, and `uptime`.

load: Characterizing the Current System Load

The system command `uptime` (actually a link to the `w` command, equivalent to `w -t`) displays a line of system statistics containing the elapsed time since system boot, the current number of users, and the system CPU load (as the number of jobs in the run-queue) averaged out over the last 1, 5, and 15 minutes. The `load` script (Listing 3.1) runs `uptime` and pipes the output into an `awk` script to extract the first of the three average load values and display a status report based on that value.

Line 11 extracts the load value based on the number of tokens detected in the `uptime` output text. The precise format of the line produced by `uptime` actually varies with the length of time the system has been up. Therefore, the `awk` script sets the `val` variable to the value of the third-to-last token. Then, lines 13 and 14 strip the trailing comma.

The rest of the script simply displays some text based on the value of `val`. The text tells a user what impact a CPU-intensive background job is likely to have on system performance at the current load level. The user is then in a better position to weigh the potential performance impact of his/her job against the criticality of that job, and decide whether or not to run the job in the background.

A sample output of the `load` script is shown in Figure 3.1. If your computer system's horsepower differs significantly from the system used to produce this sample (a 486-33 ISA machine), then you may want to alter the load values hard-coded into the script's comparison lines to better reflect the load characteristics of your particular machine.

Figure 3.1   Sample output of the load script.

```
    SYSTEM LOAD ANALYSIS

The current system load is 1.56

This is a moderate system load. Long reports will slow
the system down a bit, but go ahead if you must.
Better yet, for low-priority reports, wait until the
system load drops below 1.00.
```

Listing 3.1   The load script.

```
 1: #
 2: # load: Display system load, with suggestions as to how appropriate a
 3: #       time it is to run a CPU-intensive process.
 4: #
 5:
 6: echo
 7: echo " SYSTEM LOAD ANALYSIS"
 8: echo
 9:
10: uptime | awk '{
11:     val = $(NF - 2)
12:
13:     if (substr(val, length(val), length(val)) == ".")
14:         val = substr(val, 1, length(val)-1)
15:
16:         printf "The current system load is %s\n\n", val
17:
18:     if (val < 1) {
19:         print "This is a very light system load."
20:         print "It is a good time to run a report."
21:     }
22:     else if (val < 1.5) {
23:         print "This is a relatively light system load. It is OK to run"
24:         print "a report now."
25:     } else if (val < 2) {
26:         print "This is a moderate system load. Long reports will slow"
27:         print "the system down a bit, but go ahead if you must."
28:         print "Better yet, for low-priority reports, wait until the"
29:         print "system load drops below 1.00."
30:     } else if (val < 3) {
31:         print "This is a medium-to-heavy load. Please do not run long reports"
32:         print "unless you really have to. They WILL slow the system down somewhat."
33:     } else if (val < 4) {
34:         print "This is a heavy load. Please do not run reports unless they are"
35:         print "very urgent."
36:     } else if (val < 5) {
37:         print "This is an EXTREMELY HEAVY system load. Please defer running any"
38:         print "reports at least until the load drops down under 3.00,"
39:         print "preferably under 2.00. Thank you."
40:     }
41:     else if (val < 7) {
42:         print "At this rate, the CPU may soon have a meltdown..."
43:         print "Please, PLEASE do NOT run any reports until the load"
44:         print "settles down below 3.00 !! THANK YOU!"
45:     }
46:     else {
47:         print "This is a ridiculously heavy load; there may be"
48:         print "something wrong with the system. Please contact a Tech"
49:         print "person immediately, and, of course, do not run any reports."
50:     }
51: }'
```

a: *Displaying System and User Processes Statistics*

One very powerful window into the system process table is the ps command. I wrote the a shell script (Listing 3.2) to analyze data provided by ps and display a summary containing some basic statistics otherwise difficult to glean from the raw ps output.

When extracting data about user patterns and trends from the system process table, it is useful to first separate the "signal" from the "noise." Therefore, a breaks the list of all system processes down into three categories: root processes, printer processes, and user processes. Root processes (getty, cron, other daemons, etc.) and printer processes (the master scheduler and intermittent printer request handlers) are not large contributors to the system load, and are therefore segregated from explicit user applications when collecting user process data.

Listing 3.2   The a script.

```
 1: #
 2: # a: Analyze number of system/user processes and system load.
 3: # Written by Leor Zolman, 3/91
 4: #
 5: # usage:
 6: # a
 7: #
 8: # assumes:
 9: # 1) "uptime" command (equivalent to "w -t") is available
10: # 2) printer processes are all run with user-id "lp"
11: #
12:
13: echo
14: uptime
15: echo16: echo Analyzing...
17:
18: rootpros=`expr \`ps -u root | wc -l \` - 1`
19: lppros=`expr \`ps -u lp | wc -l \` - 1`
20:
21: otherpros=`expr $rootpros + $lppros`
22: totpros=`expr \`ps -e | wc -l \` - 3`
23:
24: userpros=`expr $totpros - $otherpros`
25: shpros=`ps -ef | awk '{
26: if (($8 == "-sh" || $8 == "-ksh" || $8 == -csh) && $1 != root)
27: print
28: }' | wc -l`
```

The a script recognizes one further dichotomy: shell interpreters are distinguished from other kinds of user processes. Generally, shell processes tend to be dormant while their subprocesses are executing. This is certainly not always the case, so I've included a feature to summarize the user process statistics both with and without shell interpreter instances taken into consideration.

The output from a sample a run is shown in Figure 3.2. All analysis is performed in lines 18–34 of Listing 3.2. There is some tricky coding involved, so I'll annotate what I've done.

Listing 3.2 (continued)

```
29: nonshpros=`expr $userpros - $shpros`
30: nusers=`expr \`who | awk '{print $1}' | sort | uniq | wc -l\``
31: int=`expr $userpros / $nusers`
32: mod100=`expr \`expr $userpros '*' 100 / $nusers\` % 100`
33: intnonsh=`expr $nonshpros / $nusers`
34: mod100nonsh=`expr \`expr $nonshpros '*' 100 / $nusers\` % 100`
35: echo
36:
37: echo "User processes................. $userpros ($nusers distinct users)"
38: echo "Avg processes per user......... $int.$mod100"
39: echo "Avg non-shell procs per user... $intnonsh.$mod100nonsh"
40: echo "Root processes................. $rootpros"
41: echo "Printer processes............. $lppros"
42: echo "---------------------------------"
43: echo "TOTAL PROCESSES............... $totpros"
44:
```

Figure 3.2   Sample output of the a script.

```
10:35am up 2 days, 18:58, 36 users, load average: 0.40, 0.25, 0.02

Analyzing...

User processes................. 85 (22 distinct users)
Avg processes per user......... 3.86
Avg non-shell procs per user... 2.18
Root processes................. 27
Printer processes............. 1
---------------------------------
TOTAL PROCESSES............... 113
```

In line 18, the innermost in-line statement

```
ps -u root
```

generates a list of all processes owned by root. This list is piped to

```
wc -l
```

to produce a single number representing a count of the number of lines in the ps output. Finally, this number is reduced by 1 (using the expr command) to compensate for the header line produced by ps, and the result is assigned to the rootpros environment variable. The next line repeats the same procedure to count lp processes, and then the sum of the root and lp process counts is assigned to the otherpros variable.

In line 22, a total system process count is computed by running ps -e, counting the output lines, and subtracting 3 (one for the header line and two for the processes spawned by invocation of the a command itself). To get the number of user processes, I subtract the value of otherpros from totpros. The result is assigned to userpros.

Lines 25–28 count up the number of user shell interpreters currently active, and assign that value to shpros. Since root processes have already been counted in a class of their own, any shell interpreters owned by root are excluded from the shpros count.

To calculate the total number of nonshell user processes, the value of shpros is subtracted from userpros and the result is assigned to nonshpos (line 29).

To calculate the processes-per-user averages, it is first necessary to find out how many "distinct" users are currently logged in to the system, since a single user may be logged in on multiple terminals or have several multiscreen sessions active on a single terminal. Line 30 calculates the number of distinct users by listing the user ID of all processes, sorting by the ID, eliminating duplicates, and counting the number of lines in the output. The resulting value is assigned to nusers.

The final calculations in lines 31–34 produce the averages to two decimal places, applying a standard multiplication and modulus kludge useful with integer-only math. The integer and fractional portions of the average values are calculated separately.

sysload.sh: Recording a Periodic System Load History

The load and a scripts provide instantaneous process information, but contain no provisions for maintaining a history. The last script is a facility for recording long-term process load history information into a set of log files. These files may be inspected periodically in order to seek out cyclical trends or patterns of light and heavy system usage.

sysload.sh (Listing 3.3) writes to three log files, given the symbolic names DAYLOG, LOADLOG, and AVGLOG. You fill in the actual pathnames for these files in lines 26–28, and the pathnames for the debugging versions in lines 30–32.

Listing 3.3   The sysload.sh script.

```
 1: #
 2: # sysload.sh: log system load
 3: # (called from cron table)
 4: #
 5: # Written by Leor Zolman, 6/17/91
 6: #
 7: # usage:
 8: # sysload.sh daily (run periodically throughout the day)
 9: # sysload.sh final (run once at the end of the day)
10: #
11: # When $1 is "daily": adds a line to DAYLOG with the current 15-minute
12: # load average.
13: #
14: # When $1 is "final": computes average of all daily entries in DAYLOG. An
15: # entry noting this average is appended to AVGLOG. The contents of DAYLOG
16: # and the average are then appended to LOADLOG, and DAYLOG is deleted.
17: # Then, if this is Friday, the average of the 5 daily averages is
18: # also computed and appended to AVGLOG.
19: #
20: #
21:
22: debug=N
23: ADMINGRP=tech # System administration group id on your system
24:
25: if [ $debug = N ]; then
26: DAYLOG=/u3/General/Ltmp/sysload.day
27: LOADLOG=/u3/General/Ltmp/sysload.log
28: AVGLOG=/u3/General/Ltmp/sysload.avg
29: else 30: DAYLOG=day
31: LOADLOG=log
32: AVGLOG=avg
33: fi
34:
35: [ $# -ne 1 ] && echo "usage: $0 {daily | final}" >&2 && exit 1
36:
37: case $1 in
38: daily)
39: if [ ! -r $DAYLOG ]; then
40: touch $DAYLOG
41: chmod 664 $DAYLOG
42: chgrp $ADMINGRP $DAYLOG
43: fi
```

The DAYLOG file is used when the call to sysload.sh has the form

sysload.sh daily

You decide how often to sample the system load, and create a cron table entry that schedules the command accordingly. For example, the script could run every fifteen minutes between 8 A.M. and 5:45 P.M. Monday through Friday. The cron table entry appears as

0,15,30,45 8-17 * * 1-5/usr/local/sysload.sh daily

where /usr/local is the location of the sysload.sh script. Figure 3.3 shows the entire contents of a system's DAILY log file. Each one-line entry contains the date, the time, and the system load. In Listing 3.3, these daily runs are processed in lines 38–50.

After all sampling for the day is complete, sysload.sh must be run one more time with the argument final instead of daily. Several things happen at that point.

1. The entire contents of DAYLOG are appended onto LOADLOG. LOADLOG thus contains a cumulative record of all daily load samples ever taken.

2. The average load for the day (as per all entries in DAYLOG) is computed, and a line containing this information is appended onto LOADLOG. The same line is also appended onto AVGLOG.

3. On Friday of each week, the five most recent daily averages from AVGLOG are themselves averaged, and a line containing this weekly average is appended onto AVGLOG.

4. The DAYLOG file is deleted, and the next weekday's daily averages are thus written to a new DAYLOG file.

Figure 3.3   Sample contents of a DAILY log file.

```
Tue 07/14/92 08:00:00: 0.00
Tue 07/14/92 08:15:00: 0.00
Tue 07/14/92 08:30:00: 0.00
Tue 07/14/92 08:45:00: 0.00
Tue 07/14/92 09:00:00: 0.00
Tue 07/14/92 09:15:00: 0.02
Tue 07/14/92 09:30:00: 0.00
Tue 07/14/92 09:45:00: 0.00
Tue 07/14/92 10:00:00: 0.50
Tue 07/14/92 10:15:00: 0.18
```

Listing 3.3 (continued)

```
44: echo `date +"%a %D %T"`: `uptime |
45: awk '{
46: txt = $(NR)
47: if (substr(txt, length(txt), length(txt)) == ",")
48: txt = substr(txt, 1, length(txt)-1)
49: print txt
50: }'` >>$DAYLOG
51: break;;
52:
53: final)
54: [ ! -r $DAYLOG ] && echo "$0: Cannot open $DAYLOG" >&2 && exit 1
55: if [ ! -r $LOADLOG ]; then
56: touch $LOADLOG
57: chmod 664 $LOADLOG
58: chgrp $ADMINGRP $LOADLOG
59: fi
60: if [ ! -r $AVGLOG ]; then
61: touch $AVGLOG
62: chmod 664 $AVGLOG
63: chgrp $ADMINGRP $AVGLOG
64: fi
65: tmp=`tmpname sld`
66: echo "`date +\"%a %D\"`: \c" >$tmp
67: awk '{
68: total = total + $4
69: count = count + 1
70: }
71: END { 72: printf("\tAverage for the day: %5.2f\n", total / count)
73: }' <$DAYLOG >>$tmp
74:
75: cat $DAYLOG >>$LOADLOG # update full log
76: cat $tmp >>$LOADLOG
77: echo >>$LOADLOG
78:
79: cat $tmp >>$AVGLOG # update average only log
80: if [ `date +%w` = 5 ]; then # if friday, then
81: tail -5 $AVGLOG |
82: awk '{
83: total = total + $7 }
84: END { printf "\t\tAVERAGE FOR THE WEEK: %5.2f\n",
85: total / 5
86: }' >> $AVGLOG # append weekly average
87: echo >>$AVGLOG # blank line between weeks
88: fi
89:
90: rm $DAYLOG $tmp # remove daily temp file
91: ;;
92:
93: *) echo "usage: $0 {daily | final}" >&2 && exit 1;;
94: esac
```

A sample `cron` table entry for the end-of-day `sysload.sh` invocation is

```
0 18 * * 1-5/usr/local/sysload.sh final
```

The last daily run happens at 5:45 P.M., so the final run is scheduled for 6:00 P.M. Figure 3.4 shows the tail portion of the contents of a representative `AVGLOG` file.

Conclusion

These utilities have provided several benefits to me as a system administrator. With the help of the `load` program, nontechnical users are now confident enough to diagnose aberrant system slowdowns, and often bring such events to my attention before I'm even aware of them. The `a` program, in conjunction with SCO's `vmstat` utility, gives me a fairly good, quick map of system utilization at any one given moment. `sysload.sh` allows me to report long-term system load statistics to management in order to help evaluate hardware and software requirements for the company. I hope the tools prove useful to you in your administration duties, as well.

Figure 3.4   Sample contents of a AVGLOG log file.

```
Mon 06/29/92:   Average for the day:   0.27
Tue 06/30/92:   Average for the day:   0.62
Wed 07/01/92:   Average for the day:   0.10
Thu 07/02/92:   Average for the day:   0.85
Fri 07/03/92:   Average for the day:   0.00
                AVERAGE FOR THE WEEK:  0.37

Mon 07/06/92:   Average for the day:   0.45
Tue 07/07/92:   Average for the day:   0.25
Wed 07/08/92:   Average for the day:   0.11
Thu 07/09/92:   Average for the day:   0.09
Fri 07/10/92:   Average for the day:   0.14
                AVERAGE FOR THE WEEK:  0.21

Mon 07/13/92:   Average for the day:   0.27
```

## Chapter 4

The UNIX Process Management System

Chris Hare

Various applications can monitor the system and aid in the performance-tuning process. In this chapter, I discuss something that few people understand but that UNIX users deal with constantly: the process management system. I then explain why and how I developed a command I call mon, which is a ps lookalike.

I use a System V environment (SCO UNIX) as the basis for my discussion and I assume some level of C knowledge, as I will be discussing C system header files and code.

What Is the Process Management System?

The UNIX process management system is based on a time-sharing kernel. The kernel manages placement of each process in the CPU for execution. This process management facility offers kernel routines that create processes, kernel routines that handle interrupts, and a process scheduling mechanism.

A Process Definition

A process is a program in motion. The executable code stored on the disk is not a process, but a program.

For every executing process, a process context describes the system resources. UNIX shares the system resources by switching the process contexts. Process contexts consist of text, data, and stack segments contained wholly or partially in memory and kernel process data structures.

The kernel process data structures consist of:

- The process u-area, usually two 4Kb pages, which contains information needed only when the process is swapped in and is a candidate for paging. There is one u-area for every process currently running on the system. The contents of the process u-area are listed in /usr/include/sys/user.h.

- A process table entry, which contains information used to determine scheduling. There is one entry in the process table for each process running on the system.

- Entries in the file and inode tables, which control access to the system's files and filesystems.

- A Task State Segment (TSS), which defines the registers identifying where the instructions are located in memory.

The Task State Segment

The TSS is a hardware construct that contains a copy of all of the registers needed to locate the instructions and data used by the process. These are

- the general registers,
- the segment registers,
- the flags register,
- the instruction pointer register,
- the selectors for the process's Local Descriptor Table, and the kernel's Global Descriptor Table,
- the page descriptor register, and
- the read-only stack pointers for the privileged execution levels.

The TSS is highly hardware-dependent. The TSS described here would be found in a segmented architecture machine, such as an Intel 386 or 486 machine. Nonsegmented architecture machines, such as the Motorola 680x0 series, will have a very different TSS structure. The TSS structure is listed in /usr/include/sys/tss.h.

The Binary Executable File Structure

The structure of an executable or binary file is related to the TSS because of the hardware dependence of the CPU architectures. There are several types, the two most important being the Object Module Format (OMF) and the Common Object File Format (COFF). The OMF is generally used by Microsoft and XENIX. The COFF is typical on SCO and AT&T UNIX systems, as well as others. Regardless of the binary type, each has several distinct components:

- a text segment, which contains the actual machine instructions to be executed;

- a data segment, which contains the variables and structures used by the program; and

- other tables and structures, which contain other useful information about the program, including a symbol table and a comment section.

At the beginning of every binary executable is a header describing the contents of the file. This header identifies the type of binary (e.g., 80286 vs 80386), the size and offset of the text and data segments, the size and offset of the symbol table, and the entry point of the program.

Binary programs on SCO UNIX may be of the OMF or the COFF. The layout of a binary under SCO UNIX is shown in Figure 4.1.

Creation of a Process

When a user issues a command to the command interpreter, the fork(S) system call is executed. fork() creates a new entry in the kernel process table. The process table is fixed in size. I will discuss it in more detail later in the chapter.

Through the fork() mechanism, only an existing process may create a new process. The fork() call copies the original process, known as the parent, to a new process, known as the child. fork() then executes the child process, which may use an exec(S) system call to load another program text for the desired process.

fork() gives the parent process the Process ID (PID) number of the child, and gives the child process a value of zero. By this mechanism, programmers can develop processes that behave differently depending on whether the processes perceive themselves as parent or child. The sample PERL code in Figure 4.2 illustrates a small program using fork() and exec. fork() causes the child program to be started, which prints the date. The parent continues execution and sleeps for 10 seconds, prints the message "The parent is dead", and exits.

fork() is accomplished by two kernel routines known as newproc and procdup. Collectively, these two routines allocate a new PID number and create an entry in the process table for the process, then perform the steps listed in the previous paragraph.

Figure 4.1 **The layout of a binary executable file under SCO UNIX.**

HEADER_DATA
File Header
Auxiliary Header Information
.text section header
.data section header
.bss section header

RAW_DATA
.text section data
.data section data

RELOCATION_DATA
.text section relocation data
.data section relocation data

LINE_NUMBER_DATA_(SDB)
.text section line numbers
.data section line numbers

SYMBOL_TABLE
.text, .data, and .bss section symbols

STRING_TABLE
long symbol names

Process Execution

An exec( ) system call initially handles the process execution. exec( ) creates and initializes the context for the new process. If there isn't already a copy of the process running in the system, then a process region is assigned for its text segment (executable code), data segment, and stack.

A process region is a data structure that describes the segment in memory. For example, it inludes the type of segment (text, data, or stack), how many memory pages are in the region, the number of processes sharing the region, and more. On SCO UNIX systems, the region table and associated structures are defined in /usr/include/sys/region.h.

UNIX creates four processes on system startup that exist for the lifetime of the system. These processes are the memory scheduler, the paging daemon, the buffer flushing daemon, and the init process. It is important to note that all four of these processes are running in kernel mode, not user mode.

Figure 4.2   **A)**   ***Sample code using the* fork( ) *and* exec( ) *commands.***

            B)   ***Sample output using the* fork( ) *and* exec( ) *commands.***

A) Sample PERL Program

```
if ($pid = fork() )
    {
    exec '/bin/date';
    exit;
    }
sleep(10);
print "The parent is dead\n";
exit;
```

B) Output

```
Sat Jun 11 11:13:48 EST 1994
The parent is dead
```

Kernel Mode

In kernel mode state, processes are not preemptible. The CPU is seized by the process until the process gives up the CPU voluntarily, or the time-slice has expired. While a process executes in kernel mode, signals are saved until the process exits kernel mode, whereupon the signals are processed (Figure 4.3). [Editor's note: Zombie processes and processes that hang the system are frequently those trapped in kernel mode. They can't be interrupted in kernel mode. Even signal 9 may not get through.] There are situations where the process is in such a state as to not respond to signals, such as zombie processes. These processes (and others) do not respond as they are typically stuck in kernel mode. When using the appropriate options to the ps command (ps -el on SCO and AT&T systems), the process priorities are listed.

The range for process priorities is 0 to 127, with 0 being highest priority, and 127 being the lowest. Priorities 0 to 39 indicate kernel mode, and 40 to 127 indicate user mode. It is important to note that processes whose priorities are 26 or higher can respond to signals, and processes whose priorities are less than 26 will not respond to signals. The more common signals and their values are listed in Table 4.1.

User Mode

User mode is all other states of execution. A user process can only execute instructions from its own text segment, reference its own data segment, and use its own stack.

Some instructions are privileged and require kernel mode to execute. User processes get access to kernel mode by using system calls, predefined kernel routines such as open(), read(), and write(), or loadable device driver routines. Once in kernel mode, the process can execute instructions from the kernel's text segment, access the kernel's data structures, and use a system stack in the kernel's u-area.

Switching from user to kernel mode is not a context switch, but a mode switch. The running process continues to execute after a mode switch. With a context switch, a new TSS is loaded and a new process begins execution.

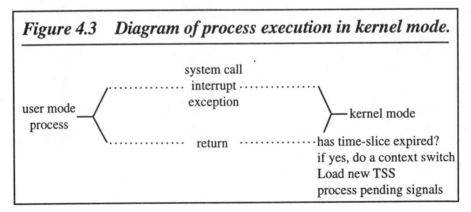

Figure 4.3   Diagram of process execution in kernel mode.

The System Processes

The memory scheduler, sched or swapper (PID 0), is responsible for swapping processes in and out of RAM according to their priority and the available memory on the system. Most UNIX systems today perform demand paging rather than swapping, as older UNIX systems did. (See the sidebar "Paging and Swapping under SCO UNIX.")

Table 4.1 **The more common kernel mode signals and their values.**

Signal Number	Receive Signals	Description
0	No	Swapper
10	No	Waiting for inode
20	No	Waiting for I/O
21	No	Waiting for Buffer
26	Yes	Waiting for pipe
28	Yes	Waiting for tty input
29	Yes	Waiting for tty output
30	Yes	Waiting for exit
40-127	Yes	User level

Paging and Swapping under SCO UNIX

The SCO UNIX operating system has two types of memory management: paging and swapping. Greg Oetting at SCO Support explains the differences.

Paging occurs when the system is low on memory, and is done on a page by page basis. When the amount of free memory reaches the value of the kernel parameter GPGSLO, the system goes through all of the pages in memory to see if any of them are old. Old pages will then either be thrown away, as in the case of program text, or written to the swap area, as in the case of data pages. This process continues until the amount of memory reaches the value of the kernel parameter GPGSHI, at which point processing continues.

Swapping occurs when there is no memory left. For example, a process requests 300Kb of memory when there is only 150Kb remaining. In this case the system goes through memory, swaps out to disk any data regions and throws away text regions. The main difference between paging and swapping is that swapping is on a larger scale.

The paging daemon, typically vhand (PID 2), steals pages of memory that have not been recently referenced for use by the system or other processes. If the page contains data or stack segments, it is saved to the swap device for later retrieval. If the page contains program text, the page is simply used.

The buffer flushing daemon, usually bdflush (PID 3), flushes "dirty" buffers which have been in the cache for too long.

Finally, the init process is the first true user process that is executed. When entering multiuser mode, init creates all of the gettys used to permit login to the system.

Why does /unix not show up in a ps listing? The kernel, /unix on SCO systems, consists of four distinct parts that execute asynchronously, not as a single entity visible by name in a ps listing. These parts are

- the code to initialize the hardware and kernel data structures,

- the three system processes already mentioned,

- the system call support for user processes, and

- the exception and interrupt handling support for the hardware.

The Process Table

The process table is configured to contain a maximum number of processes that the system can handle. This maximum number may be based on the amount of RAM installed on the machine, the number of users who will use it, or other site-dependent criteria. On many machines, the size of this table is configurable, but on some it is not.

The process table is a list of process structures. A process structure on an SCO system is defined in /usr/include/sys/proc.h. The table contains an entry for every process that the system is currently executing, whether or not that process is actually running.

The configurability of the process table relates to the number of entries, which is defined by the kernel variable NPROC. This defines the maximum size of the process table. The table is full when the message "no more process" appears on the system console.

Building a Custom
Process Statistic Program: mon.c

I built mon.c (Listing 4.1), a ps command lookalike, to explore the system structures that control the creation, execution, and scheduling of processes. Sample output from mon.c is shown in Figure 4.4. The mon.c process monitor code in Listing 4.1 is specific to SCO UNIX. The major issue to be addressed when porting this code to a non-SCO system is how to get the u-area. The porting significance of the u-area is illustrated in lines 148–156 of the code, which show that the command-line arguments,

---

Listing 4.1   mon.c source code.

```
1      /*
2      * mon.c
3      * Copyright 1992, Chris Hare
4      */
5
6      #include <sys/types.h>          /* system primitives
7      #include <sys/param.h>          /* system configuration parameters
8      #include <sys/page.h>           /* system memory management
9      #include <sys/immu.h>           /* system intel memory management
10     #include <sys/region.h>         /* system process region configuration
11     #include <sys/proc.h>           /* process table structure */
12     #include <sys/var.h>            /* system configuration */
13     #include <sys/dir.h>            /* File system header */
14     #include <sys/user.h>           /* u-area information */
15     #include <sys/sysi86.h>         /* SCO UNIX SPECIFIC - this header is used
16                                        to provide support for the sysi86
17                                        function which is used to retrive the
18                                        process u-area. */
19     #include <sys/file.h>           /* system file table structure */
20     #include <stdio.h>              /* standard libary header */
21     #include <fcntl.h>              /* file control header */
22     #include <nlist.h>              /* system namelist structure */
23     #include <pwd.h>
24     #include <string.h>             /* string functions */
25     #include <memory.h>             /* memory management functions */
26
27     struct nlist names[] = {
28         "proc", 0,   0,   0,    0,    0,
29         "v",    0,   0,   0,    0,    0,
30         "file", 0,   0,   0,    0,    0,
31         0,      0,   0,   0,    0,    0,
32     };
33
```

and the process name and its arguments are found in the u-area. The issue is that the u-area is in different places on different systems, and there is no generic mechanism to gain access to the u-area.

If you can't get to the u-area, you can list the processes, but can't find out which process is what. The code section assumes that if the sysi86() function returns a negative number, then the process no longer exists other than in the process table. The process is defunct.

Listing 4.1 (continued)

```
34      proc_t p;              /* process structure */
35      struct var v;          /* namelist structure */
36      struct file file_table;    /* file table structure */
37      int NOFILES;           /* open file counter */
38
39      char *Usage = "Usage: mon\n"; /* error message */
40
41      main(argc, argv)
42          int argc;
43          char *argv[];
44      {
45
46          int k_fd; /* kernel filedescriptor */
47
48          /* call nlist(S) to fill out values in names[]; */
49          nlist( "/unix", names );
50
51          /* open /dev/kmem, readonly;*/
52          k_fd = open( "/dev/kmem", O_RDONLY );
53          if ( k_fd < 0 )
54              {
55              perror("/dev/kmem");
56              exit(1);
57              }
58          /* call domon() to read the process table and print the results;*/
59          domon(k_fd);
60
61          close( k_fd );
62          exit(0);
63
64      }
65
```

Listing 4.1 *(continued)*

```
66      /*
67       * domon()
68       *
69       * lseek, and then read the process table from /dev/kmem
70       */
71
72      domon(fd)
73      int fd;
74      {
75
76          int bytes_seek = 0;
77          int p_no = 0;
78          /*int p_used = 0;*/
79          char *Pp_used;
80          int p_used = 0;
81          struct proc p_entry;
82          long proc_table = names[0].n_value;
83          long var_table = names[1].n_value;
84
85          /* seek to the struct v, and read it; */
86          bytes_seek = lseek( fd, var_table, 0 );
87          read( fd, &v, sizeof(v) );
88          NOFILES = v.v_nofiles;
89          /*
90          calculate the current extent of the process table, based
91          on v.ve_proc;
92          */
93          p_used = ( ( (long)v.ve_proc - proc_table ) / sizeof(p_entry) );
94          /* seek to the process table; */
95          bytes_seek = lseek( fd, proc_table, 0 );
96          /*
97          print a header on the screen;
98          */
99          dohdr();
100
101         for( p_no = 0; p_no < p_used; p_no++ )
102             {
103             /* read the process table entry;*/
104             bytes_seek = read( fd, &p_entry, sizeof(p_entry) );
105
106             /*
107               if p_stat is valid,
108               call doproc() to display the proc entry;
109             */
110             if ( p_entry.p_stat > 0 )
111                 doproc( &p_entry );
112             }
113         printf( "--\nCONFIG : %d ALLOC : %d\n", v.v_proc, p_used );
114
115     }
116
```

Listing 4.1 (continued)

```
117     /*
118     * dohdr()
119     *
120     * print column headers
121     */
122
123     dohdr()
124     {
125         printf( "STATUS FLAGS PID PPID USERID PRI NI C OF TTY COMMAND\n");
126     }
127
128     /*
129     * doproc()
130     *
131     * print process table entry
132     */
133
134     doproc(pp)
135     proc_t *pp;
136     {
137         char *p_state[8] = { "", "SSLEEP", "SRUN", "SZOMB",
138                             "SSTOP", "SIDL", "SONPROC", "SXBRK" };
139
140         struct passwd *getpwuid(); /* define the subroutine */
141         struct passwd *pw; /* where to put the data */
142         struct user u_buf;
143         char pflag[6];
144         int x;
145         int ret;
146         char cmd[PSARGSZ];
147
148         /* get the real user name for this process */
149         pw = getpwuid( pp->p_uid );
150         /* get the u-block for the process and stuff it into a buffer */
151         ret = sysi86( RDUBLK, pp->p_pid, &u_buf, sizeof(u_buf) );
152         memset( cmd, 0x00, PSARGSZ );
153         if ( ret < 0 )
154             strcpy( cmd, "<defunct>" );
155         else
156             strcpy( cmd, u_buf.u_psargs );
157         /* find out how many files this process has open */
158         for (x = 0; x< NOFILES; x++ )
159             {
160             if ( u_buf.u_ofile[x] == (char *)0 )
161                 break;
162             }
```

Listing 4.1 (continued)

```
163        /* is this process in ram, or on swap? */
164        memset( pflag, 0x00, sizeof(pflag) );
165        if ( ( pp->p_flag & 0x00000001 ) == 1 )
166            strcpy( pflag, "SYS" );
167        else if ( ( pp->p_flag & 0x00000008 ) == 0x8 )
168            strcpy( pflag, "NWAKE" );
169        else if ( ( pp->p_flag & 0x00000020 ) == 0x20 )
170            strcpy( pflag, "LOCK" );
171        else if ( ( pp->p_flag & 0x00020000 ) == 0x20000 )
172            strcpy( pflag, "ASLP" );
173        else if ( ( pp->p_flag & 0x01000000 ) == 0x01000000 )
174            strcpy( pflag, "EXIT" );
175        else if ( ( pp->p_flag & 0x00000010 ) == 0x10 )
176            strcpy( pflag, "CORE" );
177        else
178            strcpy( pflag, "SWAP" );
179        /* print the process table entry described by pp;*/
180        /* STATE FLAGS PID PPID UID PRI NI C FILES CMD*/
181        printf( "%-7s %-5s %-6d %-6d %-8s %-3d %-2d %-2d %2d %-s\n",
182        p_state[pp->p_stat], pflag, pp->p_pid, pp->p_ppid,
183        pw->pw_name, pp->p_pri, pp->p_nice, pp->p_cpu, x, cmd );
184        return(0);
185    }
```

Figure 4.4   Sample output of the mon.c program.

```
STATUS  FLAGS  PID   PPID  USERID  PRI  NI  C  FILES  COMMAND
SSLEEP  SYS    0     0     root    0    20  0  0      sched
SSLEEP  CORE   1     0     root    39   20  0  5      /etc/init -a
SSLEEP  SYS    2     0     root    0    20  0  0      vhand
SSLEEP  SYS    3     0     root    20   20  0  0      bdflush
SSLEEP  CORE   1840  1     root    28   20  0  5      /etc/getty tty01 sc_m
SSLEEP  CORE   428   1     root    28   20  0  5      /etc/getty tty04 sc_m
SSLEEP  CORE   247   1     root    39   24  0  5      /etc/slattach tty2d
                                                      198.73.137.110 198.73.137.109 9600
SSLEEP  CORE   111   1     root    26   24  0  5      /etc/logger /dev/error
                                                      /usr/adm/messages/usr/adm/hwconfig
SSLEEP  CORE   175   1     root    26   20  0  5      /etc/cron
SSLEEP  CORE   239   1     root    26   20  0  5      cpd
SSLEEP  CORE   183   1     root    26   20  0  5      /usr/lib/lpsched
SSLEEP  CORE   241   1     root    39   20  0  5      slink
SSLEEP  CORE   248   1     root    28   24  0  5      strerr
SSLEEP  CORE   345   1     root    26   20  0  5      biod 8
SSLEEP  CORE   280   1     root    26   20  0  5      /usr/lib/lpd start
SSLEEP  CORE   305   1     root    28   24  0  5      /usr/lib/powerchute/upsd
SSLEEP  CORE   291   1     mmdf    39   20  0  5      /usr/mmdf/bin/deliver -b -clocal, nb -T180
SSLEEP  CORE   285   280   root    26   20  0  5      /usr/lib/lpd start
SSLEEP  CORE   294   1     mmdf    39   20  0  5      /usr/mmdf/bin/deliver -b -csmtp -T180
SSLEEP  CORE   297   1     mmdf    39   20  0  5      /usr/mmdf/bin/deliver -b -cbadusers -T180
```

Figure 4.4 (continued)

```
SSLEEP  CORE   259  1     root    26  20  0   0   inetd
SSLEEP  CORE   257  1     root    26  20  0   5   syslogd
SSLEEP  CORE   262  1     root    28  20  0   5   rwhod
SSLEEP  CORE   300  1     mmdf    39  20  0   5   /usr/mmdf/bin/deliver -b -cbadhosts -T180
SSLEEP  CORE   325  1     root    26  24  0   5   pcnfsd
SSLEEP  CORE   324  1     root    26  20  0   5   portmap
SSLEEP  CORE   312  1     root    28  20  0   5   /etc/popd
SSLEEP  CORE   341  334   root    28  20  0   5   nfsd 8
SSLEEP  CORE   327  1     root    26  20  0   5   rwalld
SSLEEP  CORE   329  1     root    26  20  0   5   rusersd
SSLEEP  CORE   332  1     root    26  20  0   5   mountd
SSLEEP  CORE   334  1     root    20  20  0   5   nfsd 8
SSLEEP  CORE   336  334   root    28  20  0   5   nfsd 8
SSLEEP  CORE   337  334   root    28  20  0   5   nfsd 8
SSLEEP  CORE   338  334   root    28  20  0   5   nfsd 8
SSLEEP  CORE   339  334   root    28  20  0   5   nfsd 8
SSLEEP  CORE   340  1     root    39  20  0   5   nfsclnt 8
SSLEEP  CORE   342  334   root    28  20  0   5   nfsd 8
SSLEEP  CORE   343  334   root    28  20  0   5   nfsd 8
SSLEEP  CORE   419  1     root    26  24  0   5   /u2/uimx/bin/uxserverd
SSLEEP  CORE   346  1     root    26  20  0   5   biod 8
SSLEEP  CORE   347  1     root    26  20  0   5   biod 8
SSLEEP  CORE   348  1     root    26  20  0   5   biod 8
SSLEEP  CORE   349  1     root    26  20  0   5   biod 8
SSLEEP  CORE   350  1     root    26  20  0   5   biod 8
SSLEEP  CORE   351  1     root    26  20  0   5   biod 8
SSLEEP  CORE   352  1     root    26  20  0   5   biod 8
SSLEEP  CORE   354  1     root    26  20  0   5   statd
SSLEEP  CORE   356  1     root    39  20  0   5   lckclnt 8
SSLEEP  CORE   358  1     root    26  20  0   5   lockd
SSLEEP  CORE   360  1     root    26  20  0   5   rexd
SSLEEP  CORE   370  1     root    28  20  0   5   snmpd
SSLEEP  CORE   427  1     root    28  20  0   5   /etc/getty tty03 sc_m
SSLEEP  CORE   2291 259   root    26  20  1   5   telnetd
SSLEEP  CORE   439  1     root    26  20  0   5   /tcb/files/no_luid/sdd
SSLEEP  CORE   1812 1     root    28  20  0   5   /etc/getty tty02 sc_m
SSLEEP  CORE   430  1     root    28  20  0   5   /etc/getty tty05 sc_m
SSLEEP  CORE   431  1     root    28  20  0   5   /etc/getty tty06 sc_m
SSLEEP  CORE   435  1     root    28  20  0   5   /etc/getty tty09 sc_m
SSLEEP  CORE   433  1     root    28  20  0   5   /etc/getty tty07 sc_m
SSLEEP  CORE   434  1     root    28  20  0   5   /etc/getty tty08 sc_m
SSLEEP  CORE   436  1     root    28  20  0   5   /etc/getty tty10 sc_m
SSLEEP  CORE   437  1     root    28  20  0   5   /etc/getty tty11 sc_m
SSLEEP  CORE   438  1     root    28  20  0   5   /etc/getty tty12 sc_m
SSLEEP  CORE   2292 2291  patc    30  20  0   5   -sh
SSLEEP  CORE   2303 2292  patc    30  20  0   5   /usr/local/xr
SSLEEP  CORE   2304 2303  patc    30  20  0   5   /usr/local/xr
SSLEEP  CORE   1786 1     root    26  24  0   5   /usr/bin/X11/scologin
SSLEEP  CORE   2305 2304  patc    30  20  0   5   /usr/local/xr
SSLEEP  CORE   2307 2305  patc    28  20  3   5   rwcrun XR
SSLEEP  CORE   2311 259   root    26  20  0   5   telnetd
SSLEEP  CORE   2312 2311  patc    30  20  0   5   -sh
SSLEEP  CORE   2323 2312  patc    30  20  0   5   /usr/local/xr
SSLEEP  CORE   2324 2323  patc    30  20  0   5   /usr/local/xr
SSLEEP  CORE   2325 2324  patc    30  20  0   5   /usr/local/xr
SSLEEP  CORE   2327 2325  patc    28  20  0   5   rwcrun XR
SSLEEP  CORE   2389 259   root    26  20  0   5   rlogind
SSLEEP  CORE   2390 2389  chare   30  20  0   5   -ksh
SSLEEP  CORE   2419 2390  root    30  20  0   5   su
SRUN    CORE   2422 2419  root    26  20  8   5   mail chare@unilabs.org
SONPROC CORE   2423 2422  root    100 20  80  5   ./mon
--
CONFIG : 1500 ALLOC : 81
```

procmon:
A Process Monitor

Chris Hare

UNIX system administrators must be concerned with ongoing processes — those that are started when the system boots and that are not intended to exit. Sometimes, however, ongoing processes die. The reasons for this include maximum parameters being reached, programming errors, or unavailable system resources.

For some processes, you can combat this situation by using the /etc/inittab file on System V systems. /etc/inittab contains a list of processes that are to be executed when the system enters a run level, and specifies what to do when the process exits.

The inittab file consists of four colon-separated fields.

```
identifier:run levels:action:command
```

A sample /etc/inittab file is shown in Figure 5.1.

inittab is a powerful mechanism, but it is found only on System V variants of UNIX. In addition, /etc/inittab and the init command give no indication that the process has exited and been restarted unless the process continuously dies. init will then print a message on the console, such as "Command is respawning too rapidly."

BSD-based operating systems, such as SunOS, BSD/OS from BSD Inc., FreeBSD, and others, do not use /etc/inittab to control processes spawned by init.

The question then becomes, "How can I provide a system-independent method of monitoring and restarting critical system processes?" The answer is procmon.

Introducing procmon

procmon is a perl script started during system boot that runs for the life of the system. It has been written to be a system daemon, and it behaves as such. The purpose of this program is to monitor the operation of a set of defined processes, and if they are not present in the process list, to restart them. It also logs its actions, noting when the process fails and when it is restarted. A sample log, which is generated through the UNIX syslog facility, is shown in Figure 5.2.

The syslog output shows procmon starting up and recording its actions. The goal is to capture as much logging information as possible about the process being monitored, in this case named.

Automatically Starting procmon

The benefit of a program such as procmon can only be realized when the program is started at system boot time. The initialization method depends upon the UNIX variant used. On System V systems, the lines shown in Figure 5.3 are added to /etc/rc2 or to a file in the /etc/rc2.d directory, which is the preferred method.

Figure 5.1   A sample /etc/inittab *file.*

```
ck:234:bootwait:/etc/asktimerc </dev/console >/dev/console 2>&1
ack:234:wait:/etc/authckrc </dev/console >/dev/console 2>&1
brc::bootwait:/etc/brc 1> /dev/console 2>&1
mt:23:bootwait:/etc/brc </dev/console >/dev/console 2>&1
is:S:initdefault:
r0:056:wait:/etc/rc0 1> /dev/console 2>&1 </dev/console
r1:1:wait:/etc/rc1 1> /dev/console 2>&1 </dev/console
r2:2:wait:/etc/rc2 1> /dev/console 2>&1 </dev/console
r3:3:wait:/etc/rc3 1> /dev/console 2>&1 </dev/console
sd:0:wait:/etc/uadmin 2 0 >/dev/console 2>&1 </dev/console
fw:5:wait:/etc/uadmin 2 2 >/dev/console 2>&1 </dev/console
rb:6:wait:/etc/uadmin 2 1 >/dev/console 2>&1 </dev/console
co:2345:respawn:/etc/getty tty01 sc_m
co1:1:respawn:/bin/sh -c "sleep 20; exec /etc/getty tty01 sc_m"
```

procmon is a daemon process. It handles all of the system signals, and disconnects itself from a controlling terminal. When procmon starts, it prints a line indicating what configuration parameters it is using, and then quietly moves to the background. All logging at this point is generated through the UNIX syslog facility. The output printed when procmon starts is shown in Figure 5.4.

Figure 5.2   A sample procmon ***log generated by*** syslog***.***

```
Feb 20 07:31:21 nic procmon[943]: Process Monitor started
Feb 20 07:31:21 nic procmon[943]: Loaded config file /etc/procmon.cfg
Feb 20 07:31:22 nic procmon[943]: Command File: /etc/procmon.cmd
Feb 20 07:31:22 nic procmon[943]: Loop Delay = 300
Feb 20 07:31:22 nic procmon[943]: Adding named to stored process list
Feb 20 07:31:22 nic procmon[943]: Monitoring : 1 processes
Feb 20 07:31:22 nic procmon[943]: named running as PID 226
Feb 20 07:36:22 nic procmon[943]: named running as PID 226
Feb 20 07:41:23 nic procmon[943]: named running as PID 226
```

Figure 5.3   Additional code used to initialize procmon
at boot on System V systems.

```
echo "Starting System Process Monitor"
/usr/local/bin/procmon &
```

Figure 5.4   A. procmon ***startup output when using the***
procmon. cmd ***file.***
B. procmon ***startup output when using the***
program defaults.

A.) Found /etc/procmon.cfg ... loading ...

B.) no config file... using defaults ...

The *procmon* Files

procmon uses two configuration files: procmon.cfg and procmon.cmd. Of the two, only procmon.cmd is absolutely necessary. If procmon.cfg exists, it will be used to alter the base configuration of the program.

The *procmon* Configuration File

The default configuration file is /etc/procmon.cfg. If procmon does not find this file at startup, it uses the default parameters built into the program. This configuration file provides a mechanism for the system administrator to change the location of the procmon.cmd file and the delay between checking the commands in the list.

   If no /etc/procmon.cfg file is found, then the program looks in the /usr/local/bin directory for procmon.cmd and uses a delay of five minutes between checks. The sample procmon.cfg file shown in Figure 5.5 illustrates using a 15-minute delay (900 seconds), and a configuration directory of /etc. Notice that the delay value is in seconds, not minutes.

   The /etc/procmon.cfg file is not processed by procmon; if it exists, it is loaded into procmon by perl. This means that comments using the # symbol are supported, and the last line of the file must contain the command 1; to signify the end of the the loaded file.

Figure 5.5   A sample *procmon.cfg* file using a
**   15-minute delay.**

```
#
# Configuration file for procmon.
#
#
# 15-minute delay
#
$delay_between = 900;
#
# where is the process list file?
#
$ConfigDir = "/etc";
#
# --- DO NOT REMOVE THIS LINE ---
1;
```

This configuration file is used because the parameters of the program can be modified without affecting the source code. The `delay_between` variable is used to define the amount of delay between processing the list of commands. For example, if the `delay_between` variable is 900, then there will be a pause of 900 seconds between processing.

The `ConfigDir` variable defines the location of the `procmon.cmd` file for `procmon`. The program's default search is in `/usr/local/bin`. The sample in Figure 5.5 places the file in `/etc`.

If you look at the `procmon` source code (see the companion code disk), you will see

```
require "/etc/procmon.cfg";
```

which is how the configuration file is loaded into `procmon`. The perl `require` command causes perl to read the named file, `procmon.cfg`, into the current program. This is a powerful feature of perl, and it allows developers the freedom to concentrate on the problem they are trying to solve, rather than on the mundane task of processing configuration files.

The *procmon* Command File

The `procmon` command file contains the list of processes that are to be monitored. It contains two exclamation mark (!) separated fields: the pattern to search for in the process list and the name of the command to execute if the pattern is not found. A sample file is shown in Figure 5.6.

With this command file, procmon will be watching for named and cron. If named is not in the process list, then the command `/etc/named` is started. The same holds true for the cron command. Again, the purpose of using a configuration file for this information is to allow the system administrator to configure the file on the fly. If the contents of the file change, then the `procmon` daemon must be restarted to read the changes.

Figure 5.6   A sample *procmon.cmd* **file.**

```
named !/etc/named
cron!/etc/cron
```

procmon **Messages**

The `syslog` facility records several messages. The two categories of messages, startup and monitoring, are discussed in the following sections.

Startup Messages

Startup messages are recorded by `syslog` when `procmon` starts up. The appropriate value is substituted for `<value>`. `<timestamp>` is replaced by the current time through `syslog`. `<PID>` is replaced by the process identification number of the `procmon` process and `<system_name>` is replaced by the name of the system, as recorded by `syslog`. The following sample shows the form of a startup message.

```
<timestamp> <system_name> procmon[<PID>]: Process Monitor started
<timestamp> <system_name> procmon[<PID>]: Loaded config file
<value> <timestamp> <system_name> procmon[<PID>]: Command File:
<value> <timestamp> <system_name> procmon[<PID>]: Loop Delay=
<value> <timestamp> <system_name> procmon[<PID>]: Adding
<value> to stored process list <timestamp> <system_name>
procmon[<PID>]: Monitoring : <value> processes
```

Monitoring Messages

Monitoring messages are printed during the monitoring process; they represent the status of the monitored processes. If a `procmon` check finds that a monitored process is running (i.e., the process is on the process list), the following message is printed.

```
<timestamp> <system_name> procmon[<PID>]: <process> running as PID <PID>
```

If a `procmon` check finds that a monitored process is not running (i.e., the process is not on the process list), the following message is printed.

```
<timestamp> <system_name> procmon[<PID>]: <process> is NOT running
```

`procmon` prints the following message to record the time of the last (previous) failure of a process.

```
<timestamp> <system_name> procmon[<PID>]: Last Failure of <process> @ <time>
```

`procmon` prints the following message before an identical command (`<start_command>`) is executed.

```
<timestamp> <system_name> procmon[<PID>]: issuing <start_command> to system
```

procmon prints the following message after an identified command has been issued to the system (returns <return_code>).

```
<timestamp> <system_name> procmon[<PID>]:<start_command> returns <return_code>
```

The syslog may give you clues regarding the status of things after the command has been issued.

Enhancements and Deficiencies

The procmon code (see the companion code disk) was written to run on System V systems. It has been in operation successfully since December 18, 1994. However, some enhancements would be useful. For example, it would be wise to report a critical message in syslog if the command returns anything other than 0, since a non-zero return code generally indicates that the command did not start. Additionally, it would be better to include a BSD option to parse the ps output, and add an option in the configuration file to choose System V or BSD.

Conclusion

The procmon script helps to ensure that operation-critical applications remain in operation. While a similar mechanism is available through /etc/inittab and the init command, not all systems support that method. Moreover, init provides no logging or history mechanism to determine if there is a significant problem to be reviewed.

## Chapter 6

Monitoring Performance with *iostat and* vmstat

William Genosa

As a system administrator, I use a variety of tools, including sar, ps, trace, iostat, and vmstat, to identify problems related to system performance. In learning to use iostat and vmstat, I saw that both could be more useful if they could archive reports in the same fashion as sar. I could then use iostat and vmstat to monitor applications that run for several hours to see where I could improve performance.

sar produces reports based on data collected from the sadc command, which must be set up to run in cron at the desired interval. (I run sadc every 15 minutes on my systems.) The data files are stored in the directory /var/adm/sa. The name of each data file includes the day of the month, such that sa15 would be the data file for the fifteenth of the month. With this scheme in mind, I have written a shell program, sysstat, to collect statistics from iostat and vmstat. This chapter explains how sysstat works, provides examples of the output files, and reviews the iostat and vmstat commands.

Listing 6.1   The *sysstat* program.

```
#!/bin/sh
#-------------------------------------------------------------------------#
#- Author of this Program: William Genosa                                -#
#- Program Name and Release: @(#)sysstat 1.4                             -#
#- File Name Used by SCCS: s.sysstat                                     -#
#- Date and Time of Release: 1/3/94 10:05:52                            -#
#-                                                                       -#
#- Description and Usage:                                                -#
#-        This script should be run from CRON every 15 minutes to create -#
#- reports based on statistics gathered from the VMSTAT and IOSTAT      -#
#- commands.  VMSTAT is used to report about processes, virtual memory  -#
#- usage, paging, interrupts, and cpu utilization.  IOSTAT is used to   -#
#- report about disk I/O activity and throughput.                       -#
#-----------------------BEGIN PROGRAM----------------------------------#
#- We need to define locations where the reports are to be archived. The -#
#- format used is similar to the  format used by SAR.  Each report will -#
#- have the day of the month appended to it, (io15 and vm15 for the 15th -#
#- of the month).  This  scheme  automatically creates reports which are -#
#- overwritten every month.  The TIME variable is used to timestamp the -#
#- output each time the script is run.                                   -#
#----------------------SOME VARIABLE ASSIGNMENTS----------------------#
IO_OUT=/var/adm/stat/io`date +%d`              #- IOSTATs out file. -#
VM_OUT=/var/adm/stat/vm`date +%d`              #- VMSTATs out file. -#
TIME=`date +%H:%M`                              #- Format of DATE is -#
                                                #- 22:30 = 10:30 pm. -#
#-----------------------SET UP THE OUPUT FILES-----------------------#
#- If the two  output  files do not exist, then they need to be created -#
#- with the header information in the file. If the time is midnight, the -#
#- output files need to be  truncated to remove the information recorded -#
#- from a previous month, and to have the header information re-created. -#
#-------------------------------------------------------------------------#
if [ ! -f "${IO_OUT}" -o "${TIME}" = "00:00" ]     #- Set up the output -#
then                                               #- file for  IOSTAT. -#
echo "Time Disks:        % tm_act   Kbps        tps    msps\
    Kb_read Kb_wrtn" > ${IO_OUT}
fi


if [ ! -f "${VM_OUT}" -o "${TIME}" = "00:00" ]     #- Set up the output -#
then                                               #- file for  VMSTAT. -#
echo "
Time  Procs  Memory                Page            Faults       Cpu
----  -----  -----------  -----------------------  -----------  -----------
         r  b  avm  fre  re pi po fr  sr cy  in   sy  cs us sy id wa\
\n" > ${VM_OUT}
fi
```

`sysstat`

`sysstat` (Listing 6.1) has a `cron` entry to run the script every 15 minutes. `sysstat` begins by defining where the output files will be stored in the filesystem. (Avoid hard-coding file names in your code; instead, assign filenames to variables so that your code can be easily modified.) I chose to place the output files in the directory

---

Listing 6.1 *(continued)*

```
#---------------------COLLECT IOSTAT STATISTICS----------------------#
#- This program is being run on an RS-6000.  The  LSPV command generates -#
#- a line of output for each  physical disk drive on the system with the -#
#- first field containing the name of the physical disk.  The  FOR  loop -#
#- runs iostat on each physical disk four times,  every two seconds. The -#
#- first line of output from  IOSTAT  provides cumulative averages since -#
#- the last reboot.  This line is filtered out by TAIL and the remaining -#
#- three lines are piped into AWK which splits each field into an array. -#
#- The values stored in each array are summed and assigned to variables. -#
#- Then each variable is  divided by  three to get an  average  which is -#
#- output by AWK and assigned to the variable IOSTRING which is appended -#
#- to the output file.   Note that the  timestamp is shown only once for -#
#- each stanza of output.                                                -#
#------------------------------------------------------------------------#

for DISK in `lspv | awk '{print $1}'`            #- Begin  FOR  loop. -#
do
    IOSTRING=`iostat ${DISK} 2 4 | grep hdisk | tail -3 | awk '
     {                                           #- Begin AWK script. -#
        for (i = 1; i <= 3; ++i)                 #- 4 samples  taken. -#
        {                                        #- Begin AWK FOR. -#
        disk = $1                                #- For each disk get -#
        split($2,act," ");act[i]                 #- % disk is active, -#
        split($3,kbp," ");kbp[i]                 #- Number kbyte/sec, -#
        split($4,tps," ");tps[i]                 #- Number xfers/sec, -#
        split($5,kbr," ");kbr[i]                 #- Kbytes/sec  read, -#
        split($6,kbw," ");kbw[i]                 #- Kbytes/sec wrote, -#
        acttot += act[i]                         #- Total % activity, -#
        kbptot += kbp[i]                         #- Total kbytes/sec, -#
        tpstot += tps[i]                         #- Total  xfers/sec, -#
        kbrtot += kbr[i]                         #- Total  kb/s read, -#
        kbwtot += kbw[i]                         #- Total kb/s wrote, -#
        actavg  = acttot / 3                     #- Average activity, -#
        kbpavg  = kbptot / 3                     #- Ave   kbytes/sec, -#
        tpsavg  = tpstot / 3                     #- Ave    xfers/sec, -#
        kbravg  = kbrtot / 3                     #- Ave  kb/sec read, -#
        kbwavg  = kbwtot / 3                     #- Ave kb/sec wrote. -#
        }                                        #- End AWK FOR loop. -#
     }                                           #- End  AWK  script. -#
    END { printf ( "%s %13.1f %9.1f %9.1f %17d %9d\n", \
    disk, actavg, kbpavg, tpsavg, kbravg, kbwavg) }'`
```

Listing 6.1 (continued)

```
    if echo ${IOSTRING} | grep "hdisk0" > /dev/null  #- The first line of -#
    then                                             #- output  each time -#
        echo "\n${TIME} ${IOSTRING}" >> ${IO_OUT}    #- the script is run  -#
    else                                             #- will  contain the -#
        echo      " ${IOSTRING}" >> ${IO_OUT}        #- timestamp.         -#
    fi
done                                                 #- End FOR loop.      -#

#---------------------COLLECT VMSTAT STATISTICS------------------------#
#- As with  IOSTAT,  the first  line of  output  from  VMSTAT  provides -#
#- cumulative averages since the last reboot.  This line is filtered out -#
#- with TAIL and the remaing output is piped into  AWK which splits each -#
#- field into an  array.  The values stored in the  array are summed and -#
#- assigned to variables.  Then each variable is divided by three to get -#
#- an  average  which  is  output  by  AWK  and assigned to the variable -#
#- VMSTRING  which  is  appended  to  the  output  file.  Note  that the -#
#- timestamp is shown for each stanza of output.                        -#
#----------------------------------------------------------------------#
VMSTRING=`vmstat 2 4 | tail -3 | awk '
{                                                #- Begin AWK script. -#
    for (i = 1; i <= 3; ++i)                      #- 4 samples  taken. -#
    {                                            #- Begin   AWK FOR. -#
        split($1,p_r," ");   p_r[i]              #- Get process runq, -#
        split($2,p_b," ");   p_b[i]              #- Blocked  process, -#
        split($3,m_avm," ");m_avm[i]             #- Free pg space 4K, -#
        split($4,m_fre," ");m_fre[i]             #- Free real mem 4K, -#
        split($5,p_re," ");  p_re[i]             #- Pages  reclaimed, -#
        split($6,p_pi," ");  p_pi[i]             #- Pages  paged  in, -#
        split($7,p_po," ");  p_po[i]             #- Pages  paged out, -#
        split($8,p_fr," ");  p_fr[i]             #- Pages     freed, -#
        split($9,p_sr," ");  p_sr[i]             #- Pages   scanned, -#
        split($10,p_cy," "); p_cy[i]             #- Page Table scans, -#
        split($11,f_in," "); f_in[i]             #- Device interupts, -#
        split($12,f_sy," "); f_sy[i]             #- System     calls, -#
        split($13,f_cs," "); f_cs[i]             #- Context switches, -#
        split($14,c_us," "); c_us[i]             #- CPU in user mode, -#
        split($15,c_sy," "); c_sy[i]             #- CPU in  sys mode, -#
        split($16,c_id," "); c_id[i]             #- CPU   idle  time, -#
        split($17,c_wa," "); c_wa[i]             #- CPU  waiting I/O, -#
        p_rtot   +=  p_r[i]                      #- Total   runqueue, -#
        p_btot   +=  p_b[i]                      #- Total    blocked, -#
        m_avmtot += m_avm[i]                     #- Total page space, -#
        m_fretot += m_fre[i]                     #- Total  free  mem, -#
        p_retot  +=  p_re[i]                     #- Total   reclaims, -#
        p_pitot  +=  p_pi[i]                     #- Total  page  ins, -#
        p_potot  +=  p_po[i]                     #- Total  page outs, -#
        p_frtot  +=  p_fr[i]                     #- Total freed page, -#
        p_srtot  +=  p_sr[i]                     #- Total pages scan, -#
        p_cytot  +=  p_cy[i]                     #- Total  PT  scans, -#
```

/var/adm/stat. The TIME variable is used to create a timestamp of each record that is appended to the output files. It is also used to check for midnight, which is the first time cron will run sysstat. If the output files do not exist, sysstat creates them. If the output files do exist, the data in them will be from a prior month. That data must be truncated before sysstat appends the data for the current day.

The program then uses a for loop to collect statistics on every drive on the system. The lspv command (list physical volume) builds the list, and awk extracts the first field, which is the name of the physical volume. The iostat command is run for four iterations, sampling every two seconds. I kept the sampling rate short because there are ten drives on this system. If your machine has fewer disks, you may want to

---

Listing 6.1 (continued)

```
        f_intot  +=  f_in[i]              #- Total dev intrpt. -#
        f_sytot  +=  f_sy[i]              #- Total  sys calls. -#
        f_cstot  +=  f_cs[i]              #- Total context sw. -#
        c_ustot  +=  c_us[i]              #- Total CPU in usr. -#
        c_sytot  +=  c_sy[i]              #- Total CPU in sys. -#
        c_idtot  +=  c_id[i]              #- Total  CPU  idle. -#
        c_watot  +=  c_wa[i]              #- Total waiting IO. -#
        p_ravg   = p_rtot / 3            #- Ave size of runq. -#
        p_bavg   = p_btot / 3            #- Ave proc blocked. -#
        m_avmavg = m_avmtot / 3          #- Ave  page  space. -#
        m_freavg = m_fretot / 3          #- Ave  free memory. -#
        p_reavg  = p_retot / 3           #- Ave reclaimed pg. -#
        p_piavg  = p_pitot / 3           #- Ave    page   ins. -#
        p_poavg  = p_potot / 3           #- Ave   page  outs. -#
        p_fravg  = p_frtot / 3           #- Ave  pages freed. -#
        p_sravg  = p_srtot / 3           #- Ave page scanned. -#
        p_cyavg  = p_cytot / 3           #- Average PT scans. -#
        f_inavg  = f_intot / 3           #- Ave # of dev int. -#
        f_syavg  = f_sytot / 3           #- Ave #  sys calls. -#
        f_csavg  = f_cstot / 3           #- Ave context swts. -#
        c_usavg  = c_ustot / 3           #- Ave CPU usr mode. -#
        c_syavg  = c_sytot / 3           #- Ave CPU sys mode. -#
        c_idavg  = c_idtot / 3           #- Ave   idle  time. -#
        c_waavg  = c_watot / 3           #- Ave  waiting I/O. -#
      }                                  #- End AWK FOR loop. -#
    }                                    #- End   AWK  script. -#
END { printf ( "%3d %2d %5d %5d %3d %3d %3d %3d %4d %3d %3d %4d %3d \
%2d %2d %2d %2d\n", p_ravg, p_bavg, m_avmavg, m_freavg, p_reavg, \
p_piavg, p_poavg, p_fravg, p_sravg, p_cyavg, f_inavg, f_syavg, f_csavg, \
c_usavg, c_syavg, c_idavg, c_waavg) }'`

echo "${TIME} ${VMSTRING}" >> ${VM_OUT}         #- Append time+data. -#
#----------------------------------END PROGRAM----------------------------------#
```

increase the sampling interval to five seconds. The output of iostat is piped into grep to extract only the disk information. There will be four lines of information for each disk, one for each iteration of iostat. The first line is discarded by the tail command (see the following description of iostat). The remaining three lines are piped into awk, which splits each field into an array. Each array will hold three values that must be summed and then divided by three to get an average. awk outputs the average, using the printf statement to preserve the correct number of spaces between fields and to ensure the correct number of digits to the right of the decimal. The TIME variable is output for the first line in each stanza (hdisk0). Note that the same logic applies to the collection of vmstat statistics. Figure 6.1 is a sample output report for iostat. Figure 6.2 is a sample output report for vmstat.

Figure 6.1   A sample output report for iostat.

Time	Disks:	% tm_act	Kbps	tps	msps	Kb_read	Kb_wrtn
00:00	hdisk0	0.5	1.7	0.6		4	0
	hdisk1	0.0	0.0	0.0		0	0
	hdisk2	0.0	0.0	0.0		0	0
	hdisk3	0.0	0.0	0.0		0	0
	hdisk4	0.0	0.0	0.0		0	0
	hdisk5	0.0	0.0	0.0		0	0
	hdisk6	0.0	0.0	0.0		0	0
	hdisk7	0.3	1.3	0.3		0	2
	hdisk8	0.0	0.0	0.0		0	0
	hdisk9	0.0	0.0	0.0		0	0

Figure 6.2   A sample output report for vmstat.

Time	Procs		Memory		Page						Faults			Cpu			
	r	b	avm	fre	re	pi	po	fr	sr	cy	in	sy	cs	us	sy	id	wa
00:00	0	0	37413	85198	0	0	0	0	0	0	138	41	51	1	1	98	0
00:15	1	0	37413	85196	0	0	0	0	0	0	140	38	49	4	1	95	0
00:30	1	0	37413	85190	0	0	0	0	0	0	141	40	56	2	2	96	0

iostat

The syntax of iostat is

iostat [sampling interval[number of iterations]]

Thus the command iostat 3 4 samples and produces output every three seconds for four iterations. The first report always provides cumulative statistics since the last system reboot and should be ignored, as it does not accurately represent the current system activity. The remaining reports provide statistics gathered between the sampling intervals and will provide a more accurate snapshot of how the system is currently managing its resources. The iostat command produces output in a two-part report. The first part reports on CPU activity and the second part reports on disk I/O activity. My program uses only the disk I/O statistics because the vmstat command produces a more comprehensive report of CPU statistics. The following text describes each field output by the disk I/O section of an iostat report.

%tm_act   The percent of time the disk was active or the bandwidth utilization of the drive.

Kbps   Amount of data read and written in Kilobytes per second for the drive.

tps   The transfers (I/O requests) per second made to the disk. A single I/O request can be made up of several logical requests.

msps   The average milliseconds per seek. Most disks do not report this data.

Kb_read   The number of kilobytes read from the drive.

Kb_wrtn   The number of kilobytes written to the drive.

These statistics can be used to identify disk I/O delays due to poor load balancing. You may see that the disk containing the operating system shows higher activity than other disks on the system. This is normal and to be expected, but perhaps applications running on your system can be spread across physical volumes that are separate from the operating system. Strategic placement of executables, data, and temporary work areas can significantly improve system performance. One final note: in order for iostat to function under AIX, the operating system attribute to "continuously maintain disk i/o history" must be set to true. You can check your system with the following command, which will list the effective attribute iostat for logical device sys0.

```
lsattr -l'sys0' -E -a 'iostat'
```

If this attribute is set to false on your system, you can set it to true with the following command, which changes logical device attribute iostat.

```
chdev -l 'sys0' -a'iostat=true'
```

vmstat

The syntax for vmstat is the same as for iostat. The first report from vmstat also contains cumulative statistics from the last system reboot and should be ignored, as with iostat. vmstat reports on 17 statistics grouped under five categories. The categories and statistics are listed in the following text, along with a description.

Processes

The AIX operating system is a multitasking operating system that allows all processes to compete for use of the CPU. The scheduler determines when processes will run. Each process is assigned a priority and a slot in the process table. Processes must be in real memory to run. If a process is scheduled to run but a memory page for part of that process is not in real memory, that process is blocked and placed in the wait queue. Processes ready to run are placed in the run queue. vmstat reports on processes in the run queue and in the wait queue. The following text describes each field output by the processes section of a vmstat report.

r   The number of processes in the run queue. This number should be a single-digit number on a healthy and stable system.

b   The number of processes in the wait queue, waiting for the virtual memory manager to page the part of the process on disk into real memory. This number should also be a single digit on a healthy and stable system.

Memory

Memory is controlled by the virtual memory manager. Virtual memory includes all of real memory as well as all the paging space. Disk paging space allows the virtual memory manager to overbook real memory. Virtual memory addresses must be translated into real memory addresses by the Virtual Memory Manager (VMM). Address translations take time to resolve, so the VMM caches frequently used memory addresses in Translation Lookaside Buffers. A page fault occurs when the VMM attempts to access a memory page that is not in real memory. Real memory that is not used is placed in the free list. The VMM is responsible for maintaining the free list. The following text describes each field output by the memory section of a vmstat report.

avm   The number of active 4Kb disk blocks being used for page space or back store.

fre   The number of available 4Kb real memory frames. This number should be high right after you reboot your system. As applications require memory, the VMM will allocate real memory from the free list to those applications. The VMM will try to maintain the free list above the operating system parameter MINFREE. If the VMM needs to free memory, it will page out real memory frames to disk back store.

Paging

Virtual memory address space is partitioned into segments of 256Mb of contiguous space. Segments are further partitioned into pages. There are different types of segments. A *persistent segment* is used to permanently store pages that are part of files and executables. A *working segment* uses the paging space or back store for transitory pages with no permanent storage space. Process stack and data regions, as well as shared library text regions, will be paged out to working segments. The following text describes each field output by the paging setion of a vmstat report.

re   The number of currently unused frames reclaimed by the system after they were returned to the free list. The number of frames accessed as a result of a read ahead pre-fetch from disk is also reported under this column.

pi   The number of page-ins from disk.

po   The number of page-outs to disk.

fr   The number of frames freed to replenish the free list.

sr   The number of frames examined for page-out. The VMM uses various criteria when selecting the frames that can be returned to the free list. The idea is not to page out frames that may soon be needed again.

cy   Real memory frames are referenced by the VMM through a Page Frame Table (PFT). This statistic indicates the number of cycles the VMM made while scanning the entire PFT in search of candidates to be returned to the free list.

Faults

A fault is defined as an interrupt. Interrupts can either be hardware or software interrupts. A disk interrupt would be an example of a hardware interrupt. A system call is an example of a software interrupt implemented with a software interrupt instruction that branches to the system call handler routine. The following text describes each field output by the faults section of a vmstat report.

in   The number of device or hardware interrupts. This number will never be less than 100 due to the 10-millisecond system clock.

sy   The number of system calls. System calls allow user processes to exchange data with the kernel and use system resources, such as disk I/O.

cs   The number of context switches. Because AIX is a multitasking operating system, all processes appear to run simultaneously. In actuality, CPU time is given to each process in time slices. When a process has used up its time slice, it must relinquish the CPU to another process. The CPU must save the working environment of the current process and load in a new working environment for the next process to be executed. This is known as a *context switch*. AIX, in combination with the RS/6000 architecture, handles context switches very efficiently.

CPU

A process that executes within its own code and does not require the system or kernel resources is operating in user mode. While a process is executing system calls, it is operating in kernel or system mode. The following text describes each field output by the CPU section of a vmstat report.

us   The percent of time the CPU is operating in user mode.

sy   The percent of time the CPU is operating in kernel mode.

id   The percent of time the CPU is idle with no processes available for execution and no pending I/O.

wa   The percent of time the CPU is idle with no processes available for execution but with pending I/O requests.

Conclusion

I want to conclude with the advice that it is always easier to diagnose problems if you have a profile of normal system activity. Understanding how your system performs before trouble occurs can help immeasurably in the determination of performance problems.

Bibliography

IBM. "Performance Monitoring and Tuning Guide." IBM Publication SC23-2365-01.

Loukides, Mike. *System Performance Tuning*. Sebastopol, CA: O'Reilly & Associates, 1991. ISBN 0-937175-60-9.

Heise, Russell. "The vmstat Tool," *IBM AIXtra*: September/October 1993.

## Chapter 7

Configurable Subscription-Based Scripts for System Monitoring

Jeffrey Soto and Ravindra Nemleker

Large networks of distributed systems are continuously producing events or entering states that are of interest to various groups or individuals. The operating system, back-ups, databases, batches, and communication gateways all produce logged messages. Filesystems, processes, file transfers, and print and mail queues all generate copious amounts of information that must be monitored.

Monitoring and reporting intelligently on these events is a significant challenge. Obtaining information that can be used to provide support depends on being able to gather the information, filter it, and distribute it to the interested parties. Integrating these various logs with commercial SNMP-based event monitors is difficult. SNMP-based event monitors offer only a limited class of threshold monitors and net-work-oriented events traps and provide little flexibility in defining notification policy. Furthermore, such monitors often furnish metrics that are of marginal interest to application or systems administrators.

Log reports can easily overwhelm you with information. Out of all the available data, only a small subset is meaningful. Such reporting results in messages being ignored. Separating the important events from the noise is key to managing enterprise-wide distributed systems. However, there is no standard means of managing this data. There is no standard way of logging messages, and there are no daemons that work for all types of error logs.

The bright side is that all these disparate systems do have a common denominator — flat ASCII text. UNIX commands that report in ordinary ASCII text can be used to generate information on most system facilities. By first identifying key parameters and substrings that correspond to specific, high-interest events, and then filtering and distributing those events according to a predefined notification policy, you can significantly improve the quality of the information you receive.

Specific information on various conditions can be obtained by interrogation scripts, polled at various frequencies. Logs of any kind can be scanned using string searches. Once information on a condition or event has been obtained, it must be dispatched according to interest and priority. Polling can be distributed to scale. Events can be pulled from the host by the monitor or pushed by the host's local process monitors, such as a batch monitor.

At Donaldson, Lufkin and Jenrette, we have developed a simple, yet effective, set of scripts to gather and distribute these events.

Our subscription-based system monitoring facility provides fine-grained reporting of system events and conditions. The system uses only native monitoring facilities and scripts and a message paging service. It does not require any form of sophisticated daemon for monitoring or reporting events.

Systems, monitoring services, and contacts are maintained through subscription lists. A separate notification facility manages administrator notification, providing host reports on a by-condition, by-user basis. You can target any host for many kinds of system events, and notify any person or group, by mail or page, at various levels of urgency. Monitoring can be distributed to scale on large networks. In addition, the system can automatically notify on problem resolution — a feature that is not found even in expensive system management tools.

The tool contains about 500 lines of Korn shell code and is free of the intricacies of different UNIX versions over heterogeneous platforms. Systems can be monitored irrespective of their hardware and operating system details. This tool is currently being used at Donaldson, Lufkin and Jenrette in New York to monitor over 100 UNIX and Novell servers.

Monitoring Services Types

Two types of monitoring services are Log-based and State-based.

Log-based   reporting applies to system events that are singular in nature. Notification is once per occurrence. An example would be a SCSI disk error or a system reboot. Information on these events is generally parsed from system logs. These events are of interest primarily to system administrators. The Log Monitor (Listing 7.1) is a stand-alone script that parses the system log searching for predefined error strings.

Listing 7.1   The Log Monitor script — `event_log.ksh`

```ksh
#!/bin/ksh
#
# "@(#)event_log.ksh"
#
# This scripts accesses all the NIS and Sybase servers to find out if there
# are any messages in the /var/adm/messages file. This script should be run
# from the server as user root.
#
# Parameters : None
#
# Calling mechanism :
#     Should be called from cron after every unit of time equal to the
#     reporting time. For example if you want notifications to be sent every
#     15 minutes, then the cron entry should be
#     0,15,30,45 * * * * /usr/local/admin/bin/event_log.ksh
#
# Author : Ravindra Nemlekar and Jeffery Soto
#
#

BASEDIR=/usr/local/admin/scripts
HOST_DIR=$BASEDIR/hosts
PATH=$PATH:/usr/5bin
HOST_LIST=/tmp/hosts.$$
TMPFILE=/tmp/file.$$
MAILFILE=/tmp/mail.$$
NIS_LIST=/usr/local/admin/scripts/NIS_SERVERS
SYBASE_LIST=/usr/local/admin/scripts/SYBASE_SERVERS

server_list=/tmp/list.$$
mask_list=/tmp/mask.$$
```

State-based reporting deals with states or conditions. These services keep track of conditions and report on entry as well as on exit from particular conditions; thus, they are stateful in nature. An example would be an unreachable host or a file system that was over capacity. Knowing about a change in the condition (i.e., that the host is now reachable or that the filesystem is now safely within operating parameters) allows support groups to coordinate their activities. If multiple parties simultaneously receive an urgent page, they may be unable to reach each other to find out if the problem is being addressed. Automatic notification on problem resolution means that on-call administrators don't have to log in to find out whether or not a problem has already been resolved. The scripts presented in Listings 7.2 through 7.10 (the Condition Monitor) manage the state-based reporting.

Listing 7.1 (continued)

```
# Combined unique list of servers with comments stripped.
cat $NIS_LIST $SYBASE_LIST | grep -v '^#' | sort -u > $HOST_LIST

# Create a msg directory for each server if it doesn't already exist.
for host in `cat $HOST_LIST`
do
    if [ ! -d $HOST_DIR/$host ]; then
        mkdir $HOST_DIR/$host
        chmod 777 $HOST_DIR/$host
        touch $HOST_DIR/$host/EVENT_FILE
    else
        touch $HOST_DIR/$host
    fi
done

# Check if the host is alive.
# If yes, then
#     grep for error messages
# else
#     page sa for at the most 3 times.
#
for host in `cat $HOST_LIST`
do
    $BASEDIR/check_in_master_list.ksh $host $BASEDIR/MASTER_LIST
    if [ 0 -ne $? ] ; then
    # Host not in master list. Ignore it.
    continue
    fi
```

Listing 7.1 (continued)

```
STATUS=`/usr/etc/ping $host | awk '{print $3}'`
count_file=$HOST_DIR/$host/countfile
if [ "$STATUS" != "alive" ]; then
    sleep 3
    STATUS=`/usr/etc/ping $host | awk '{print $3}'`
        fi
        if [ "$STATUS" != "alive" ]; then
        # Have we beeped before If we have, increment the counter,
        # beep up to 3 times, then suspend the beep
            integer count=0
            if [ ! -f $count_file ]
            # Is it the first iteration?
            then
                echo "1" > $count_file
            else
                # Just increment the count.
                count=$(cat $count_file)
                count=count+1
                echo "$count" > $count_file
                if (( count > 2 )) ; then
                    if (( count == 3 )) ; then
                        /usr/local/bin/beep sa \
                        "${host}: Host unreachable by event logger - Final"
                    fi
                    continue
                fi
            fi
            /usr/local/bin/beep sa "${host}: Not reachable by event logger"
            continue
        fi

if [ -f $count_file ]; then
        /usr/local/bin/beep sa \
            "${host}: Host OK, reachable from event logger"
        /bin/rm -f $count_file
    fi
    # Escape all the formatting characters from "rsh"
    rsh -l root $host egrep -i "\(error\|bad\|\panic\|fatal\|full\| \
        REPEATED\ LOGIN\ FAILURES\|\copyright\)" /var/adm/messages | \
        fgrep -v sendmail\ > $TMPFILE
    if [ $? -ne 0 ] ; then
        continue ;    # rsh failed for some reason
    fi
```

Listing 7.1 (continued)

```
            cat $HOST_DIR/$host/EVENT_FILE $TMPFILE | sort -u > /tmp/tmpfile.x
            cat /tmp/tmpfile.x $HOST_DIR/$host/EVENT_FILE | sort | \
                uniq -u > $MAILFILE
        mv -f $TMPFILE $HOST_DIR/$host/EVENT_FILE
        /bin/rm -f /tmp/tmpfile.x
        if [ -s $MAILFILE ]; then
            cat $MAILFILE >> $HOST_DIR/$host/log.event
            cut -f4- -d' ' $MAILFILE | sort | \
                uniq -c | Mail -s "$host: Error condition reported" sa dba
            /usr/local/bin/beep sa "${host}:`/usr/ucb/head -1 $MAILFILE `"
            /bin/rm -f $MAILFILE
        fi
done
/bin/rm -f $HOST_LIST $TMPFILE $MAILFILE
```

Figure 7.1   A diagram of the Subscription Monitor System illustrates how the Event/Log Monitor and the Condition Monitor work together from two separate systems.

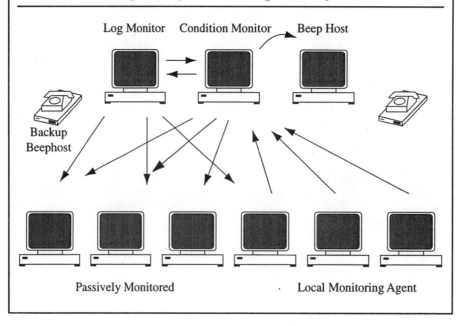

Log Monitor   Condition Monitor   Beep Host

Backup
Beephost

Passively Monitored   Local Monitoring Agent

As we have implemented it, the Log Monitor and the Condition Monitor are on two separate systems (Figure 7.1). This allows the two monitor systems to independently keep an eye on each other. It also provides some protection against human error, as the two systems are configured separately and both are capable of independently reporting on a down host (Figure 7.2). If one monitor server is malfunctioning or is misconfigured, the other will report the down host.

Each host receiving any monitoring service gets a dispatch directory entry on the monitor hosts (Figure 7.3). A separate subscription list is maintained for each service. The following is a list of current probe services.

- Network Connection Monitor
- Filesystem Capacity Monitor
- System Log Monitor
- Database Log Monitor
- Uptime Monitor

**Figure 7.2   *A diagram of the Connection Service
illustrates how either the Log Monitor
system or the Condition Monitor system
is able to detect and report a down host.***

Log Monitor   Condition Monitor   Beep Host

loghost   monhost

sysmon/mhost1/state.CONNECT

Notifier

config.state.CONNECT
beepcontacts=SA.DBA
Beepcount=2
Mailcontacts=Joe.D.Manager

mhost1   mhost2   mhost3

beep SA "sysmon@monhost:mhost1: Unreachable"
beep DBA "sysmon@monhost:mhost1: Unreachable"

mail Joe.D.Manager
Subject : mhost1: *Connection Error Condition *

1) Connection monitor detects the down host and logs the state in the dispatch directory.
2) The notifier picks up the error ticket and performs the notification specified in the configuration file for that problem for that host.

Each monitor service obtains configuration information for the problem type from a generic problem configuration file that contains defaults for all monitored hosts. More specific behavior can be set at the individual host level. Each monitor service may require different parameters. For example, the Disk Monitor will have a default warning threshold of 85 percent. Some systems may require a higher or lower threshold or may only be interested in some filesystems and not others. Monitored hosts are listed in a minimum of two lists: a specific monitor service list, which controls access to a particular monitor service, and a master monitor list, which controls access to all monitor services. The master monitor list allows you to turn off all monitoring services for a host without having to remove the name from multiple specific monitor service lists.

Figure 7.3   A sample directory structure for the monitor hosts.

```
Directory structure for the notifier host

/usr/local/admin/sysmon/
    /config.generic
    /config.Condition.FILE_SYSTEM_FULL/
        /monlist
        /config.generic
        /config.filesystems
    /config.Condition.LOW_FILE_LIMIT/
        /config.generic
    /config.Condition.HIGH_FILE_LIMIT/
        /config.generic
    /config.Condition.NO_CONNECT/
        /config.generic
    /config.<Conditionnames>/
    /hosts/
        /hosta/
            /config.Condition.NO_CONNECT
            /config.Condition.HIGH_FILE_LIMIT
            /config.filesystems
        /hostb/
            /config.Condition.LOW_FILE_LIMIT
            /config.Condition.HIGH_FILE_LIMIT
        /hostc/
            /novell_hostd/
            /config.Condition.NO_CONNECT
        /hoste/
            ...
```

Once an error condition in a given host exists, a named condition or event problem ticket is created in the dispatch directory established for that host. The event is simultaneously logged for inclusion in daily and weekly reports.

The Notifier

Notification of events and conditions is handled by a separate process that cycles through the host dispatch directories looking for event tickets. When one is found, the notifier consults the hierarchical configuration files for contact information and notification options. The name of the file determines its type and whether it is stateful or not. The actual error message is contained in the file. In this way the notifier is generalized, and can provide this service for any type of ticket. The monitoring service that created a stateful ticket must remove it by creating an "OK" ticket. This signals the notifier to send the "all clear" message, as defined by the monitoring service. Unresolved tickets trigger a daily reminder message, so that outstanding problems aren't forgotten or overlooked. Singular event tickets are removed by the notifier, since they do not require follow-up.

Figure 7.3 (continued)

```
If the base directory is /usr/local/admin/sysmon, the configuration file
for a condition can be found under one or more of the following:
    config.generic
    config.<Condition_Name>/config.generic
    <hostname>/config.<Condition_Name>


A host directory under /usr/local/admin/sysmon/hosts/<hostname>
contains the following
    <Condition_Name>
    -Message of the condition
        e.g.Condition.NO_CONNECT
    config.<Condition_Name>
    -Configuration file for condition
        e.g.config.Condition.NO_CONNECT
    count.<Condition_Name>
    -Number of iterations by notification since the condition has occurred
        e.g.count.Condition.NO_CONNECT
    End.<Condition_Name>
    -End of a condition
        e.g.End.Condition.NO_CONNECT
    log.Condition
    -Log for all conditions
```

Conditions can optionally trigger a script listed in the configuration file. This script will be invoked once on entry into the condition and can perform advanced diagnostics or execute a contingency option. For example, an over-capacity filesystem could trigger an e-mailed disk usage report to facilitate the clean-up, and a down host could trigger a router diagnostic to check the network environment.

This structure allows new types of monitoring services to be added while using the same back-end notification mechanism. A host with its own process monitor can create and send a problem ticket to a relay host to be picked up by the notifier. This eliminates the need to reinvent the subscription, configuration, and reporting back-end. Also, if the relay host is used, it isn't necessary to rsh to a trusted host to deposit tickets, so polling is reduced. The monitor host needs only to poll the relay hosts.

Further enhancements will include a network named pipe to transport events directly to the monitor host using a socket. This would facilitate local process monitoring and eliminate the latency associated with the relay host. It would also permit high-priority events to be asynchronously logged to the dispatch directories. The process would resemble the print spooler in structure.

The end result is reliable and consistent system event monitoring and a consolidated log regardless of the subsystem source. Notification policy can be defined very precisely and the system can be easily administered. Nothing needs to be done to the actively monitored host, so there is no licensing or need for a local agent. This is an important cost consideration in large networks. Since only generic scripting and plain vanilla TCP/IP utilities are used, portability across heterogeneous platforms is assured.

Services

The following is a description of the files, scripts, and directories used as part of the monitor system.

Service Subscription Lists and Configuration Directories

Service subscription lists are maintained for each service in a file called monlist. This file contains the names of all the machines that are to be monitored. Each machine is listed on a separate line. Comments should be preceded by a # sign and should occur only at the start of the line. The monitor lists are maintained for each monitor service. The master monitor list provides the method to enable or disable all monitoring services for a particular host. Figure 7.3 shows the configuration directories used by these scripts.

The Log Monitor Script

event_log.ksh (Listing 7.1) polls all monitored systems and performs a string search on each system log. The strings are carefully selected to report on the most serious error events. This is the key to filtering the information and reporting only critical events. The script first performs a ping to the system to ensure that it's connected. The script is capable of distinguishing new events from previously reported ones.

The Connection Monitor Script

check_alive.ksh (Listing 7.2) is used for checking if the server is alive on the network. It uses an RPC version of ping, called newping, which checks if the machine can respond to a connection request. For non-UNIX based machines (like Novell and Tandem), the PING variable should be set to the generic ping command. The value of

Listing 7.2   The Connection Monitor script — *check_alive.ksh.*

```
#!/bin/ksh
#=========================================================
# "@(#)check_alive.ksh"
#
# Check if a particular machine is alive by pinging it. If the machine does
# not respond we try once more. Log an error if the system does not respond.
# If the system responds, log an okay message. The ping command can be set
# to a particular command depending on the OS. "newping" is used for UNIX
# machines and is the default.
#
# Author : Ravindra Nemlekar
#
# Parameters : (Optional)
#     Systems which are to be monitored.
#     If no parameters, then problem specific monitor or the generic monitor list is used.
#
# Calling mechanism :
#     Can be called from cron after every unit of time equal to the reporting time.
#     For example if you want servers to be checked every 15 minutes, then the cron
#     entry should be 0,15,30,45 * * * * /usr/local/bin/check_alive.ksh
#     Can also be called from other scripts to check if the server is alive before
#     executing any command on it.
#
# Return value :
#     0 - Host is alive and rsh'able
#     1 - Cannot connect to host
#     2 - Host connected but not responding
#     3 - Connection refused by host
#     4 - Network problem
#     5 - Host unreachable
#     254 Host alive but not rsh'able (i.e. non-UNIX host).
#     255 Unknown Error
#=========================================================
```

this variable is the command that will be used for checking the connectivity of the system. If the machine does not respond, the script waits for some time (the default is three seconds) before making the next attempt. If the second attempt fails, the script responds with an error. This reduces the number of false alarms.

If an error is detected, a file named `Condition.NO_CONNECT` is created in the `${BASEDIR}/hosts/<hostname>` directory. This file contains the specific error message generated by the `ping` or `newping` command. If the machine responds to a polling, then the script checks for the presence of a previously generated `Condition.NO_CONNECT` file. If one exists, the script then creates an `End.Condition.NO_CONNECT` file. The presence of this file signals the notifier to remove the condition files and, optionally, send an all-clear message.

Listing 7.2 (continued)

```
BINDIR=/usr/local/admin/sysmon
BASEDIR=/usr/local/admin/sysmon
CONDITION_NAME=Condition.NO_CONNECT
HOST_DIR=$BASEDIR/hosts
PATH=/usr/local/admin/bin:$PATH        # required for newping
tmpfile=/tmp/hostlist.$$
# Wait time (in seconds) between 2 tries
SLEEP_TIME=3
# Avoid permission problems
umask 0

# Pick up the condition specific data
if [ -d $BASEDIR/config.$CONDITION_NAME ] ; then
    CONFIGDIR=$BASEDIR/config.$CONDITION_NAME
else
    CONFIGDIR=$BASEDIR
fi
# File contains list of hosts monitored
HOST_LIST=$CONFIGDIR/monlist
# Arguments is present are the hosts which are to be checked
if [ $# -ne 0 ] ; then
    echo "$*" > $tmpfile
    HOST_LIST=$tmpfile
fi

#=========================================================
# Create a msg directory for each server if it doesn't already exist.
for host in `cat $HOST_LIST | grep -v \# `
do
    if [ ! -d $HOST_DIR/$host ]
    then
        mkdir $HOST_DIR/$host
        chmod 777 $HOST_DIR/$host
    else
        touch $HOST_DIR/$host
    fi
done
```

This script accepts parameters and can be used as a stand-alone script or incorporated into other scripts. If no parameters are passed, all the machines present in `monlist` are checked. System names can also be passed as parameters for checking.

Listing 7.2 (continued)

```
# We ping each host. If the host does not respond, we wait for some time
# and then try again. It it fails, we log an error. If the host is responding,
# log an okay if there was previously a problem.

for host in $(cat $HOST_LIST | grep -v \#)
do
    # Process the host only if it is present in the master list.
    $BASEDIR/check_in_master_list.ksh $host $BASEDIR/MASTER_LIST
    if [ 0 -ne $? ] ; then
        continue # Ignore this host
    fi

    unset PING
    # Read this for each host so that each gets the initialized parameters
    # Read the global config file, then local config files would override the
    # parameters which are to be reset for each. Each parameter is initialized
    # to some default value so that even if no config files are present,
    # The script does not misbehave.
    if [ -f $BASEDIR/config.generic ] ; then
        # read the global file first
        . $BASEDIR/config.generic
    fi
    if [ -f $BASEDIR/config.$CONDITION_NAME/ config.generic ] ; then
    # read the condition specific global file
    . $BASEDIR/config.$CONDITION_NAME/config.generic
    fi
    if [ -f $BASEDIR/hosts/$host/config.$CONDITION_NAME ] ; then
        # read the condition specific file for the problem on that host.
        . $BASEDIR/hosts/$host/config.$CONDITION_NAME
    fi
    TIME_NOW=$(date "+%h-%d %H:%M")
    EXIT_VALUE=1
    # Default ping is the rpc based ping.
    PING=${PING:-newping}
    $PING $host
    status=$?
    if [ "$status" -ne 0 ] ; then
        sleep $SLEEP_TIME
        $PING $host
        status=$?
    fi
```

The Disk Monitor Script

dskmon.ksh (Listing 7.3) is the Disk Monitor script. It calls check_filesystem_limit.ksh (Listing 7.4) to check for two limits, a low-water mark and a high-water mark. The low-water mark can be used for warning messages and the high-water mark for more serious reporting. The low-water mark is called the LOW_FILE_LIMIT and is set by default to 80

Listing 7.2 (continued)

```
    case "$status" in
        0)  # Host is up. Log the host as OK if
            # previous error existed
            if [ -f $HOST_DIR/$host/$CONDITION_NAME ]
            then
                echo "$TIME_NOW: $host now reachable" > \
                    $HOST_DIR/$host/End.$CONDITION_NAME
            fi
            ;;

        1)  MSG="CAN'T CONNECT" ;;

        2)  MSG="CONNECTED but NO RESPONSE" ;;

        3)  MSG="CONNECTION REFUSED" ;;

        4)  MSG="NETWORK PROBLEM" ;;

        5)  MSG="HOST UNREACHABLE" ;;

        255) MSG="UNKNOWN ERROR" ;;

    esac # End of case loop

    EXIT_VALUE=$status
    if [ $status -ne 0 ] ; then
        echo "$TIME_NOW: $host: $MSG" > $HOST_DIR/$host/$CONDITION_NAME
    else
        # Host alive but cannot be rsh'ed
        if [ "$PING" != "newping" ] ; then
            EXIT_VALUE=254
        fi
    fi
done    # End of Host Check

# Hosts were passed from the command line
if [ $# -ne 0 ] ; then
    /bin/rm -f $tmpfile
fi

# Return the exit value of the last server.
# This is [more] meaningful when the check is done on one server only.
exit $EXIT_VALUE
```

Listing 7.3   *The Disk Monitor script —* `dskmon.ksh.`

```ksh
#!/bin/ksh
#==============================================================
# "@(#)dskmon.ksh"
#
# Checks filesystems and logs any that exceed the specified percentage used.
# There are 2 limits provided, the low file limit and the high file limit.
# Separate configuration parameters can be set for each of the limits.
#
# Author : Ravindra Nemlekar and Jeffrey Soto
#
#==============================================================
BINDIR=/usr/local/admin/sysmon
BASEDIR=/usr/local/admin/sysmon
CONDITION_NAME=Condition.FILE_SYSTEM_FULL
CONDITIONDIR=$BASEDIR/Condition.FILE_SYSTEM_FULL
# Pick up the Condition specific data
if [ -d $BASEDIR/config.$CONDITION_NAME ] ; then
    CONFIGDIR=$BASEDIR/config.$CONDITION_NAME
else
    CONFIGDIR=$BASEDIR
fi
SERVER_LIST=$CONFIGDIR/monlist
tempfile=/tmp/dskmon.$$
umask 0

touch $tempfile

cd $BASEDIR/hosts
for server in `cat "$SERVER_LIST" | grep -v \#`
do
    # Process machine only if it is present in
    # the master list.
    $BASEDIR/check_in_master_list.ksh $server $BASEDIR/MASTER_LIST
    if [ 0 -ne $? ] ; then
        continue       # Ignore this host
    fi
    # Check if the server is reachable
    $BINDIR/check_alive.ksh $server
    if [ "$?" != 0 ]
    then
        # Server cannot be rsh'ed. Don't proceed !!
        continue
    fi    # Check the filesystems
    if [ 4 = "$(uname -r | cut -c1)" ] ; then
        # SunOS 4.x
        rsh -n $server df -t 4.2 | awk '{ \
            printf("%s:%s:%s:%d\n", $1, $5, $6, NR) }' > $tempfile
    else
        # Solaris
        rsh -n $server df -k | awk '{ \
            printf("%s:%s:%s:%d\n", $1, $5, $6, NR) }' \> $tempfile
    fi
```

Listing 7.3 (continued)

```
CONFIGS=/dev/null
# Read this for each host so that each one gets the initialized parameters
if [ -f $BASEDIR/config.generic ] ; then
    # Read the global file first
    . $BASEDIR/config.generic
fi
if [ -f $BASEDIR/config.Condition.FILE_SYSTEM_FULL/config.generic ] ; then
    # read the condition specific global file
    . $BASEDIR/config.Condition.FILE_SYSTEM_FULL/config.generic
fi
# Global level Configuration for each filesystem
if [ -f $BASEDIR/config.Condition.FILE_SYSTEM_FULL/config.filesystems ] ; then
    CONFIGS="$BASEDIR/config.Condition.FILE_SYSTEM_FULL/config.filesystems $CONFIGS"
fi
# Low water mark for filesystem full
if [ -f $BASEDIR/config.Condition.LOW_FILE_LIMIT/config.generic ] ; then
    . $BASEDIR/config.Condition.LOW_FILE_LIMIT/config.generic
fi
# High water mark for filesystem full
if [ -f $BASEDIR/config.Condition.\HIGH_FILE_LIMIT/config.generic ] ; then
    . $BASEDIR/config.Condition.HIGH_FILE_LIMIT/config.generic fi
    # Read the condition specific host specific files
    if [ -f $server/config.Condition.LOW_FILE_LIMIT ] ; then
        . $server/config.Condition.LOW_FILE_LIMIT
    fi
    if [ -f $server/config.Condition.HIGH_FILE_LIMIT ] ; then
        . $server/config.Condition.HIGH_FILE_LIMIT
    fi
    # Configuration for each filesystem for host
    if [ -f $server/config.filesystems ] ; then
        CONFIGS="$server/config.filesystems $CONFIGS"
    fi
    LOW_FILE_LIMIT=${LOW_FILE_LIMIT:-80}
    HIGH_FILE_LIMIT=${HIGH_FILE_LIMIT:-95}
    # Store these two values since they will be
    # reset for each Filesystem.
    LOW=$LOW_FILE_LIMIT
    HIGH=$HIGH_FILE_LIMIT
    # Process the output of "df". Check the usage of each filesystem
    # and check whether it exceeds the low or high limit.
    for filesystem in $(cat $tempfile | grep -v Filesystem)
    do
        LOW_FILE_LIMIT=$LOW
        HIGH_FILE_LIMIT=$HIGH
        filesys=`echo $filesystem | awk -F: '{print $1}'`
        pct_dsk_used=`echo $filesystem |awk -F: '{print $2}' | awk -F% '{print $1}'`
        mount_point=`echo $filesystem | awk -F: '{ print $3}'`
        LOW_LIMIT=$($BINDIR/check_filesystem_limit.ksh "LOW" $mount_point $CONFIGS)
        if [ "$LOW_LIMIT" ] ; then
            LOW_FILE_LIMIT=$LOW_LIMIT
        fi
        HIGH_LIMIT=$($BINDIR/check_filesystem_limit.ksh "HIGH" $mount_point $CONFIGS)
        if [ "$HIGH_LIMIT" ] ; then
            HIGH_FILE_LIMIT=$HIGH_LIMIT
        fi
```

percent. The high-water mark is called the HIGH_FILE_LIMIT and defaults to 95 percent filesystem full. The error messages are contained in the files, Condition.LOW_FILE_LIMIT and Condition.HIGH_FILE_LIMIT, for the respective cases. Limits can be set on a per-filesystem basis in the file config.filesystems.

config.filesystems can be present at a global level for all hosts or for each individual host. The format of the file is

```
<filesystem> <low_filesystem_limit> <high_filesystem_limit>
```

Listing 7.3 (continued)

```
            low_dsk_stat=`expr $pct_dsk_used -$LOW_FILE_LIMIT`
            high_dsk_stat=`expr $pct_dsk_used - $HIGH_FILE_LIMIT`
            file_id=`echo $filesystem | awk -F: '{ print $4}'`
            if [ "$high_dsk_stat" -gt 0 ] ; then
                echo "$(date "+ %H:%M") $server $filesys $mount_point\
                $pct_dsk_used% full" > $BASEDIR/hosts/$server/Condition.HIGH_FILE_LIMIT
                elif [ "$low_dsk_stat" -gt 0 ] ; then
                echo "$(date "+ %H:%M") $server $filesys $mount_point \
                $pct_dsk_used% full" > $BASEDIR/hosts/$server/Condition.LOW_FILE_LIMIT
                if [ -f $BASEDIR/hosts/$server/Condition.HIGH_FILE_LIMIT ] ; then
                    fgrep "$filesys" $BASEDIR/hosts/\
                        $server/Condition.HIGH_FILE_LIMIT >/dev/null
                    if [ $? -eq 0 ] ; then
                        echo "$server: $mount_point under ${HIGH_FILE_LIMIT}%"\
                            > $BASEDIR/hosts/$server/End.Condition.HIGH_FILE_LIMIT
                    fi
                fi
            else    # Filesystem within limit
                if [ -f $BASEDIR/hosts/$server/Condition.HIGH_FILE_LIMIT ] ; then
                    fgrep "$filesys" $BASEDIR/hosts/\
                        $server/Condition.HIGH_FILE_LIMIT >/dev/null
                    if [ $? -eq 0 ] ; then
                        echo "$server: $mount_point under ${HIGH_FILE_LIMIT}%"\
                            > $BASEDIR/hosts/$server/End.Condition.HIGH_FILE_LIMIT
                    fi
                fi
                if [ -f $BASEDIR/hosts/$server/Condition.LOW_FILE_LIMIT ] ; then
                    fgrep "$filesys" $BASEDIR/hosts/\
                        $server/Condition.LOW_FILE_LIMIT >/dev/null
                    if [ $? -eq 0 ] ; then
                        echo "$server: $mount_point under ${LOW_FILE_LIMIT}%"\
                            > $BASEDIR/hosts/$server/End.Condition.LOW_FILE_LIMIT
                    fi
                fi
            fi
        done    # End of processing of server's filesystems
        /bin/rm -f $tempfile    # Clean up
done    # End of processing this server
```

An example of this file format is

```
/usr 85 95
```

This specifies that the low limit for the /usr filesystem is 85 percent and the high limit is 95 percent.

Listing 7.4   *The script called by the Disk Monitor to check for low and high file limits*
— *check_filesystem_limit.ksh.*

```
#!/bin/ksh
#=========================================================
# "@(#)check_filesystem_limit.ksh"
#
# Usage : check_filesystem_limit.ksh mount_point file1 ...
#
# This script returns the (high or low) limit set for
# that filesystem. Returns nothing if no limit is
# set. The file contains the filesystem name
# followed by the low limit and the high limit.
#
# Author : Ravindra Nemlekar
#=========================================================

if [ $# -lt 3 ] ; then
    echo "Usage: $0 LOW|HIGH mount_point file_from_which_to_be_checked"
    exit 1
fi

# Check for lower limit else it's the high file limit
if [ "LOW" = "$1" ] ; then
    mount_point=$2
    shift 2
    awk ' $1 == FILE_SYS { value = $2 ; exit 0 }
        END             { if (value != 0)
                            print value } ' FILE_SYS=$mount_point $*
else
    mount_point=$2
    shift 2
    awk ' $1 == FILE_SYS { value = $3 ; exit 0 }
        END             { if (value != 0)
                            print value } ' FILE_SYS=$mount_point $*
fi
```

Generic Event Notification Scripts

logevent.ksh (Listing 7.5) is used to log events and conditions onto a single host, called as loggerhost with user id loguser. logevent.ksh requires a filename as its parameter. It copies this file to the system loggerhost with user id loguser as Condition.EVENT_TYPE, where EVENT_TYPE is the filename passed to the script. The filename identifies the event. The contents of the file consist of a description of the event. For example,

```
logevent.ksh
/tmp/SYBASE_SERVER_NOT_RESPONDING
```

Listing 7.5   The script used to log events and conditions — logevent.ksh.

```
#!/bin/ksh
#
# "@(#)logevent.ksh"
#
# This script is used to log a condition. It can be
# a condition or an event. It should be specified
# in the configuration files if its an event. It
# should be run on the host which wants to log
# the condition or event.
#
# Parameters : (only one)
# arg1 : Name of the message file (along with path)
# Contents of this file should be the message
#
# Author : Ravindra Nemlekar
#
#

if [ $# -ne 1 ] ; then
    echo Usage: $0 MESSAGE_FILE_NAME
    exit 1
fi
rsh loggerhost -l loguser mkdir -p hosts/$(hostname) >/dev/null 2>&1
rcp -p $1 loguser@loggerhost:hosts/$(hostname)/Condition.$(basename $1)
```

Listing 7.6 The script used to log error-resolved messages — `logok.ksh`.

```
#!/bin/ksh
#============================================================
# "@(#)logok.ksh"
#
# This script is used to log an end of condition state. It should
# be run from the host which want to log the end of a condition.
#
# Parameters : (only one)
# arg1 : Name of the okay file (along with path)
#     Contents of this file should tune the message
#
# Author : Ravindra Nemlekar
#
#============================================================
if [ $# -ne 1 ] ; then
    echo Usage: $0 OK_FILE_NAME
    exit 1
fi
rsh loggerhost -l loguser mkdir -p hosts/$(hostname) >/dev/null 2>&1
rcp $1 loguser@loggerhost:hosts/$(hostname)/End.Condition.$(basename $1)
```

Listing 7.7 `notification.ksh` — the heart of the monitoring system.

```
#!/bin/ksh
#============================================================
# "@(#)notification.ksh"
#
# This script notifies the user(s) about the conditions and events. Currently
# only two notification styles are supported : paging and mail. Mail and page
# contacts can be configured separately in the configuration files. If the
# message is a state, the message file is retained and will be deleted when
# the end of condition message is received. In case of an event, the messages
# file is deleted after the user(s) are notified of the event.
#
# Parameters : None
#
# Calling mechanism :
# Should be called from cron after every unit of time equal to the reporting time.
# For example if you want notifications every 15 minutes, then the cron entry should
# be 0,15,30,45 * * * * /usr/local/bin/notification
#
# Author : Ravindra Nemlekar and Jeffrey Soto
#
#============================================================
BINDIR=/usr/local/admin/sysmon
BASEDIR=/usr/local/admin/sysmon
integer ok_value=-1 no_ok_required=-2
umask 0

cd ${BASEDIR}/hosts
```

logok.ksh (Listing 7.6) is used to log error-resolved messages. These messages are logged onto a single host, called as loggerhost, with user id loguser. logok.ksh requires a filename as its parameter. It copies this file to the system loggerhost with user id loguser as End.Condition.CONDITION_TYPE, where CONDITION_TYPE is the

---

Listing 7.7 (continued)

```
# Search for a Condition file. If found, read the generic config file,
# the condition specific config file and the condition specific config
# file for that host. Each notification style can be turned on or off.
for file in $(find . -type f -name "Condition.*" -print)
do
    host=$(dirname $file)
    condition_type=$(basename $file)
    count_file=$host/count.$condition_type
    ok_file=$host/End.$condition_type
    host_log_file=$host/log.Condition
    integer count=0
    # Is it the first iteration?
    if [ ! -f $count_file ] ;then
        echo "0" > $count_file
    else
        # Just increment the count.
        count=$(cat $count_file)
        count=count+1
        echo "$count" > $count_file
    fi

    if [ -f $ok_file ] ; then
        count=ok_value
    fi

    # Default is a stateful condition not an event
    EVENT_FLAG=0
    # Send an Okay message also
    OK_FLAG=1
    # Read this for each host so that each gets the initialized parameters
    # Read the global config file, then local config files would override the
    # parameters which are to be reset for each. Each parameter is initialized
    # to some default # value so that even if no config files are present,
    # the script does not misbehave.
    if [ -f $BASEDIR/config.generic ] ; then
        # read the global file first
        . $BASEDIR/config.generic
    fi
    if [ -f $BASEDIR/config.$condition_type/config.generic ] ; then
        # read the condition specific global file
        . $BASEDIR/config.$condition_type/config.generic
    fi
    if [ -f $host/config.$condition_type ] ; then
        # read the condition specific file for the problem on that host.
        . $host/config.$condition_type
    fi
```

Listing 7.7 (continued)

```
# Send a mail by default
MAIL_FLAG=${MAIL_FLAG:-1}
# Mail "sa" by default
mail_contacts=${MAIL_CONTACTS:-sa}
if [ "$MAIL_FLAG" -eq 1 ] ; then
    if (( count == 0 )) ; then
        cat $file | /usr/ucb/Mail -s "Error on $(basename $host)" $mail_contacts
        elif (( count == ok_value )) ; then
            if [ "$OK_FLAG" = 1 ] ; then
                cat $ok_file | /usr/ucb/Mail -s \
                    "$(basename $host) is ok" $mail_contacts
            fi
    fi
fi

# Number of beeps to be sent for a particular condition.
BEEP_COUNT=${BEEP_COUNT:-0}
# Beep "sa" by default
beep_contacts=${BEEP_CONTACTS:-sa}
# Don't beep by default
do_beep=False
if (( count < $BEEP_COUNT )) ; then
    do_beep=True
fi

if [ "$OK_FLAG" = 0 -a $count -eq $ok_value ]
then
    do_beep=False
    echo $(date) $(cat $ok_file) >> $host_log_file
fi

# Do the actual beeping
if [ "$do_beep" = "True" ] ; then
    if [ -f $ok_file ] ; then
        msg=$(cat $ok_file)
    else
        msg=$(cat $file)
    fi
    if (( count == 0 || count == $ok_value ))
    then
        echo $(date) $msg >> $host_log_file
    fi
    for name in $beep_contacts
    do
        /usr/local/bin/beep $name $msg
    done
fi
# Execute a script when the condition is encountered first.
# This enables automated response to the condition.
if (( count == 0 )) ; then
    if [ "$SCRIPT" ] ; then
        # don't wait for the script to complete
        $SCRIPT      &
    fi
fi    # Remove the condition and Okay files, so
# that they are not sent again.
if (( count == $ok_value || $EVENT_FLAG == 1 ))
then
    /bin/rm -f $ok_file $count_file $file
fi
done
```

filename passed to the script. The filename identifies the event. The contents of the file consist of a description of the okay message. The filename CONDITION_TYPE must be the same as that used for logging the condition. For example,

```
logok.ksh
/var/tmp/SYBASE_SERVER_NOT_RESPONDING
```

collect_events.ksh (Listing 7.9) gathers the condition and okay files from the loggerhost system. collect_events.ksh then deletes the condition and okay files from loggerhost to prevent duplicate logging of messages.

Notification Script

notification.ksh (Listing 7.7) is the heart of the monitoring system. It picks up all the errors, events, and conditions deposited by the monitor services or collected by collect_events.ksh script and sends them to the subscribed users and groups. The users and groups to which notification should be sent can be configured in config.generic (Listing 7.10). The types of notification currently supported are mailing and paging, which can be configured differently. Parameters

---

Listing 7.8   check_in_master_list.ksh — *called by* event_log.ksh *and* diskmon.ksh.

```
#!/bin/ksh
#
# check_in_master_list.ksh :
# Used for checking whether a host is present in the master list.
#
# Parameters :
#    arg1    hostname
#    arg2    Filename of master list
#
# Return value :
#    0    host is present in the master list
#    1    host not present or commented out
#    2    invalid parameters
#
if [ $# -ne 2 ] ; then
    echo "Usage: $0 <hostname> <master_list>"
    exit 2
fi

awk '           { exit_value = 1 ; }
    $1 == HOST  { exit_value = 0 ; exit ; }
       END      { exit (exit_value) ; }
    ' HOST=$1 $2
```

can be set for each condition or event type at the global level by editing the global
config.generic file. Further tuning can be done within the configuration file
present per host for each condition or event type. For example

```
#global config file.
config.generic
#event/cond specific file.
<CONDITION or EVENT>/config.generic
# condition per host
hosts/<host>/config.<CONDITION or EVENT>
```

The format of the configuration files for all the conditions is the same. These files
make up the basis of the subscription system. The format is as follows.

```
<parameter_name>=<parameter_value>
```

Listing 7.9   `collect_events.ksh`*— gathers the
condition and okay files, then deletes
them to prevent duplication.*

```
#!/bin/ksh
#=================================================================
# "@(#)collect_events.ksh"
#
# A Script that will copy the condition files from "loggerhost"
# (the relay host) and to the notifying system.
#
# Author : Ravindra Nemlekar
#
#=================================================================

BINDIR=/usr/local/admin/sysmon
BASEDIR=/usr/local/admin/sysmon
umask 0

# Copy the messages from the loggerhost and remove them from loggerhost,
# so that they are not repeated again. Logevent.ksh and logok.ksh
# will take care or re-creating directories if not present.
cd ${BASEDIR}
rcp -r loguser@loggerhost:hosts . > /dev/null 2>&1
rsh -l loguser loggerhost /bin/rm -rf hosts > /dev/null 2>&1
```

White spaces are not supported in `parameter_name`. White spaces in `parameter_value` should be enclosed in double quotes. There should be no white spaces on either side of the = sign. The following `parameter_names` are supported.

`BEEP_CONTACTS` The argument to this parameter consists of the names of the users and groups who should be paged for conditions, events, and ends of condition. If there are multiple arguments to this parameter, they should be enclosed within double quotes.

`BEEP_CONTACTS="sa dba" # Page sa and dba.`

`BEEP_COUNT` The argument to this parameter is the number of times the `BEEP_CONTACTS` will be paged. For events that do not maintain a state, this parameter is ignored.

`BEEP_COUNT=2 # Beep only twice on a Condition.`

`BEEP_DAILY` This parameter turns the paging of daily reminders on or off. Setting this value to 1 turns it on. Any other value turns it off.

`BEEP_DAILY=0 # Turn off paging of daily reminders.`

`MAIL_CONTACTS` The argument to this parameter consists of the names of the users or groups who should be mailed for conditions, events, and ends of conditions. If there are multiple arguments to this parameter, they should be enclosed in double quotes.

`MAIL_CONTACTS="sa dba" # Mail sa and dba.`

Listing 7.10   A sample `config.generic` **file used by** `notification.ksh.`

```
MAIL_FLAG=1
MAIL_CONTACTS=sa
BEEP_DAILY=0
MAIL_DAILY=1
BEEP_COUNT=1
BEEP_CONTACTS=sa
OK_FLAG=1
```

MAIL_FLAG This parameter turns the mail sending option on or off. Setting this value to 1 turns mail on. Any other value turns mail off.

```
MAIL_FLAG=1 # Turn on mail sending option.
```

MAIL_DAILY This parameter turns the mailing of daily reminders on or off. Setting this value to 1 turns it on. Any other value turns it off.

```
MAIL_DAILY=1 # Turn on mailing of daily reminders.
```

OK_FLAG This parameter sends an okay message when the condition changes. Setting the value to 1 sends an okay. Any other value does not send an okay.

```
OK_FLAG=1 # Send an okay message.
```

EVENT_FLAG This parameter indicates whether the item is a condition or an event. Setting this value to 1 indicates a condition. Setting this value to 0 indicates an event. Events require no follow-up. The notifier removes the event after notification.

```
EVENT_FLAG=1 # Default is an event, not a statful condition.
```

SCRIPT This parameter specifies a program that is to be run when the condition or event is encountered for the first time. For example, in the case of a full filesystem, a find command can be run to delete all the core dumps.

```
SCRIPT="find / -name core -exec /bin/rm -f {} \; "
```

This feature lets you extend the monitoring system to perform extended diagnostics, execute contingencies, kick off back-ups, or perform some other job as a result of a monitored condition.

Conclusion

With some planning, the system presented here can be configured to monitor and report on your site's events and states. You'll need to consider what kind of information you want and decide who should receive the information. Once you've installed it, you'll find that it provides both a highly useful information filter and a reliable means of notifying interested parties of system conditions.

## Chapter 8

Setting Priorities

Larry Reznick

nice(1) is nice. By prefixing a command line with the word "nice," SVR4 users can reduce the impact of their programs by 10 levels of priority. If users don't run nice, the system's default priority, which is set to level 20 out of 40 total levels, applies. Increasing the niceness of user programs by 10 can make a real difference to system performance. But just try to get your users to do that regularly.

renice(1) is nicer. This BSD extension to SVR4 lets users change the priority of their own jobs, making the job take more of the system's attention. Only the system administrator can reduce any job's niceness, but users can make their own jobs nicer to the system by setting one of the 20 niceness levels for any or all of their processes. renice has no default priority, though. Users must explicitly name some priority change amount to apply to all of the Process ID numbers (PIDs) named. Again, this doesn't happen automatically. It's a dirty job and the system administrator is probably going to get stuck with it.

On SVR4, renice's work is done with priocntl(1). As with renice, all users can apply priocntl to their own jobs, but only a root user can apply it to any job. priocntl has more control over process scheduling than nice or renice. System administrators can also change the scheduler's priorities for handling all jobs using dispadmin(1M).

Some of this process priority information is available from ps(1). SVR4's version of ps shows detailed information when used with the -elf option. However, two other options show additional ps information useful for priocntl: -j gives Process Group ID numbers (PGIDs) and Session ID numbers (SIDs), and -c gives scheduling classes and global priority levels. Figure 8.1 shows the information generated when these two options are added to the -elf option. Notice that -elf shows the PID, the Parent PID (PPID), the CPU's utilization percentage (C), the process priority (PRI), and the nice number (NI). The priority numbers in the PRI column show niceness — that is, the higher the number, the lower the priority — but on a larger scale than the NI numbers, which are constrained into the nice command's range.

ps's -j option adds the PGID and SID numbers between the PPID and the C columns. These numbers are useful in priocntl when you want to display (priocntl -d option) or set (priocntl -s option) priorities by specific group or SIDs (by adding the -i pgid option or the -i sid option to priocntl's command line).

ps's -c option is more significant when using priocntl. Using -c replaces the C column with a class (CLS) column and changes the form of the PRI column to show the system's global priority levels. The CLS column shows abbreviations for the three job scheduling classes.

Global priority levels in the PRI column are very different from niceness numbers in two ways. First, the numbers show priority, not niceness; that is, the higher the global priority number, the higher the priority. Second, the global priority numbers go much higher than any niceness numbers. Figure 8.2 shows an abbreviated sample output of ps -elf, while Figure 8.3 shows a similarly abbreviated sample of ps -elfjc. In those figures, the ADDR, SZ, WCHAN, STIME, TTY, and TIME fields have been cut.

Figure 8.1 ***The differences in the process priority information fields generated by SVR4's version of ps(1) when used with the -elf, -i, and -c options.***

```
$ ps -elf | head -1
 F S      UID  PID PPID C PRI NI      ADDR    SZ WCHAN     STIME      TTY TIME COMD

$ ps -elfj | head -1
 F S      UID  PID PPID PGID    SID C PRI NI    ADDR SZ WCHAN STIME TTY TIME COMD

$ ps -elfc | head -1
 F S      UID  PID PPID CLS PRI      ADDR    SZ WCHAN     STIME      TTY TIME COMD

$ ps -elfjc | head -1
 F S      UID  PID PPID PGID    SID CLS PRI    ADDR SZ WCHAN STIME TTY TIME COMD
```

Job Scheduling Classes

While many system administrators are familiar with niceness levels, not all may be familiar with global priority levels. These levels are configurable in the kernel. On SVR4, jobs are in one of three classes: time-sharing, system, and real-time. Altogether, these three classes comprise the 160 default global priorities.

Time-sharing processes are the typical processes run by every UNIX system. These processes vary their priorities, sharing their use of the CPU with other processes. Time-sharing processes have the lowest global priority levels, ranging from 0 to 59.

Figure 8.2 An abbreviated sample output of SVR4's ps -elf. In this case, the PRI field shows niceness.

```
F  S   UID   PID  PPID  C  PRI  NI  COMD
39 S   root    0     0  0    0  SY  sched
10 S   root    1     0  0   39  20  /sbin/init
39 S   root    2     0  0    0  SY  pageout
39 S   root    3     0  1    0  SY  fsflush
39 S   root    4     0  0    0  SY  kmdaemon
10 S   root  187     1  0   26  20  /usr/lib/saf/sac -t 300
10 S   root  153   144  0   26  20  lpNet
10 S   root  127     1  0   26  20  /usr/sbin/cron
10 S   root  168     1  0   26  20  /usr/lib/mail/surrcmd/smtpd -H rezb
10 S   root 2096     1  0   28  20  /sbin/getty vt01 19200NP
10 S   root  183     1  0   28  20  /usr/lib/mousemgr
10 S   root  139     1  0   26  20  /usr/sbin/rpcbind
10 S   root  144     1  0   26  20  /usr/lib/lpsched
10 S   root 2095     1  0   28  20  -sh 10 S root 170 1 0 26 20 /usr/lib/netsvc/rusers/rpc.rusersd
10 S   root  166     1  0   26  20  /usr/lib/netsvc/rwall/rpc.rwalld
10 S   root 2123     1  0   28  20  /sbin/getty vt02 19200NP
10 S   root  179     1  0   28  20  pciconsvr.eth -D0000 -L0000 -n4 -IO
10 S   root  174     1  0   26  20  /usr/lib/netsvc/spray/rpc.sprayd
10 S   root  177     1  0   28  20  pcimapsvr.eth -D0000 -n4 -IO.0.0.0.
10 S   root  191     1  0   28  20  /sbin/getty vt03 19200NP
10 S   root 4085     1  0   28  20  /sbin/getty vt04 19200NP
10 S   root  193     1  0   28  20  /sbin/getty vt05 19200NP
10 S   root  194     1  0   28  20  /sbin/getty vt06 19200NP
10 S   root 8813     1  0   28  20  /sbin/getty vt07 19200NP
10 S   root  196     1  0   28  20  /sbin/getty vt08 19200NP
10 S   root  197     1  0   28  20  /sbin/getty vt09 19200NP
10 S   root 3278     1  0   28  20  /sbin/getty vt10 19200NP
10 S   root 3280     1  0   28  20  /sbin/getty vt11 19200NP
10 S   root  200   187  0   26  20  /usr/sbin/inetd
10 S   root  201   187  0   26  20  /usr/lib/saf/listen tcp
10 S reznick 8955    1  1   39  20  -csh
10 S   uucp  435   433  0   28  20  UUCICO -r1 -scustcon
10 O reznick 9392 8955 34   50  20  ps -elf
10 S   uucp  433     1  0   30  20  /usr/lib/uucp/uusched
```

System processes are the processes run by the kernel, such as those run by init(1M) and configured in /etc/inittab(4). Unlike the time-sharing class, system processes don't vary their priorities. User processes are never in the system class, even when they call the kernel to do some work. System processes have global priority levels ranging from 60 to 99, so the lowest system class priority level is higher than the highest time-sharing class process.

Real-time processes are critical processes run by the kernel. Like the system class, and unlike the time-sharing class, real-time processes use a fixed priority scheme. Global priority levels for real-time processes range from 100 to 159, so the lowest

---

Figure 8.3 An abbreviated sample output of SVR4's ps -elfjc. In this case, the PRI field shows the global priority level.

F	S	UID	PID	PPID	PGID	SID	CLS	PRI	COMD
39	S	root	0	0	0	0	SYS	99	sched
10	S	root	1	0	0	0	TS	60	/sbin/init
39	S	root	2	0	0	0	SYS	98	pageout
39	S	root	3	0	0	0	SYS	79	fsflush
39	S	root	4	0	0	0	SYS	74	kmdaemon
10	S	root	187	1	187	187	TS	73	/usr/lib/saf/sac -t 300
10	S	root	153	144	144	144	TS	73	lpNet
10	S	root	127	1	127	127	TS	73	/usr/sbin/cron
10	S	root	168	1	168	168	TS	73	/usr/lib/mail/surrcmd/smtpd -H rezb
10	S	root	2096	1	2096	2096	TS	71	/sbin/getty vt01 19200NP
10	S	root	183	1	0	0	TS	71	/usr/lib/mousemgr
10	S	root	139	1	139	139	TS	73	/usr/sbin/rpcbind
10	S	root	144	1	144	144	TS	73	/usr/lib/lpsched
10	S	root	2095	1	2095	2095	TS	71	-sh
10	S	root	170	1	170	170	TS	73	/usr/lib/netsvc/rusers/rpc.rusersd
10	S	root	166	1	166	166	TS	73	/usr/lib/netsvc/rwall/rpc.rwalld
10	S	root	2123	1	2123	2123	TS	71	/sbin/getty vt02 19200NP
10	S	root	179	1	179	179	TS	71	pciconsvr.eth -D0000 -L0000 -n4 -I0
10	S	root	174	1	174	174	TS	73	/usr/lib/netsvc/spray/rpc.sprayd
10	S	root	177	1	177	177	TS	71	pcimapsvr.eth -D0000 -n4 -I0.0.0.0,
10	S	root	191	1	191	191	TS	71	/sbin/getty vt03 19200NP
10	S	root	4085	1	4085	4085	TS	71	/sbin/getty vt04 19200NP
10	S	root	193	1	193	193	TS	71	/sbin/getty vt05 19200NP
10	S	root	194	1	194	194	TS	71	/sbin/getty vt06 19200NP
10	S	root	8813	1	8813	8813	TS	71	/sbin/getty vt07 19200NP
10	S	root	196	1	196	196	TS	71	/sbin/getty vt08 19200NP
10	S	root	197	1	197	197	TS	71	/sbin/getty vt09 19200NP
10	S	root	3278	1	3278	3278	TS	71	/sbin/getty vt10 19200NP
10	S	root	3280	1	3280	3280	TS	71	/sbin/getty vt11 19200NP
10	S	root	200	187	200	200	TS	73	/usr/sbin/inetd
10	S	root	201	187	187	187	TS	73	/usr/lib/saf/listen tcp
10	S	reznick	8955	1	8955	8955	TS	60	-csh
10	S	uucp	435	433	127	127	TS	71	UUCICO -r1 -scustcon
10	0	reznick	9395	8955	9395	8955	TS	49	ps -elfjc
10	S	uucp	433	1	127	127	TS	69	/usr/lib/uucp/uusched

real-time priority level is higher than the highest system class process. Once a real-time process enters the scheduler, no other process — not even a system process — will get control again until the real-time process finishes or relinquishes its time slice.

/etc/conf/cf.d/mtune(4) contains several tunable parameters for the scheduler. Figure 8.4 shows default settings for some of the scheduler's parameters. RTMAXPRI defines the real-time class's maximum priority within the class. TSMAXUPRI defines the time-sharing class's maximum user-settable priority, which users may change using priocntl. The value in the default column, 20, represents both the minimum and maximum applied, ranging from −20 to +20. MAXCLSYSPRI identifies the maximum number of system class priorities. RTNPROCS and TSNPROCS identify the number of process levels for the real-time and time-sharing classes, respectively.

Scheduling Priorities

Once a process has used up or voluntarily given up its time slice, the scheduler is free to give another process a time slice. Ideally, the system's CPU resources are spread evenly across all jobs, but the scheduler rewards nice jobs and penalizes piggy jobs in the time-sharing class. There is no reward and penalty scheme for the system class and the real-time class. The system class is off limits to all users — even system administrators, unless they're changing the kernel. priocntl gives users control over their own time-sharing and real-time processes, and gives administrators control over all time-sharing and real-time processes. dispadmin gets or sets a class's priority tables, although only a root user can set the tables.

Figure 8.4 ***The default settings for some of the scheduler's tunable parameters in the file /etc/conf/cf.d/mtune(4).***

---

* Name	Dflt	Min	Max
RTMAXPRI	59	59	59
RTNPROCS	60	60	60
TSMAXUPRI	20	10	30
TSNPROCS	60	60	60
MAXCLSYSPRI	99	99	99

Figure 8.5 shows the time-sharing table's data, as output by the command

```
dispadmin -g -c TS
```

Detailed information about the time-sharing dispatcher parameter table is in ts_dptbl(4). Each row represents one priority level.

Figure 8.5 An abbreviated time-sharing priority table set by dispadmin.

```
# Time Sharing Dispatcher Configuration
RES=1000
```

# ts_quantum	ts_tqexp	ts_slpret	ts_maxwait	ts_lwait	PRIORITY	LEVEL
1000	0	10	5	10	#	0
1000	0	11	5	11	#	1
1000	1	12	5	12	#	2
1000	1	13	5	13	#	3
1000	2	14	5	14	#	4
1000	2	15	5	15	#	5
1000	3	16	5	16	#	6
1000	3	17	5	17	#	7
1000	4	18	5	18	#	8
1000	4	19	5	19	#	9
800	5	20	5	20	#	10
800	5	21	5	21	#	11
800	6	22	5	22	#	12
800	6	23	5	23	#	13
800	7	24	5	24	#	14
800	7	25	5	25	#	15
800	8	26	5	26	#	16
800	8	27	5	27	#	17
800	9	28	5	28	#	18
800	9	29	5	29	#	19
600	10	30	5	30	#	20
...						
200	39	54	5	54	#	49
100	40	55	5	55	#	50
100	41	55	5	55	#	51
100	42	56	5	56	#	52
100	43	56	5	56	#	53
100	44	57	5	57	#	54
100	45	57	5	57	#	55
100	46	58	5	58	#	56
100	47	58	5	58	#	57
100	48	59	5	59	#	58
100	49	59	5	59	#	59

The first column in any row is the `quantum`, which is the number of time slices given to a process at that row's priority level. The *RES* value shown at the top of the `dispadmin` output indicates the resolution of the quantum column in fractions of a second. The quantum is set at 1000 by default, and the quantum column shows milliseconds. Each time slice is defined by HZ in `/usr/include/sys/param.h` and is echoed in `/etc/default/login`. *HZ* is the real resolution of your system in clock ticks per second. The tables may show millisecond, microsecond, or even nanosecond resolution, but any quanta with greater resolution than HZ are rounded up to the next HZ value.

For example, my Esix SVR4 system and a client's SCO system both use HZ=100. On those systems, priority level 0 uses 1000 milliseconds (1 second) and priority level 59 uses 100 milliseconds (.1 second). If any quantum showed less than 100 milliseconds or had a remainder less than HZ when divided by HZ, such as the 24 in 1024 because HZ is 100, the system would round it up to the next HZ increment. So, 83 milliseconds would round up to 100 milliseconds, 257 milliseconds would become 300 milliseconds, and 1024 milliseconds would become 1100 milliseconds. To see the resolution in HZ rather than in the default milliseconds, add the `-r` option.

```
dispadmin -g -c TS -r $HZ
```

Using `-r` changes the resolution, and in this case would set it to the HZ value.

Recall that the dispatcher table's priority level numbers show higher numbers for higher priorities. That means processes running at 0, the lowest priority in the 60 time-sharing levels, are allowed the most time, and processes running at 59, the highest priority, are given the least time. Processes that don't run often are allowed to run for a long time when they finally do run. High priority processes run frequently but briefly.

The second column identifies the priority level to use the next time the process gets its turn if its current time slice expires. A process's time slice expires when the process runs without sleeping and exhausts its time. Other interruptions pause the process's clock. Returning from the interrupt continues the process's clock right where it left off.

Notice that in Figure 8.5 the expired processes have their priorities reduced by 10 levels if they're high-priority, but by half if their priority is lower than 20. Level 59, the highest priority level in the time-sharing class shown, gets a quantum of 100 milliseconds. If a process at that level uses up all of its time without sleeping, next time the process will run at level 49, allowing any higher priority process to run first. At that new level, the process gets a 200-millisecond slice, but if the process uses all of that up next time, it will be reduced to level 39 (400 milliseconds — not shown on the abbreviated table), then to level 29 (600 milliseconds — also not shown), then to level 19 (800 milliseconds), then to levels 9, 4, 2, 1, and finally 0 (all 1000 milliseconds each). Such a voracious process would get big time slices, but with decreasing frequency, so as to avoid dragging the system down.

The third column names the priority level assigned to the process if it sleeps. Processes voluntarily giving up their time slices get rewarded with a higher priority. When a process is blocked, waiting for I/O, this return-from-sleep column also applies. In Figure 8.5, sleeping processes with low priority have their priorities raised by increments of 10 levels. Starting with level 40, priorities are raised half the previous increment. So, sleeping processes that initially run occasionally, but with a large quantum, eventually rise to become frequently run processes, although with a small quantum.

A process at any priority level may have to wait for other, higher-priority processes. Column four sets the maximum time in seconds a process may wait for its turn to execute. If any process waits longer than this number of seconds, the process is compensated for being so patient. Column five contains the new priority level given to the delayed process. Typically, column five contains the same level numbers as column three, the sleep return column. In Figure 8.5, every priority level has a five-second maximum wait time. If any low-priority process is busy waiting for more than five seconds, its priority is increased 10 levels. The process will not necessarily execute right away if there are still many higher-priority processes, but this change increases its likelihood of getting executed. If the process is again forced to wait longer than five seconds, its level will increase by another 10. Eventually, such a process will rise to a top priority and execute, falling or rising from there according to its CPU usage.

Use the command

```
dispadmin -g -c RT
```

to see the real-time dispatcher parameter table. This table is described in rt_dptbl(4). An abbreviated version of it is shown in Figure 8.6. This table is far simpler than the time-sharing table. As before, each row represents one priority level, but there is only one column. Real-time processes are explicitly assigned one level and they stay there unless someone manually changes them.

Remember that the lowest priority real-time process, level 0, is higher than every other system and time-sharing process. Once a real-time process starts, little else on the system will get a chance. At real-time level 0, a process has a 1000 quantum. When that expires without sleeping or blocking, the scheduler will look to see if there's another real-time process above or at the same level. If not, this same real-time process will execute again because no system or time-sharing process is at a higher priority. Thus, once any real-time process starts, it drags the system away from any other work. The down side is, of course, that other system work suffers. On the up side, real-time processes get the full attention of the CPU and finish soon, as they should; otherwise, they shouldn't use real-time priority. Ongoing real-time processes shouldn't run on the same system as other time-sharing processes.

***Figure 8.6   An abbreviated real-time priority table set
           by*** dispadmin.

```
# Real Time Dispatcher Configuration
RES=1000

# TIME QUANTUM                        PRIORITY
# (rt_quantum)                         LEVEL
       1000                    #          0
       1000                    #          1
       1000                    #          2
       1000                    #          3
       1000                    #          4
       1000                    #          5
       1000                    #          6
       1000                    #          7
       1000                    #          8
       1000                    #          9
        800                    #         10
        800                    #         11
        800                    #         12
        800                    #         13
        800                    #         14
        800                    #         15
        800                    #         16
        800                    #         17
        800                    #         18
        800                    #         19
        600                    #         20
...
        200                    #         49
        100                    #         50
        100                    #         51
        100                    #         52
        100                    #         53
        100                    #         54
        100                    #         55
        100                    #         56
        100                    #         57
        100                    #         58
        100                    #         59
```

If you want to tune your time-sharing or real-time dispatcher parameter table, use dispadmin -g to get the current table's settings and redirect the output to a file. Edit that file to use whatever settings you prefer. Don't add any new priorities because the new table must have the same number of priority levels as the original table the -g option showed. If you want a different number of priorities, you must change the relevant tunable parameters in the kernel or in the space.c file in either /etc/conf/pack.d/ts or /etc/conf/pack.d/rt, and then rebuild the kernel. When you're finished editing the dispatcher table file, use the dispadmin -s option.

For instance, if you want to edit the time-sharing table, you might execute

```
dispadmin -g -c TS >ts_dptbl.new
```

After editing the file, you can set the new table in the kernel's space with the command

```
dispadmin -s ts_dptbl.new -c TS
```

Changing Priorities

The most important issue to decide when changing a process's priorities is probably the easiest to decide. Should the process be a time-sharing process or a real-time process? Typically, the answer to that question is time-sharing. But if you need to set an occasional real-time process, check whether your system is currently configured for real-time processing. Both dispadmin and priocntl can tell you this with their -l options. If you use dispadmin -l, only the class names appear. priocntl -l gives slightly more information, as shown in Figure 8.7.

Figure 8.7   Sample priocntl -l output showing the system's current scheduling classes.

```
CONFIGURED CLASSES
==================

SYS (System Class)

RT (Real Time)
    Maximum Configured RT Priority: 59

TS (Time Sharing)
    Configured TS User Priority Range: -20 through 20
```

If your system doesn't have the real-time class and you want it, you must remake the kernel. Edit /etc/conf/pack.d/ts/space.c and find a line reading

EXCLUDE:RT

SVR4 automatically includes the real-time class by default. If someone excluded it, find out why before you reenable it. To enable the real-time class, replace the EXCLUDE line with

INCLUDE:RT

Rebuild the kernel and reboot. The class should appear in the next dispadmin -l or priocntl -l option output. You can do the same thing to eliminate the time-sharing class for systems that you want to dedicate to real-time processing, but given real-time's privileged priorities, there are not many reasons for eliminating the time-sharing class.

priocntl has three primary options: -d, to display scheduling parameters; -s, to set scheduling parameters; and -e, to execute a command using specific scheduling parameters. Anyone may display process parameters, but users can set only their own processes. Of course, the administrators may set other users' processes when they have root permission.

When displaying or setting scheduling parameters, using an -i option followed by a keyword identifies which kinds of process information to apply to the list. After the keyword comes a list of ID numbers associated with that keyword. The obvious keywords use the PID or the PPID, but PGID and SID come into play here also. This is where adding the ps -j option, which shows those values, may be helpful. Most of the time, select processes are changed using one of these keywords, but you could use the UID or GID keywords to change all of the processes associated with a particular user or a group of users. Use the ID numbers as they appear in the /etc/passwd(4) or /etc/group(4) files, not the user or group names.

Use a -c option to specify RT or TS class. If you don't use the -c option, all of the ID numbers named must be in the same class. Each of those -c classes have special options associated with them. RT class options let you set the process's priority level and quantum. TS class options let you set the priority level and the user-changeable limit for the processes identified. Using the -c option, you can change a running process from one class to another.

   Finally, the -e option lets you execute processes in either the TS or RT class, applying other class options as needed. This is identical to the nice command's operation but you have more control. With the -s option simulating renice but exceeding renice's control, the priocntl program puts all of the scheduling operations into one place. Use priocntl to adjust priorities where necessary or launch programs with the appropriate priority. Programmers at your site may use the priocntl(2) function to embed this identical control in their programs. Judicious use of priocntl and sleep will improve your system's performance.

Chapter 9

Understanding Run Levels

Emmett Dulaney

UNIX systems, as well as BSD flavors, have only two run levels — single user and multiple user. Under SV, run levels have become to a machine what permissions are to a user. Operating at one run level restricts a machine from performing certain tasks (such as networking), while running at another enables these functions. Which functions are enabled at each run level has changed over the years. (For example, run level 1 used to be equivalent to multi-user state on many older machines.) Under current definitions, there are eight accepted run levels.

0   Shutdown state requiring a manual reboot. When you change to this level, files are synchronized with the disk and the system is left in a state in which it is safe to power off. This level is also known on some systems as Q or q.

Q or q   On systems where these are not equal to zero, they force the system to reread the inittab files and take into account any changes that have occurred since last boot.

1   Single user mode, also known as S or s mode on many systems. This allows only one user (traditionally the root user) to access the system and prevents anyone else from getting in. Additionally, it allows only one terminal to login. If the change is to level 1, then the one terminal allowed to login is the one defined as the console (and this command can be given only at the console). If the change is to S or s, then the only terminal allowed to login is the one that changed the run level. This is the level used when performing kernel rebuilds, installing software that rebuilds the kernel, performing troubleshooting, etc.

2   Multiple user mode, the traditional state allowing more than one user to login at a time. This is the level in which background processes (daemons) startup and additional file systems, if present, are mounted. (Note: the root file system is always mounted.)

3   Network mode. This is the same as level 2, but with networking or remote file sharing enabled.

4   User defined.

5   Hardware state.

6   Shutdown and automatic reboot. This performs the same action as changing to run level 0 and then rebooting the machine. This can be called a "warm boot" (in the language of the DOS world), because power is never removed from the components. Run levels 0 and 5 represent a "cold boot," since power must be turned off and then restored.

An easy way to summarize the run levels is that 2, 3, and 4 are operational states of the computer — it is up and running and users are allowed to conduct business. All other run levels involve some sort of maintenance or shutdown operation that prevents users from processing.

Identifying and Changing Run Levels

The -r parameter of the who command gives you your machine's current run level, as well as the two most recent previous run levels. For example

```
$ who -r
   . run level 2 May 4 10:07    2   1   0
$
```

shows that the current run level is 2 and that that has been the run level since May 4th at 10:07. On some systems, the three numbers to the right show the current run level, the previous run level, and the next previous run level. On other systems, the three numbers represent the process termination status, process id, and process exit status.

Changing levels requires root permission and can be done with either the init or shutdown command. Depending upon your vendor and system, the init utility is located in either /etc or /sbin. The shutdown command is traditionally in /usr/sbin. The init utility is very simple: it allows you to specify a number and the machine then changes to that run level. Thus

```
# init 3
```

would immediately change the machine to run level 3.

The shutdown command interacts with init and offers substantially more parameters and options. A -g option allows you to specify a grace period of seconds to use before beginning the operation (the default is 60), -i signifies which run level you want to go to, and -y carries out the action without asking for additional confirmation. To change to run level 3 in 15 seconds, the command would be:

```
# shutdown -g15 -i3 -y
```

Once the command is typed, a warning message is broadcast telling users that the run level is changing (this is true with init as well). The system then waits the specified number of seconds — allowing users to save files and logoff — before making the change. By contrast, init would tell users the run level is changing and would immediately begin changing it without giving the users time to protect their work.

Actions Defined in inittab

The inittab file, located in /etc or /sbin, is an initialization table. It contains a list (or table) of the actions that take place when a machine changes to a different run level. Figure 9.1 shows a section of an inittab file from an SCO system. The line numbers to the left have been added to aid this discussion. Each entry is a colon-delimited field consisting of four entries.

```
id:rstate:action:process
```

Figure 9.1 A sample section of an inittab file on an SCO system.

```
1    tcb::sysinit:/etc/smmck </dev/console >/dev/console 2>&1
2    mt:23:bootwait:/etc/brc </dev/console >/dev/console 2>&1
3    is:S:initdefault:
4    r0:056:wait:/etc/rc0 1> /dev/console 2>&1 </dev/console
5    r1:1:wait:/etc/rc1 1> /dev/console 2>&1 </dev/console
6    r2:2:wait:/etc/rc2 1> /dev/console 2>&1 </dev/console
7    r3:3:wait:/etc/rc3 1> /dev/console 2>&1 </dev/console
8    co:2345:respawn:/etc/getty tty01 sc_m
9    co1:1:respawn:/bin/sh -c "sleep 20; exec /etc/getty tty01 sc_m"
10   c02:2:respawn:/etc/getty tty02 sc_m
11   c03:2:respawn:/etc/getty tty03 sc_m
12   c04:2:respawn:/etc/getty tty04 sc_m
13   c05:2:respawn:/etc/getty tty05 sc_m
14   c06:2:respawn:/etc/getty tty06 sc_m
15   c07:2:respawn:/etc/getty tty07 sc_m
16   Sela:2:off:/etc/getty ttyla m
```

id   is the identification of the process, usually only two or three characters in length — one to four is the allowable range.

rstate   is the required state, or run level, necessary for the process to execute.

action   is a keyword telling init what to do with the process.

process   is the actual command to be carried out.

Line 3 of Figure 9.1 is extremely important: it is the line with the action field defined as initdefault. In this example, each time the system is rebooted, it will attempt to change to an initial state of S — single user. It could just as easily be 2 — multi-user. The file is plain text, so you can change this line using any text editor to make the system boot to a different level. The inittab file is not required for the operating system to boot — it is only a convenience. On most systems, if the file is erased or damaged, the system will boot to single user and any attempt to change to another state can cause it to hang. On other systems, if the entry or file is missing, a prompt will ask the console what the run level should be.

As line 3 of Figure 9.1 illustrates, there is only one line in the inittab file with the action field defined as initdefault. Other actions that can be specified are described in the following text.

boot   The entry is processed only on bootup and is not restarted if it dies. init does not wait for the entry to complete running before continuing with the next command, and can run many entries defined as boot simultaneously. This action is rarely used.

bootwait   The entry is processed only on bootup. init waits for the entry to finish running and then die before continuing with the next command. init does not restart the process once it finishes or dies off. Line 2 of Figure 9.1 uses this option with a utility to mount and check file systems.

off   If the process is currently running, a warning signal is sent, and after 20 seconds the process is killed with a kill -9 command. Line 16 shows that when the run level is changed to 2 (multiple user) terminal 1 is killed. This has the effect of logging that user off; it adds a level of security that protects against the possibility of the root user changing run levels and walking away from the terminal, thus allowing access to anyone who happens to sit there.

once   When the specified run level is reached, the process is started. init does not wait for the process to terminate before continuing, and does not restart it if it dies. Like boot, this option is not used very often.

ondemand   This option has the same meaning as respawn but is used mostly with a, b, and c levels (user defined). (See respawn for more information.)

powerfail   The action is triggered only when a power failure is at hand. A signal 19 is the most common indication of a power failure. A powerfail typically calls a sync operation.

powerwait   When a power failure occurs, this process is run and init waits until the processing finishes before processing anymore commands. Again, sync operations are the main purpose of the action.

respawn   If the process dies after it has been started, it is restarted. init does not wait for the process to complete execution before continuing with other commands. As lines 8–15 in Figure 9.1 show, respawn is associated with terminals; once a terminal is killed, you want it to respawn and allow another login.

syncinit   This option is not available on all systems. It tells init to reset the default sync interval (i.e., the number of seconds until modified memory disk buffers are written to the physical disk). Default time is 300 seconds, but the interval can be set to anything between 15 and 900.

sysinit   Before init tries to access the console, it must run this entry, which is usually reserved for devices that must be initialized before run levels are determined. Line 1 in Figure 9.1 shows that the Trusted Computing Base, which is used for user login and authentication, is initialized even before the console is made active, allowing any user to login.

wait   This option starts the process at the specified run level and causes init to wait until the process completes before moving on. This option is associated with scripts that perform the run level changes. Lines 4–7 in Figure 9.1 use this option for every run level change.

Line 2 of Figure 9.1 shows that the same processes will be carried out for run level changes to 2 or 3. Similarly, line 4 shows that the same processes will be carried out for changes to run levels 0, 5, or 6. The process carried out by line 4 is a shell command script in the /etc directory called rc0.

Figure 9.2 shows several key routines from the rc0 script of an SCO machine. I chose to use SCO because it illustrates nicely the steps that are carried out. I added line numbers to the file for purposes of this discussion, and then stipped away those lines that were not pertinent.

Figure 9.2   The key routines of the rc0 script on an SCO system.

```
24     a=`stty -g` #save stty values for later restoration
25
26     echo 'The system is coming down. Please wait.'
27
42     if [ -d /etc/rc0.d ]
43     then
44          for f in /etc/rc0.d/K*
45          {
46               if [ -s ${f} ]
47               then
48                    /bin/sh ${f} stop
49               fi
50          }
54          for f in /etc/rc0.d/S*
55          {
56               if [ -s ${f} ]
57               then
58                    /bin/sh ${f} start
59               fi
60          }
61     fi
74     trap "" 15
75     kill -15 -1
76     sleep 10
77     /etc/killall 9 2>/dev/null
78     sleep 10
79     sync;sync;sync
80     /etc/unmountall
81     stty $a 2>/dev/null      #restore saved stty values
82     sync;  sync
83     echo '
84     The system is down.'
85     sync
```

Lines 24 and 81 of Figure 9.2 work together, first saving the terminal settings and then restoring them after completing other processes. Line 26 echoes that the system is coming down. Line 42 is where things get interesting: a test is performed to see if there is a directory called /etc/rc0.d. If there is, then any file within that directory that begins with a K is executed (lines 44–50). Next any file within that directory beginning with an S is executed (lines 54–60). Line 74 effectively ignores the standard kill signal by mapping it to nothing — theoretically, up until this point, it is still possible to stop the shutdown. A killall is performed to kill all processes with a signal of 9, then three sync operations are performed. Finally, drives are unmounted (line 80), two more syncs are done (line 82), and a message is echoed that the system is down. One last sync rounds out the change to run level 0.

Similar scripts exist under the names of rc1, rc2, and rc3. Each performs similar operations. For example, rc1 checks to see if there is an rc1.d subdirectory. If there is, it executes any scripts within that subdirectory starting with K, then any scripts within that subdirectory starting with S.

About K and S Scripts

On older systems, all executable scripts are kept in a single directory, with each script combining the S* and K* action (hard links point to the relevant script). On newer systems, script files within each rcx.d subdirectory that begin with a K kill a process that is already running; those that begin with an S start a process that is not yet running. The names of these scripts typically begin with the K or S, followed by a two-digit number and a name for the operation. Figure 9.3 shows a listing of the rc0.d and rc2.d subdirectories. The two-digit number has no special significance, and can fall anywhere between 00 and 99. The numbers need not increment in any certain order, and a newly-created script can take any number not already in use within that directory. The only thing to bear in mind is that the scripts are called for execution with K* and S*; thus they are executed in numerical order with 00 (providing it exists) executed first and 99 executed last.

Figure 9.3   *Script files from* rc0.d *and* rc2.d *subdirectories.*

```
rc0.d:
total 16
-rwxr--r--   2 root      sys          630 Mar 15  1993 K00ANNOUNCE
-rwxr--r--   3 root      sys          742 Mar 15  1993 K70uucp
-rwxr--r--   3 root      sys         1027 Mar 15  1993 K75cron
-rwxr--r--   3 root      sys         1397 Mar 15  1993 K80lp
-rwxr--r--   3 root      sys         1078 Mar 15  1993 K86mmdf
```

It is relatively simple to understand what most of the scripts do, since to their names are descriptive. The files displayed in Figure 9.3 have the following consequences:

K00ANNOUNCE   simply echoes "System services are now being stopped."

K70uucp   cleans up miscellaneous uucp locks (/usr/spool/uucp/LCK.*).

K75cron   links to S75cron. Depending upon which way K75cron is called, it will either kill the cron PID, or start /etc/cron. The same script is capable of doing both.

K80lp   links to S80lp. K80lP will either summon /usr/lib/lpshut or start /usr/lib/lpsched. K80lP will also remove a printer lock (/usr/spool/lp/SCHEDLOCK), if one exists.

Figure 9.3 (continued)

```
rc2.d:
total 42
-rwxr--r--  2 root     sys       779 Mar 15  1993 S00SYSINIT
-rwxr--r--  2 root     sys      1085 Mar 15  1993 S01MOUNTFSYS
-rwxr--r--  2 root     sys       796 Mar 15  1993 S03RECOVERY
-rwxr--r--  2 root     sys       794 Mar 15  1993 S04CLEAN
-rwxr--r--  2 root     sys       617 Mar 15  1993 S05RMTMPFILES
-rwxr--r--  2 root     sys       767 Mar 15  1993 S15HWDNLOAD
-rwxr--r--  2 root     sys       767 Mar 15  1993 S16KERNINIT
-rwxr--r--  2 root     sys      1081 Mar 15  1993 S20sysetup
-rwxr--r--  2 root     sys       933 Mar 15  1993 S21perf
-rwxr--r--  3 root     sys       742 Mar 15  1993 S70uucp
-rwxr--r--  3 root     sys      1027 Mar 15  1993 S75cron
-rwxr--r--  3 root     sys      1397 Mar 15  1993 S80lp
-rwxr--r--  3 root     sys      1078 Mar 15  1993 S86mmdf
-rwxr--r--  2 root     sys       768 Mar 15  1993 S87USRDAEMON
-rwxr--r--  2 root     sys       768 Mar 15  1993 S88USRDEFINE
-rwxr--r--  2 root     sys       767 Mar 15  1993 S90RESERVED
```

`K86mmdf` links to `S86mmdf`. Depending upon how `K86mmdf` is called, it will either start the `mmdf` daemon or kill its associated PID. Like several of these scripts, `K86mmdf` uses the following syntax to find the PID:

```
pid=`/bin/su root -c "/bin/ps -e" | grep whatever | sed -e 's/^ *//' -e 's/.*//'
```

`S00SYSINIT` runs additional scripts in `/etc/rc.d/0` and `/etc/rc.d/1`. This is used only for historical purposes and to maintain compatibility with older UNIX and XENIX versions.

`S01MOUNTFSYS` performs a `mountall` to bring up the filesystems and initiate auditing.

`S03RECOVERY` provides crash recovery after a boot.

`S04CLEAN` removes temporary and lock files. This is the script used to empty `/tmp`.

`S05RMTMPFILES` cleans up any other existing temporary files.

`S15HWDNLOAD` performs a hardware download.

`S16KERNINIT` performs a kernel initialization.

`S20sysetup` prints system ID information, if it exists; creates the information by sending the output of `uname -n` to `/etc/systemid`.

`S21perf` fires up the administrative utility `sadc`.

`S87USRDAEMON` starts up the user daemons.

`S88USRDEFINE` provides a location in which system-specific routines can be placed.

`S90RESERVED` sets several variables and mails information about the boot to the root user's mail file.

You can start and stop additional processes when you change to one of the predefined run levels simply by creating a shell script, preceding it with K or S, and placing it in the appropriate `rcx.d` subdirectory.

Creating a Run Level

Using the information presented here, you can easily create your own run level. Run level 4 is, by default, not used by the UNIX operating system. As mentioned earlier, you can use it to customize your system. To do so, follow these four steps.

1. Create an entry in /etc/inittab that resembles the following example.

    ```
    r4:4:wait:/etc/rc4 1> /dev/console 2>&1 </dev/console
    ```

2. Create a script in /etc called rc4 by copying rc0 to rc4, then changing all references from rc0.d to rc4.d. The only references should be as shown in Figure 9.1 on lines 42, 44, and 54. Comment out lines 26, 76–80, 82, and 85. Then change the echo statement on line 84 to say "Change to Run Level 4 completed."

3. Make an rc4.d subdirectory below /etc.

4. Within /etc/rc4.d, create your command scripts. If, for example, you want to start a database process when you change to this run level, call the script S00DATABASE, and place the command to start it within that script. Then create a corresponding K script to close the database when you change from that run level.

Significant Files

Several files maintain run level information. /etc/default/boot is an SCO-specific file that maintains information on the console keyboard. /etc/wtmp and /etc/utmp work as opposite log files to each other. /etc/wtmp keeps a record of all processes that are spawned, while /etc/utmp keeps a record of all processes that have died. These log files do tend to grow and should be routinely trimmed.

Summary

Changing run levels simply entails calling an additional set of scripts. Those scripts can either start processes that are not running or kill processes that are running. Run levels 2, 3, and 4 are operational states allowing users to interact with the operating system. Run levels 0, 1, 5, and 6 involve downing the computer or performing maintenance operations. Run level 4 is available for administrator definition and can easily be used to stop and start additional processes.

Chapter 10

Reporting Memory Data with *sar*

Chris Hare

To properly manage system performance, system managers and capacity planners must monitor the usage of the various system resources regardless of the operating environment. The UNIX utility sar, short for System Activity Reporter, supplies a low-cost method of collecting that data. sar is bundled with nearly all forms of UNIX systems; although sar is readily available, you might still opt to avoid it. sar easily qualifies as one of those rather esoteric commands for which UNIX is often criticized. sar is difficult to use, difficult to interpret, and it lacks the interactive user interface that many people want. For those willing to make the effort, sar will deliver important performance information.

   sar has two forms: that of the data collector and that of the data viewer. The command line formats for the data collector form are in Figure 10.1. The options and explanations for the data viewer form are in Table 10.1.

What Will sar Monitor?

sar is capable of monitoring the following list of system components.

CPU Utilization   The portion of time spent in user mode, system mode, idle and waiting for block I/O, and idle.

Buffer Activity   The number of transfers per second between system buffers and disk, accesses of system buffers, cache hit rations, and physical device data transfers.

Disk/Tape Devices   The busy and queue requests, number of transfers to and from the devices, and average wait times.

TTY Devices   The input and output character processing.

System Calls   The counts for some specific system calls and for the aggregate of all calls.

System Swapping   The tansfers made for swapping and process switching.

File System Access   The number of calls to routines like igets and namei.

Report on Run Queue   The number of processes in the run queue.

File/Inode and Process Tables   The number of entries and the size of each table.

Message/Semaphores   The number of primitives per second.

Paging Activities   The number of page faults and protection errors.

Unused Memory   The amount of free memory and free space on the swap device.

Remote File Sharing and Server/Request Queue   The statistics on RFS services.

   In collection mode, sar places its output in the file /usr/adm/sa/sa??, where ?? is replaced with the day's date. For example, the file created for June 26 would be sa26.

Figure 10.1   The command line formats for sar, sadc, sa1, **and** sa2.

```
sar [-ubdycwaqvmnprDSAC] [-o file] t [ n ]
sar [-ubdycwaqvmnprDSAC] [-s time] [-e time] [-i sec] [-f file]
/usr/lib/sa/sadc [t n] [ofile]
/usr/lib/sa/sa1 [t n]
/usr/lib/sa/sa2 [-ubdycwaqvmnprDSAC] [-s time] [-e time] [-i sec]
```

Table 10.1   The sar **command line options and their explanations.**

Option	Instructions to sar
-A	Report on *all* of the following options.
-a	Report the utilization of the file access routines, iget, namei, and dirblk.
-b	Report on the buffer activity, which includes the transfers per second of data between the system and block devices, system buffer accesses, buffer cache hits, and data moved through the physical or raw device mechanism.
-C	Report RFS buffer caching overhead.
-c	Report on system call usage, both from a generic point of view consisting of all system calls, and a specific set, as well as the number of characters transfered through the system call interface.
-D	Report on Remote File Sharing activity, including the average number of RFS servers, percentage of time which the servers are idle, and the average number of receive descriptors. This will be availble *only* if your system is running RFS.
-d	Report on activity for each block device on the system. This feature, which may not be available on all systems, reports on the portion of time a device has spent servicing a transfer request, the average number of requests waiting to be processed during that interval, number of transfers to and from the device, the average period of time that a request waits on the queue before being serviced.
-m	Report on the message and semaphore activities, in primitives per second.
-n	Report name cache statistics, including; c-hits, the number of name cache hits; cmisses, the number of name cache misses; and hit%, the hit ratio as a percentage.
-p	Report on the system paging activities, including address translation page faults (page not in memory) and protection faults (illegal access).
-q	Report the average queue length while occupied and the percent of time occupied for the run queue and the swap queue.
-r	Report on the current unused memory and disk blocks, including the available free memory, and available free swap space.

How It Works

sar samples a series of kernel counters at given intervals to provide a sense of what is happening on the system during peak hours. The actual data collection is typically handled by shell scripts that are scheduled by cron, as in Listing 10.1.

This example, which is fairly representative of common practice, uses shell scripts, namely sa1 and sa2. Both of these commands are in /usr/lib/sa, while sar is in /usr/bin.

The sa1 shell script causes sar's output to be saved to the file mentioned earlier, namely /usr/adm/sa/sa??. The first two entries in the crontab of Listing 10.1 cause information to be gathered every 20 minutes during normal working hours, and hourly otherwise. This cross-section provides a "reasonable" view of the system utilization. If this level of granularity is not appropriate to your installation, you can change the parameters defining when the sa1 command is run.

The sa2 shell script takes the output from sa1 and builds a daily report, which is stored in /usr/adm/sa/sarDD, where DD is the day of the month.

sa1 uses the separate command /usr/lib/sa/sadc, which is the actual data collector for the facility, while sa2 uses the facilities of sar to build the report. The command line arguments for sadc are also shown in Figure 10.1. sadc writes a binary record to standard output or to the named output file. The structure of this binary record (Figure 10.2) is documented in the sar manual pages, but is not part of any system header file.

Table 10.1 (continued)

Option	Instructions to sar
-S	Report RFS server and request queue status.
-u	Report on the CPU utilization. This is the default option, which shows the time spent in kernel, mode user mode, idle with a process waiting for block I/O to complete, or just idle.
-v	Report on the status of the inode, file, and process tables, including the configured size and actual usage at the time of sampling.
-w	Report on the system swapping and switching performance, consisting of the number of blocks read for swap-ins and swap-outs and the number of process switches.
-y	Report on the TTY activity on the system, providing information on the number of characters being processed by the raw input, canonical input, and output systems, as well as transmit, receive, and modem interrupt rates.

Listing 10.1   A sample crontab ***illustrates shell scripts scheduled by*** cron ***to handle actual data collection for*** sar.

```
#
# The sys crontab should be used to do performance
# collection. See cron # and performance manual pages
# for details on startup.
#
0 * * * 0-6 /usr/lib/sa/sa1
20,40 8-17 * * 1-5 /usr/lib/sa/sa1
5 18 * * 1-5 /usr/lib/sa/sa2 -s 8:00 -e 18:01 -i 1200 -A
```

Figure 10.2   A sample binary record written to standard output by sadc.

```
struct sa {
    struct sysinfo si;          /* see /usr/include/sys/sysinfo.h */
    struct minfo mi;            /* defined in sys/sysinfo.h */
    struct dinfo di;            /* RFS info defined in sys/sysinfo.h */
    struct rcinfo rc;           /* Client cache info defined in sys/sysinfo.h */
    struct bpbinfo bi;          /* Co-processor info defined in sys/sysinfo.h */
    int bpb_utilize             /* Co-processor utilize flag */
    int minserve, maxserve;     /* RFS server low and high water marks */
    int szinode;                /* current size of inode table */
    int szfile;                 /* current size of file table */
    int szproc;                 /* current size of proc table */
    int szlckf;                 /* current size of file record header table */
    int szlckr;                 /* current size of file record lock table */
    int mszinode;               /* size of inode table */
    int mszfile;                /* size of file table */
    int mszproc;                /* size of proc table */
    int mszlckf;                /* maximum size of file record header table */
    int mszlckr;                /* maximum size of file record lock table */
    long inodeovf;              /* cumulative overflows of inode table */
    long fileovf;               /* cumulative overflows of file table */
    long procovf;               /* cumulative overflows of proc table */
    time_t ts;                  /* time stamp, seconds */
    long devio[NDEVS][4];       /* device unit information */
    int cachehits;              /* number of name cache hits */
    int cachemisses;            /* number of name cache misses */
    #define IO_OPS 0            /* cumulative I/O requests */
    #define IO_BCNT 1           /* cumulative blocks transferred */
    #define IO_ACT 2            /* cumulative drive busy time in ticks */
    #define IO_RESP 3           /* cumulative I/O resp time in ticks */
};
```

If sadc is executed with no arguments, no syntax error is reported. Instead, the command will write a special record to the binary file, indicating that the system counters have been reset. Typically this special mode is used at boot time by one of the /etc/rc2.d scripts, usually /etc/rc2.d/S21perf.

sa2 uses the sar command to build the readable report. The options used on the sa2 command line are passed directly to sar, as shown in Figure 10.1.

The remainder of this chapter illustrates how to interpret sar's various reports. sar gives the system and node names, version number, the date, and selected averages in the first line of each report. The example reports were generated on a Motorola 8000 UNIX system, which was deliberately loaded to create some interesting output.

Monitoring CPU Utilization

The -u option, which is also the default if no option is provided, instructs sar to report on the CPU utilization. Figure 10.3 shows a sample report, including the line giving the system and mode names, version number, the date, and selected averages. The remaining sample reports in figures throughout this chapter will omit this line.

The CPU utilization report summarizes four data fields.

- %usr is the percentage of time operating in user mode.

- %sys is the percentage of time operating in system or kernel mode.

- %wio is the percentage of time the CPU is idle because it was waiting for a process's block I/O to complete.

- %idle is the percentage of time when the system wasn't doing anything at all.

Note that Figure 10.3 indicates a potential CPU bottleneck: there are no remaining CPU cycles (0 %idle). Remember that an %idle of 0 indicates that this machine has nothing left to give the users in the area of raw computing power. Similarly, the report in Figure 10.4 indicates a problem with the disk subsystem. A consistently large %wio (say greater than 10 percent) could indicate that the disk subsystem is incapable of

---

Figure 10.3   A sample report from sar -u *on a system with a potential CPU bottleneck.*

17:38:41	%usr	%sys	%wio	%idle
17:38:46	58	41	1	0
17:38:51	50	50	0	0
17:38:56	58	42	0	0
Average	54	46	0	0

meeting demands. This problem can be lessened by using a second or alternate disk for some of the data or upgrading the disk subsystem. Figure 10.5 shows an example from a loaded-down SCO UNIX system.

Buffers, Swapping, and Memory

The -b option instructs sar to report on the next potential problem area, system buffer usage. Figure 10.6 shows a sample report. Values in a column with a /s in the heading are in "hits" per second. The most critical values are the percentages %rcache and %wcache, which are the hit rates for disk reads and writes, respectively. For optimum

---

Figure 10.4   A sample report from sar -u **on a system with a potential problem in the disk sybsystem.**

22:50:35	%usr	%sys	%wio	%idle
22:50:40	5	27	8	60
22:50:45	3	46	5	46
22:50:50	5	84	11	0

Figure 10.5   A sample report from sar -u **on a loaded-down system.**

10:29:02	%usr	%sys	%wio	%idle
10:29:04	18	41	41	0
10:29:05	4	14	83	0
10:29:06	3	20	77	0
10:29:07	30	60	10	0
10:29:08	20	61	18	0

Figure 10.6   A sample report from sar -b **on a system with a potential problem in system buffer usage.**

22:53:51	bread/s	lread/s	%rcache	bwrit/s	lwrit/s	%wcache	pread/s	pwrit/s
22:53:56	3	150	98	0	1	100	0	0
22:54:01	2	172	99	15	19	24	0	0
22:54:06	3	281	99	0	1	100	0	0

performance, the hit ratio for both reads and writes should be as close to 100 percent as possible. If %rcache is less than 90 percent or if %wcache is less than 70 percent, then the size of the buffer cache should be increased. Remember that dramatic increases in the size of the buffer cache remove RAM from the system and may increase the swapping or paging traffic on your system.

To get a full picture of memory performance, you must also examine paging and swapping statistics. While you can always improve cache hit ratios by increasing the number of buffers, increases beyond a certain level will actually have an adverse effect on overall performance. The excess buffers will decrease the amount of available memory for processes and data.

The -w option instructs sar to report on paging and swapping activity (Figure 10.7).

The pswch/s value is the number of process switches per second, which is the number of processes which have been through the CPU. In the not-too-busy system shown in Figure 10.7, two process switches took place in the first two five-second intervals and none in the last. (This is an example of a "lightly-loaded" system.) If the system doesn't have enough RAM, it will do some paging and swapping to manage its memory deficiency. On systems running at or near the maximum potential, the paging and swapping components may also reach maximums.

Many systems report how much RAM is really available after all of the kernel requirements are satisfied at boot time. You can get similar information anytime with sar's -r option. This option will report the amount of free RAM and free swap space at the moment when the command was executed.

```
# sar -r 1 1

00:03:05 freemem freeswp
00:03:06 486 25696
```

The freemem value is the number of currently free 4Kb pages. On my 4 Meg system, sar reports 486 * 4096 or 1,990,656 free bytes. The freeswp value is the number of disk blocks available for swapping, in 512-byte blocks. The freeswp value raises or lowers to show the level of free swap space.

Figure 10.7 **A sample report from** sar -w **on a lightly-loaded system.**

00:00:28	swpin/s	bswin/s	swpot/s	bswot/s	pswch/s
00:00:33	0.00	0.0	0.00	0.0	2
00:00:38	0.00	0.0	0.00	0.0	2
00:00:43	0.00	0.0	0.00	0.0	0

On systems that show the freeswp value raising and lowering, but show no swapping activity with the -w option, vhand is running to collect memory pages.

Because RAM is such a vital resource, it is common to combine the -rwp options to show the free RAM available, paging, and swap utilization.

Device Activity

The -d option instructs sar to report only on the hard disk and tape subsystems. The names of the devices are very system specific, so the -d option does not work on all systems. For example, my Motorola 8000 UNIX system does not report any information when I use the -d option; however, my SCO 3.2v4 UNIX does.

The example is shown in Figure 10.8 is from an SCO UNIX 3.2v4 system, which has a 425Mb IDE hard disk. The wd-0 device name refers to the first hard disk on the Western Digital-style disk controller. In this case, the controller and disk processed 49.77Mb of data (r+w/s) in 212.14 blocks (blks/s). This calculates to

```
212.14 / 49.77 = 4.26 Megabytes per transfer approximately
```

This figure indicates that the disk subsystem may not be fast enough to cope with large data transfers. In this output, the reports were on a per second basis, so a 4.26Mb per second transfer may be quite sufficient.

Figure 10.8   *A sample report from* sar -d *on a system with a disk subsystem that may not be fast enough to cope with large data transfers.*

15:52:14	device	%busy	avque	r+w/s	blks/s	avwait	avserv
15:52:15	wd-0	37.50	1.00	41.35	165.38	0.00	9.07
15:52:16	wd-0	33.33	1.44	38.24	172.55	3.85	8.72
15:52:17	wd-0	45.19	1.32	47.12	188.46	3.06	9.59
15:52:18	wd-0	57.55	2.44	56.60	324.53	14.67	10.17
15:52:19	wd-0	50.00	1.86	58.82	239.22	7.33	8.50
15:52:20	wd-0	26.47	1.26	21.57	86.27	3.18	12.27
15:52:21	wd-0	28.57	1.23	29.29	117.14	2.20	9.76
15:52:22	wd-0	67.65	1.26	53.92	211.76	3.27	12.55
15:52:23	wd-0	76.64	1.41	61.68	250.47	5.15	12.42
15:52:24	wd-0	84.31	1.53	96.08	396.08	4.69	8.78
Average	wd-0	50.05	1.51	49.77	212.14	5.18	10.06

This report has two additional important fields.

- avwait is the average time in milliseconds before the request is passed to the controller.

- avserv is the average time in milliseconds before the request is processed by the controller.

These two fields are significant because they represent how well your disk controller is responding to the requests. The lower the number, the faster the request was processed and returned to the application.

TTY Activity

After memory performance, the next most common performance concern is terminal I/O load. As intelligent serial interface hardware becomes more common, TTY activity impacts the overall system performance much less than when systems still relied on the main CPU to process all character input.

The -y option instructs sar to report on the TTY activity (see Figure 10.9). Each of the columns reports the number of characters through the system per second. On the example system, the values are usually zero, but because a backup and a UUCP call to a neighboring machine were in progress when Figure 10.9 was generated, the numbers are much higher. rawch and canch are the number of characters per second processed through the raw and canonical interfaces, respectively. outch is the output character rate in characters per second.

Figure 10.9   A sample report from sar -y ***on a system showing high character throughout.***

	rawch/s	canch/s	outch/s	rcvin/s	xmtin/s	mdmin/s
16:23:51						
16:23:52	136	0	84	122	84	0
16:23:53	141	0	12	121	8	0
16:23:54	94	0	81	122	85	0
16:23:55	141	0	858	122	629	0
16:23:56	94	0	900	121	928	0
16:23:57	141	0	880	121	842	0
16:23:58	141	0	966	123	944	0
16:23:59	94	0	803	121	852	0
16:24:00	141	0	850	121	934	0
16:24:01	88	0	951	122	929	0
Average	121	0	639	122	624	0

System Calls

The -c option instructs sar to report on the system call utilization, summarized by these subgroups: all system calls (scall), read(S), write(S), fork, and exec. An example report appears in Figure 10.10.

The scall field counts all system calls in the interval. sread, read(S), fork, and exec report the number of calls to each respective routine. While you may enjoy marvelling at these call counts, you probably won't find it to be very useful.

Files, Inodes, and Processes

The process, file, and inode tables are fixed in size, and are adjusted by following the kernel configuration instructions for your particular version of UNIX. The -v option instructs sar to report on the usage of these resources. (You can get similar information from crash.)

Figure 10.11 is a sample of the sar -v output on my Motorola UNIX system. Since I am the primary (and usually the only) user on this machine, I can say that this is a single-user system.

Figure 10.10   A sample report from sar -c showing a system's call utilization.

23:48:44	scall/s	sread/s	swrit/s	fork/s	exec/s	rchar/s	wchar/s
23:48:49	117	21	33	0.00	0.00	17497	1394
23:48:54	122	23	34	0.00	0.00	18477	1343
23:48:59	170	27	29	0.40	0.40	18475	944

Figure 10.11   A sample report from sar -v on a single-user system.

17:01:12	proc-sz	ov	inod-sz	ov	file-sz	ov	lock-sz	fhdr-sz
17:01:13	26/128	0	61/200	0	42/200	0	0/ 50	0/ 0
17:01:14	26/128	0	61/200	0	42/200	0	0/ 50	0/ 0
17:01:15	26/128	0	61/200	0	42/200	0	0/ 50	0/ 0
17:01:16	26/128	0	61/200	0	42/200	0	0/ 50	0/ 0
17:01:17	26/128	0	61/200	0	42/200	0	0/ 50	0/ 0

For each of four resources (proc-sz, process table; inod-sz, inode table; file-sz, file table; lock-sz, file locks), the -v option reports the number currently allocated followed by the maximum configured. For example, the proc-sz field in Figure 10.11 shows 26 processes out of a maximum of 128. The ov column reports the number of overflows during the sampling period.

Figure 10.12 shows the same report for a multi-user SCO UNIX system. Even though the system in Figure 10.12 was fairly idle, half of the process, inode, and file tables are already consumed. Although it is possible for the users on this system to cope with these parameters, this configuration is potentially dangerous. Running out of any of these resources will result in work being "lost" or in some aspect of the system not working correctly.

Evaluating the Data

Making sense out of the information provided from any system performance and analysis tool can be difficult, but here are some things to watch for when evaluating the data.

Maintain a %wio below 10. If the %wio is consistently higher than 10, the disk subsystem may not be able to meet demands; if so, I suggest that both swapping and buffers be examined.

Keep an eye on swapping. Consistent and prolonged swapping indicates a memory deficiency, and may eventually lead to *thrashing*, a condition indicated by almost constant disk activity and very high levels of swapping.

Monitor the number of buffers. An overabundance of buffers will decrease the amount of RAM available to the user and system processes, thereby increasing the likelihood of swapping. This problem can be overcome by adding more RAM to the system or by decreasing kernel tunables, such as buffers.

Figure 10.12 **A sample report from sar -v on a multi-user system with a potentially dangerous configuration.**

17:11:51	proc-sz	ov	inod-sz	ov	file-sz	ov	lock-sz
17:11:52	59/100	0	173/300	0	177/300	0	0/100
17:11:53	59/100	0	173/300	0	177/300	0	0/100
17:11:54	59/100	0	173/300	0	177/300	0	0/100
17:11:55	59/100	0	173/300	0	177/300	0	0/100
17:11:56	59/100	0	173/300	0	177/300	0	0/100

The performance of the system can also be affected if there aren't enough buffers. If the ratios reported in the buffer analysis are less than 80 percent for writes and 90 percent for reads, I suggest creating a kernel with more buffers. SCO UNIX and XENIX will automatically calculate a buffer setting based upon the amount of available RAM, but this calculated default can be over-ridden.

Rectify and record any kernel error messages.   For example, "file table overflow" indicates that the file table isn't large enough. Be warned, however, that making the kernel tables too large also removes needed RAM from the system by assigning it to the kernel.

In assessing performance, remember that some factors may be inherent in the design of the software or the hardware, such as different data paths on the bus and the controller (e.g., an 8-bit ISA card in a 32-bit bus machine). Also keep in mind that typically, only a small increase in system performance can be achieved by adjusting kernel parameters. Depending upon what is adjusted, and to what levels, this may make things worse.

The End

While the art (or science) of performance tuning is somewhat shaded in mist, a little common sense will help you see better performance. When adjusting kernel parameters, go small — too big may be too much!

Chapter 11

Managing Disk Space

Marty Leisner

Managing disk space efficiently entails making rational decisions about storage. Backups are useful for protecting against catastrophe, but backups aren't always very useful in daily work. Anything online is at your fingertips and easy to work with; anything on tape is harder to access, and therefore is often ignored. Whenever possible, it's better to leave files you and your users may need in the future online. This chapter explores several tactics for maximizing your disk utilization through efficient storage techniques and presents some scripts that help implement those tactics.

The chapter contains a great deal of benchmark information to help you make logical choices. All the benchmarks were done on a DX4/100 machine running Linux v1.2.8. Size statistics are hardware independent (bytes are the same on all platforms). The absolute timing information is hardware dependent (faster computers will run faster). The relative times should be more meaningful to you (what's faster on my setup should be faster on all setups). I do a lot of benchmarking on two distributions: gawk v2.15.6 and gdb v4.14 for the following reasons.

- They are fairly large (but gdb is an order of magnitude bigger than gawk).

- They are representative of the type of file that system administrators often use.

- You can freely get them to compare your results with mine.

- I had them handy.

Eliminate Stale Files

Your first step should be to determine which files are of use and which are not. If you still have distributions of software that you've built on your system, you can check the makefiles for one of the following flavors of clean.

- clean
- realclean
- distclean
- nuke
- clobber

Most makefiles include one of the above; the choice depends on the flavor of the makefile and the author's preferences. After using clean, you can see how much space you saved and how much space is consumed. Then you are ready for other tactics covered here.

Identifying Files

Disks accumulate files. Often, it's impossible to tell from the filename what type of file a given file may be, especially when you're dealing with binaries from multiple architectures on NFS-mounted filesystems. You can use ls(1) to help you identify what files are there. The GNU fileutils info file lists this description of ls(1) with the -F option.

```
`-F'
`_classify'
Append a character to each filename indicating the file type.
Also, for regular files that are executable, append `*'. The file
type indicators are `/' for directories, `@' for symbolic links,
`|' for FIFOs, `=' for sockets, and nothing for regular files.
```

Most versions of ls include -F, and many users use it in their Bourne-type shell initilization files:

```
alias ls='ls -F'
```

Invoking `ls -F` will give you some hint as to what the files are. Compare the output of `ls`

```
% ls
autoscan   bitcount.d   env        foo             strerror.c xdos
awk        bsdlpq       false      libXpm.so.4.5   tee        xsession
bash       dired        fdformat   libmalloc.so.1.0 who
```

with `ls -F`

```
% ls -F
autoscan*  bitcount.d  env*       foo/            strerror.c xdos@
awk@       bsdlpq*     false*     libXpm.so.4.5*  tee*       xsession*
bash*      dired*      fdformat*  libmalloc.so.1.0* who*
```

With `ls -F`, you can see immediately which files are executable, which are symbolic links, and which are directories.

Another important tool is the `file` program, which has been in existance since v6 in 1975. `file` applies heuristics and a table of "magic numbers" to guess the file type. Sometimes it's wrong, but most of the time it's right. Running `file` on a variety of machines, I found some surprising differences in the output. The following text shows four different systems' `file` output.

SunOS v4.1.3

```
leisner@gnu$ /bin/file *
autoscan:        executable /usr/gnu/bin/perl script
awk:             symbolic link to /usr/gnu/bin/gawk
bash:            sparc demand paged dynamically linked
                 executable not stripped
bitcount.d:      ascii text
bsdlpq:          sparc demand paged dynamically linked
                 set-uid executable not stripped
dired:           commands text
env:             data
false:           executable shell script
fdformat:        data
foo:             directory
libXpm.so.4.5:   data
libmalloc.so.1.0: sparc demand paged shared library executable
                 not stripped
strerror.c:      c-shell commands
tee:             data
who:             data
xdos:            symbolic link to /usr/bin/xdos
xsession:        data
```

IBM AIX v4

```
% file *
autoscan:         shell script
awk:              symbolic link to /usr/gnu/bin/gawk.
bash:             data or International Language text
bitcount.d:       ascii text
bsdlpq:           data or International Language text
dired:            vax bsd demand paged executable - version 25600
env:              vax bsd demand paged executable - version 25600
false:            shell script - sh (default shell)
fdformat:         data or International Language text
foo:              directory
libXpm.so.4.5:    data or International Language text
libmalloc.so.1.0: data or International Language text
strerror.c:       English text
tee:              data or International Language text
who:              data or International Language text
xdos:             symbolic link to /usr/bin/xdos.
xsession:         data or International Language text
```

Solaris v2.3

```
leisner@solar2$ file *
autoscan:         executable /usr/gnu/bin/perl script
awk:              Sun demand paged SPARC executable dynamically
                  linked
bash:             Sun demand paged SPARC executable dynamically
                  linked
bitcount.d:       ascii text
bsdlpq:           Sun demand paged SPARC executable dynamically
                  linked
dired:            commands text
env:              data
false:            executable shell script
fdformat:         ELF 32-bit LSB, dynamically linked, stripped
foo:              directory
libXpm.so.4.5:    ELF 32-bit LSB, dynamically linked
libmalloc.so.1.0: Sun demand paged SPARC executable dynamically
                  linked
strerror.c:       English text
tee:              ELF 32-bit MSB executable SPARC Version 1,
                  dynamically linked, stripped
who:              ELF 32-bit MSB executable SPARC Version 1,
                  dynamically linked, not stripped
xdos:             symbolic link to /usr/bin/xdos
xsession:         ELF 32-bit LSB, dynamically linked, stripped
```

Freeware `file` *v3.15*

(started by Ian Darwin, currently maintained by Mark Moraes and Christos Zoulas)

```
leisner@gnu$ file *
autoscan:           a /usr/gnu/bin/perl script text
awk:                symbolic link to /usr/gnu/bin/gawk
bash:               sparc demand paged dynamically linked
                    executable not stripped
bitcount.d:         ascii text
bsdlpq:             setuid sparc demand paged dynamically linked
                    executable not stripped
dired:              Linux/i386 demand-paged executable (ZMAGIC)
env:                Linux/i386 demand-paged executable (ZMAGIC) not
                    stripped
false:              Bourne Shell script text
fdformat:           ELF 32-bit LSB executable i386 (386 and up)
                    Version 1
foo:                directory
libXpm.so.4.5:      ELF 32-bit LSB dynamic lib i386 (386 and up)
                    Version 1
libmalloc.so.1.0:   sparc demand paged shared library not stripped
strerror.c:         C or REXX program text
tee:                ELF 32-bit MSB executable SPARC Version 1
who:                ELF 32-bit MSB executable SPARC Version 1
xdos:               broken symbolic link to /usr/bin/xdos
xsession:           ELF 32-bit LSB executable i386 (386 and up)
                    Version 1
```

With the freeware file, all the guesses were correct and reasonable (since I generated the files, I can confirm the accuracy of the guesses). The freeware version also knows about lots of binary formats; the other files only know about the native machine format and call all foreign formats "data." A current version of the freeware file is available on `ftp://tesla.ee.cornell.edu/pub/file-X.YY.tar.gz`, where X and YY are version numbers.

Shrink Binaries by `stripping`

After a binary is installed, you may be able to shrink it. If the program was compiled with the `-g` option, the symbol table will be very large (much larger than the program). If the program wasn't linked with the `-s` (`strip`) option, there is still symbol information available in the binary (typically on the order of 10 percent). This gives you enough information to produce a core dump, which produces enough information to let you determine in which routines the core dump occurred (but not enough to run the debugger).

Table 11.1 shows examples of `stripped` programs (on Linux v1.2.8), using the Elf tools based on `gcc` v2.6.3 with options `-g` `-O`. As the table shows, `stripping` will reduce the size of debuggable binaries by 80 percent. If you use `strip`, however, debugging and analyzing core dumps becomes impossible. If you want to debug, you need to be able to regenerate the binary. Also, to analyze core dumps, you need to be able to regenerate the binary exactly.

Use Shared Libraries

Most modern UNIX systems support the concept of shared libraries. Shared libraries are much like shared text, in the sense that one copy needs to be kept in core and multiple programs share this single copy. There is minor overhead on program startup (since dynamic relocations need to be performed), but the binaries are much smaller on disk and the executable image is more compact.

How many programs use `printf`? Would it help if all the programs used the same memory resident copy of `printf`? What if I want to compile `printf` with symbols for debugging? Shared libraries address these issues.

Shared libraries offer significant space savings. Table 11.2 shows some examples, in which all the programs are compiled with `-O` and are `stripped`.

If you program with libraries and if a number of programs use the libraries, it may make sense to learn how to construct shared libraries (once constructed, they're very easy to use). Another major advantage to using shared libraries is that you can install updates transparently (applications that use the shared libraries don't have to be recom-

Table 11.1	*Examples of filesize reduction achieved by `stripping` programs on Linux v1.2.8 using the Elf tools on `gcc v2.6.3` with `-g-O`.*

Program	Size (in bytes)		Reduction Percentage
	`-g-O`	`stripped`	
gawk v2.15.6	418219	134464	67.8%
make v3.74	394459	95328	75.8%
xfig v3.1.3	4952192	565784	88.6%
ctwm v3.3	1217451	224416	81.6%
bash v1.14.5	1505959	304256	79.8%

piled to be updated). This helps enormously in system administration. But be aware that the interface between the programs and the library has to remain the same for this to work. If there are subtle changes, you may be in for a head-scratching experience.

Have One Copy of the Source Code

If you are supporting a number of diverse machines, it's confusing and inefficient to have multiple copies of the source code floating around. Via NFS, you can easily have the source on one host and execute a make on another host with another architecture. Most GNU configure scripts support a -srcdir option, which allows you to specify where the source actually resides. But you must be careful — if you configure within the directory that contains the source, you can't reconfigure elsewhere; in this case, you should do a make distclean. Some configure scripts don't properly support the -srcdir option; if you have problems, try to execute the make in the source directory.

-srcdir makes it much easier to support multiple machines from one source tree. You can even write-protect the sources so they won't change (via a chmod -R -w command). Alternatively, you can export a read-only NFS filesystem, so you won't accidentally write on distributed sources.

Some distributions come in tree form on a CD-ROM. When a distribution is on CD-ROM (for example, O'Reilly sells the BSD v4.4 and X11 trees), you can leave the source there and use a tool like lndir to make links to a hard disk. You can then build off the hard disk, getting read-only files from the CD-ROM via symbolic links.

BSD v4.4 supports a layered filesystem, which takes the place of a link tree. You can structure a filesystem such that you have a read-only filesystem (normally a CD-ROM) under a hard disk. You thus have the appearance of a writable CD-ROM. I've never seen it, but it sounds clever.

| | Size (in bytes) | | Reduction |
Program	Static	Dynamic	Percentage
gawk v2.15.6	513157	134400	73.8%
make v3.74	289057	99857	73.0%
bash v1.4.5	485816	304256	37.4%

Table 11.2 **Examples of filesize reduction achieved through shared library use for programs compiled with -O and stripped.**

File Compression

File compression is another useful tactic for keeping information online and minimizing disk usage. Compression reduces filesize, and uncompressing is much quicker than recovering from tape. GNU gzip has two major advantages over compress: size and time. When I first saw this, I found it hard to believe, since compression is so commonplace. compress(1) has been standard for years and is patented (by Unisys). But gzip

- compresses better,
- uncompresses faster,
- is covered by the GNU license, but also
- compresses more slowly.

The fact that gzip compresses more slowly is not very important, since a file can only be compressed once. Once compressed, it can be uncompressed many times. Table 11.3 shows relative performance for gzip and compress.

gzip has a significant advantage in size over compress. Moreover, gzip gives you a choice of nine different levels of compression, with a tradeoff of time and space. Table 11.4 shows time and space results for selected levels of gzip. Notice that all the levels of compression are significantly better than for compress. The default compression, level 6, takes about half the time of maximum compression.

While the sizes at the different compression levels in the examples in Table 11.4 vary by less than 20 percent, the user time differs by 500 percent. You trade off a large amount of processing time for a small amount of compression. The default level (level 6) is a reasonable tradeoff.

Size isn't the only important factor: the speed of decompression is equally significant. Table 11.5 compares compression and decompression speeds for gzip and compress. gzipped files are extracted faster than compressed files. In addition, gunzip(1) can handle both gzipped and compressed files. gunzip does a quicker job of extracting compressed files than uncompress(1). The examples in Table 11.5 are run to stdout, going into /dev/null.

Table 11.3   Examples of filesize reduction achieved by using compress and gzip.

File	Sizes (in bytes)			Reduction Percentage Comparisons		
	Full Size	compressed Size	gzipped Size	compressed to Original	gzipped to Original	gzipped to compressed
gawk-2.15.6.tar	1925120	754167	520032	39%	27%	68%
gdb-4.14.tar	19179520	7006133	4527543	36%	23%	65%

There is no performance penalty for unzipping maximally gzipped files. In fact, I've seen a small performance penalty for unzipping minimally gzipped files. And there is a signficant advantage in using gunzip to deal with compressed files.

Compressing Trees

Compressing trees is also a good tactic for saving space, and it's very easy to uncompress trees when you need them. The dates are preserved, which is very important. If you're root, the ownership is also preserved. Use the command

```
gzip -r <path>
```

to compress trees and the command

```
gunzip -r <path>
```

to uncompress trees.

Table 11.4   Comparisons of filesize and usertime results for sample levels of gzip.

File	Size (in bytes)			User Time (in seconds)		
	Level 1	**Level 6**	**Level 9**	**Level 1**	**Level 6**	**Level 9**
gawk-2.15.6.tar	626408	520032	517712	6.98	25.89	40.94
gdb-4.14.tar	5595060	4557302	4527543	69	230	400

Table 11.5   Comparisons of compression and decompression times for compress and gzip.

File	Compression Time (in seconds)		Decompression Time (in seconds)		
	compress	gzip	uncompress	gunzip	gunzip compressed **Files**
gawk-2.15.6	7.11	22.66	4.03	1.66	3.36
gdb-4.14.tar	75.5	200.4	43.74	17.1	31.7

As Table 11.6 shows, a compressed tree incurs a small space penalty compared to compressed `tar` files. But the convenience factor is very high, since looking through compressed files goes very quickly if you know where to look (and uncompressing a tree takes about the same amount of work as untarring, or uncompressing, a tree). Also, you can browse compressed text files easily with `zmore` and `zcat`.

Compressing Executables

`gzip` has a companion program called `gzexe`, which creates a compressed runnable script. The script is divided into two parts.

1. A control section, which is a small script that uncompresses the program into `tmp` and runs the program.

2. The data, which is compressed and follows the script.

`gzexe` should be used carefully, because every time the program is run it uncompresses into `tmp`. In addition, multiple copies of the same program running at the same time won't share text (since each executable makes a separate image). An alternative may be to `gzip` the executable and manually `gunzip` it when you need it. `gzexe` works best when applied to `stripped` binaries; applying it to `unstripped` binaries often results in larger files than you'd get by just `stripping` them. Also, note that very short runs (i.e., get version or help) take much longer, since the executable needs to be decompressed first. Table 11.7 shows the effect of `gzexe` on the size of certain executables.

Table 11.6	*Comparisons of filezsize for `zipped` tar files and `gzipped` trees.*	
Program	**Blocks (from du)**	
	zipped tar	gzipped tree
gawk v2.15.6	511Kb	753Kb
gdb v4.14	4.5Mb	6.2Mb

Compressing man *Pages and* info *Files*

info file readers and man page readers that can deal with zipped information can be very useful, since the documentation on your system can easily consume several megabytes. When I started to run Linux, I became aware of the possibility of zipping this information, since the documentation is enormous and it's my personal hard disk. There are copies of man and info that deal with gzipped man pages and info files. However, most vendors' versions of man(1) won't handle this — you'll need to get an enhanced version of man. One site for this is

```
ftp://sunsite.unc.edu/pub/Linux/system/Manualpagers/man-1.4e.tar.gz)
```

In addition to dealing with compressed and gzipped man pages, enhanced man has a number of useful options not found in conventional versions. It was begun by John Eaton (jwe@che.utexas.edu), and has been supported and enhanced during the last five years by a number of maintainers. It's definitely worth taking a look.

texinfo is a hypertext format which is the standard for the gnu project. A texinfo master is created, which can deliver either a printed manual, via TeX, or online reference, via info (generated by a program called makeinfo). The hyptertext format is a big advantage over standard man. If you're interested, ftp to prep.ai.mit.edu and get texinfo-3.6.tar.gz. The info program is included, along with other tools to develop texinfo documents. Be aware that many tools supply both an info document and an outdated man page; if the info document is much newer than the man page, the man page shouldn't be trusted.

The tk tools (tkman and tkinfo) can both work with compressed files. They use John Ousterhout's wish (a windowing shell), generated with the Tk/Tcl toolkits. If you don't already have wish, tkman and tkinfo are excellent examples of applications to start with once you do install it.

Table 11.7   Comparisons of filesize for original and gzexed version.

Program	Initial Size	gzexe Size	Reduction Percentage
gawk v2.15.6	134400	59985	55.3%
bash v1.14.5	304256	138635	54.4%
make v3.74	99857	50875	49.6%

Dealing with Compressed `tar` *Archives*

A standard way of passing information around UNIX systems is through compressed `tar` archives. Once an archive is compressed, it is never necessary to uncompress it. To work on `foo.tar`, just execute

```
zcat foo.tar.gz | tar -xf -
```

or if you are using GNU `tar`

```
tar -xzf foo.tar.gz
```

There is a good reason to work this way. Uncompressed `tar` files can be space hogs. In fact, you may not have space for the uncompressed `tar` file and whatever it contains. This approach leaves the file as a `compress` file and uses pipes to extract the `tar` file. An even more extreme example would be listing the first few entries in a `tar` archive so you're sure of what you have; doing this in pipes is relatively fast, while having to uncompress the whole archive can be very time-consuming.

Convert `compressed` *Files to* `gzipped` *Files*

A tool called `znew` converts `compressed` files to `gzipped` files. If you have a tree of `compressed` files to convert, run this little pipeline

```
find . -name '*.Z' | xargs znew
```

An example of the effect of `znew` is in Table 11.8. Notice that converting text from `compressed` format to `gzip` format results in a space saving of about one-third.

Table 11.8 *Comparisons of distribution size after using* `znew` *to convert* `compressed` *files to* `gzipped` *files.*

Distribution	Files	Megabytes in `du`	
		`compressed`	`gzipped`
`comp.sources.unix` volume 28	450	5.63	3.632
`comp.sources.misc` volume 47	762	3.323	2.091

zip Versus gzip

The most popular DOS compression program is zip. There are a number of other compression programs (such as arc and zoo), which are less common and which I won't discuss here (except to say that there are implementations for all of them on UNIX). zip can use the same type of encoding as gzip on UNIX (along with a number of other algorithms). UNIX tends to break up compression and archival tools and use pipes to connect them (while DOS-based tools bundle them together). The major advantage of a gzipped tar archive is that it applies compression to one large file, which gives a smaller result (compression works better on one large datastream than on lots of small datastreams). zip compresses each file separately.

The Info-ZIP group has put together a freeware set of zip manipulation tools (available at ftp://ftpu.uu.net/pub/archiving/zip) that run on VMS, OS/2, MS-DOS, NT, AmigaDOS, Atari TOS, Macintosh, and almost every known flavor of UNIX. The major advantages of using unzip as a decompressor are portability and consistency of user interfaces across platforms. If you aren't concerned about portability, stick with gzip and tar; if you are, take advantage of zip and unzip.

The prune *Script*

A little script called prune (Listing 11.1) allows you to implement the recommendations I've made throughout this chapter. prune is also safe to use for removing backup files. Be careful when using backups that end in ~; if you have ever done

```
rm * ~
```

instead of

```
rm *~
```

you remember the grief it caused. prune can

- act recursively,
- erase backup files (ending with ~),
- gzip with level 9 compression,
- convert compressed files to gzip files, and
- overwrite existing files.

prune works with the GNU findutils and bash (available at prep.ai.mit.edu:/pub/gnu). I initially wrote a much more complicated bash script to work with prune, and thought I should convert prune to perl. But after I thought about the problem, I decided to really simplify prune by using find and xargs to run the commands. The only shortcoming is that the tool doesn't compare the dates between compressed and uncompressed files with the same basename. In practice, it's effective, since most install scripts leave man pages and info files uncompressed, and specifying the overwrite option allows you to replace a previously compressed file with a newer file.

Listing 11.1   *The* prune *script implements the recommendations made in this chapter.*

```
#! /bin/bash
# script to add in erasing ~ files, convert and zipping
# $Id: prune,v 1.3 1995/07/13 13:28:23 leisner Exp leisner $

# exit immediately on errors??
set -e

function echo
{
    builtin echo -e "$*"
}

function usage {
    echo $progname [ -b9Zvq ] pathname [ pathname ... ]
    echo "\t-b -- leave ~ files along"
    echo "\t-9 -- use best zip level"
    echo "\t-Z -- use znew on .Z files"
    echo "\t-v -- be verbose"
    echo "\t-z -- zip uncompressed files"
    echo "\t-f -- follow symbolic links."
    echo "\t-n -- pretend and list commands which will run"
    echo "\t-o -- overwrite"
    echo "\t-h -- generate this help screen"
    exit 1

}


function xargs {
    command xargs --no-run-if-empty $*
}
```

Listing 11.1 (continued)

```
progname=$0
# this will be echo to show commands
pretend=

# if true, don't erase ~ files
leave_backups=

# pass this to commands, -v or null
verbose=

# null or -9, pass this to gzip/znew
level9=

# if set, convert .Z files to .gz
dot_Z=

# if -follow, pass this to find.
follow=

# if -f, force compression (remove old file)
overwrite=

# if set, gzip uncompressed files.
gzip=

while getopts "bohfz9vZn" c; do
    case $c in
        b)    leave_backups=true ;;
        v)    verbose=-v ;;
        Z)    dot_Z=true ;;
        9)    level9=-9 ;;
        n)    pretend=echo ;;
        f)    follow=-follow;;
        z)    gzip=true;;
        o)    overwrite=-f;;
        \? | h)
              usage
              ;;
    esac
done

shift $[OPTIND-1]

if [ $# -ne 1 ]; then
    usage
fi
```

Holes

Most modern UNIX filesystems can handle sparse files efficiently — that is, files that contain a large amount of empty space. An example of this is a core dump. To get the actual disk space used by a sparse file, use the following command.

```
leisner@gemini$ sleep 1d
^\Quit (core dumped)
bash2 leisner@gemini$ ls -l core
-rw-r--r--  1 leisner  staff    8421808
Mar 18 15:18 core
bash2 leisner@gemini$ du -s core
104     core
```

As you can see, the sizes are radically different. And, if you move the file, you can make it normal size by using a command similar to the following example.

```
leisner@gemini$ sleep 1d
^\\Quit (core dumped)
leisner@gemini$ ls -l core
-rw-r--r--  1 leisner s dsp  8421808
Mar 18 15:23 core
leisner@gemini$ du -s core
104     core
leisner@gemini$ gzip core
leisner@gemini$ ls -l core.gz
-rw-r--r--  1 leisner  sdsp   15797
Mar 18 15:23 core.gz
leisner@gemini$ gunzip core
leisner@gemini$ du -s core
8240    core
```

Listing 11.1 (continued)

```
if [ $dot_Z ]; then
    find $* -name '*.Z' -type f $follow | xargs $pretend znew $overwrite
$level9 $verbose
fi


if [ ! $leave_backups ]; then
    find . -name '*~' -type f $follow | xargs $pretend rm $verbose
fi

# ignore any ~ files, only do files
if [ $gzip ]; then
    find . -name '*[!.gz]' -name '*[!~]' -type f $follow | xargs $pretend gzip
$level9 $overwrite $verbose
fi
```

In this example, taking the holes out of a core dump file increases the size by more than two orders of magnitude. Eight-megabyte files can quickly use up your disk space. Once the holes have been removed from a file, I don't know of a way to put them back in. I wrote a little program, `holify.c` (Listing 11.2), that can rectify this problem.

```
leisner@gnu$ sleep 1d
^\Quit (core dumped)
leisner@gnu$ du -s core
104     core
leisner@gnu$ gzip -c core >core.sleep.gz
leisner@gnu$ zcat core.sleep.gz | holify >core2
Wrote 49152 real bytes,  79725107 virtual bytes
leisner@gnu$ du -s core2 core
80      core2
104     core
leisner@gnu$ cmp core core2
leisner@gnu$
```

Listing 11.2 `holify.c` *rectifies the problem of dealing with holes.*

```
/*
 * Copyright (C) 1995
 * Marty Leisner    leisner@sdsp.mc.xerox.com.
 *
 * This program is free software; you can redistribute it and/or modify it
 * under the terms of the GNU General Public License as published by the
 * Free Software Foundation; either version 2, or (at your option) any
 * later version.
 *
 * This program is distributed in the hope that it will be useful,
 * but WITHOUT ANY WARRANTY; without even the implied warranty of
 * MERCHANTABILITY or FITNESS FOR A PARTICULAR PURPOSE. See the
 * GNU General Public License for more details.
 *
 * You should have received a copy of the GNU General Public License
 * along with this program; if not, write to the Free Software
 * Foundation, 675 Mass Ave, Cambridge, MA 02139, USA.
 */
```

Conclusion

Erasing files is a very drastic way of dealing with the disk space shortages. Dynamic linking has size advantages over static linking. Further, debugging symbols show approximately an order of magnitude difference (the size of the debugging information far outweighs the size of the program). Compression tools can also help greatly, and it takes much less time to compress and uncompress files than to find an old copy on a backup tape. The benchmarks presented here show a number of advantages of gzip over compress; if you're still using compress, you should look into gzip. The X11 font architecture uses compressed font files; using gzipped font files (which involves a change in the decompression code) would both increase performance and save space. All of the above can help you keep information available while paying a minimal storage price.

Listing 11.2 (continued)

```
#include <unistd.h>
#include <errno.h>
#include <stdio.h>
#include <assert.h>

static const char *id = "$Id: holify.c,v 1.1 1995/01/24 02:47:20 leisner Exp $";
static char *progname;

static void usage(void)
{
    exit(1);
}

/* write the last byte if its not written...
 * this makes some systems work better
 */
static void copy_file(const int input, const int output)
{
    int total_written = 0;
    int total_read = 0;
    int virtual_written;
    int holes = 0;
    /* indicates the last buffer was written */
    int did_write = 0;
```

Listing 11.2 *(continued)*

```
while(1) {
    int bytes_read;
    int bytes_written;
    char buffer[4096 + 1];
    char *cp;

    bytes_read = read(input, &buffer, sizeof(buffer) - 1);
    if(bytes_read == 0)
        break;
    if(bytes_read == -1) {
        if(errno == EINTR)
            continue;
        fprintf(stderr, "Fatal error, %s\n", strerror(errno));
        exit(1);
    }

    total_read += bytes_read;
    buffer[bytes_read] = 1;     /* sentinnel */

    for(cp = buffer; !*cp; cp++)
        ;

    if(cp == &buffer[bytes_read]) {
        /* have hole */
        int result;

        result = lseek(output, bytes_read, SEEK_CUR);
        did_write = 0;
        assert(result != -1);
        holes++;
    } else {
        bytes_written = write(output, buffer, bytes_read);
        assert(bytes_written == bytes_read);
        did_write = 1;
        total_written += bytes_written;
    }
    virtual_written += bytes_read;

}

fprintf(stderr, "Wrote %d real bytes, %d virtual bytes\n", total_written,
        virtual_written);
```

Listing 11.2 (continued)

```
#ifndef NO_LAST_WRITE
    if(!did_write) {
        const char zero = 0;

        lseek(output, -1, SEEK_CUR);    /* back up */
        write(output, &zero, 1);    /* write a zero byte */
    }
#endif
}

main(int argc, char **argv)
{
    int i;

    progname = argv[0];

    if(argc == 1) {
        /* input may be a pipe, stdout must be a file */
        if(isatty(1)) {
            fprintf(stderr, "Need to write to a file");
            usage();
        }
    }

    if(argc == 1)
        copy_file(0, 1);
    else {
        fprintf(stderr, "can't do this yet\n");
        usage();
        for(i = 1; i < argc; i++) {
        }
    }
}
```

Chapter 12

Using *fsck* to Check ufs File Systems

Tom Clark

There are several common types of UNIX file systems [1, 2], but this chapter covers only the ufs file system. The concepts presented are applicable to all UNIX file systems checked with the fsck program.

File systems are generally logically independent of the required underlying physical storage devices, although their operation is directly affected by these storage devices. (For example, errors affecting the operation of the devices commonly affect the file system structure or the files maintained by the file system.) However, not all file system errors can be related to an error reported by the underlying storage device. (Some other storage device, or source of error, may be the root cause.)

For simplicity, this chapter is limited to storage devices attached to the host computer via the SCSI (Small Computer System Interface) bus. These devices support an addressable linear array of identical logical blocks, each block containing 512 bytes of data. (Other common block sizes are 1024 and 2048). Focusing on SCSI systems dictates to some extent problem determination procedures and error recovery and restart procedures, since these procedures are designed to support the selected storage devices. The chapter also includes a script for checking multiple file systems.

The SCSI Disk Error Model

A very high percentage of SCSI disk errors occur when data is retrieved from the medium. Errors that occur when storing data are usually not detected until the data is retrieved, although the device can immediately signal a write error if it is unable to locate the proper block on a write operation.

Even though the majority of accesses to a disk are data retrieval operations, complete media testing entails both storage and retrieval operations. The device that supports defect management enables linking around defective blocks, or *bad* blocks. Typically, defect management is performed either in response to the execution of a disk maintenance command or at the direction of a disk device driver in response to read errors reported by the device. The defect management strategy used will differ for hard read errors and soft read errors.

A *hard error* exists when the device signals that it is unable to recover data (e.g., too many errors) or when successive unsuccessful attempts to correctly retrieve data (errors reported along with the data) are halted by the device driver.

The disk driver may have previously requested that the device automatically reassign a bad block during an initialization phase. If not, it may issue a separate command to the device to reassign the known bad block. It may also choose to do nothing, leaving a hole in the linear array and presenting an opportunity for another utility (e.g., some format commands) to attempt a patch of the linear array.

A *soft error* exists when successive unsuccessful attempts to retrieve data are followed by a single successful data retrieval before the device driver halts the data retrieval operations. Excessive soft errors are indicative of future problems (i.e., soft errors can evolve into hard errors) and should be corrected during preventive maintenance.

The reassignment of a data block may result in data loss even though the device performed without additional errors. This usually happens when the device is unable to correctly recover data from the bad block and transfer it to the patch block.

A device driver typically stores whatever data has been retrieved from a bad block and writes it to the patch block after completion of the reassignment. When no data is retrieved, a block of 0s is written to the patch block. Little else can be done to recover data directly; instead, restore files from recent backups.

You can use device maintenance commands such as format to perform surface analysis to detect bad blocks. You can then reassign bad blocks. You should do this analysis and maintenance periodically since the recording media degrades with time.

The ufs File System

A ufs file system can be represented simply as a large data structure composed of sequences of one or more smaller data structures (referred to as a *cylinder group*), each with the following components [1].

- Offset
- Super-block
- Cylinder Group Map
- Inodes
- Storage Blocks

The super-block contains information on the size and status of the file system, the label (obtained from block 0 of a SCSI disk), and the cylinder group. Multiple super-blocks are created and used to repair ones that are bad.

Inodes contain all the information about a file except its name (which is kept in a directory). Typically, one inode is created for every 2048 bytes of available storage. (This can be altered when the file system is built; refer to the mkfs user command). An inode contains information on the

- file type (regular, directory, block, character, symbolic link, or FIFO/pipe),
- file permissions,
- number of hard links,
- user-id and group-id,
- number of bytes,
- first 12 disk block addresses,
- three indirect pointers to additional disk block addresses, and
- file time-related data.

The majority of blocks in a cylinder group (1 to 32 cylinders per group) are allocated to storage blocks.

The fsck *Program*

fsck sequences through the following check phases.

- Check Blocks and Sizes (file system inode list)
- Check Pathnames (directory entries)
- Check Connectivity (one directory for each inode and multiple links)
- Check Reference Counts and Cylinder Groups (link count and alterations made previously)
- Check the Free List (blocks are allocated to an inode or the free block list)

(Refer to Thomas and Farrow [5] for a more detailed description of the check sequence. The information presented here has been condensed from the references listed at the end of the chapter.)

An underlying presumption regarding the use of fsck is that files with corrupted inodes should be replaced from backup copies and that the user is able to keep track of such files. The following key factors also affect the use of fsck.

- Mounted (or active) file systems may change while being examined by fsck.
- Any change that occurs in a file system while running fsck can produce inconsistencies.
- Inconsistencies may be minor enough to result in an automatic repair action by fsck.
- Major inconsistencies require user intervention.
- False inconsistencies are treated as though they were actual inconsistencies.

To avoid related problems, fsck does not work on mounted file systems, except the root (/) file system. fsck can be run on root while in single-user mode.

However, there are two interfaces to a block storage device (block and character, or raw), and it is possible to run fsck on a mounted file system through the raw interface. Doing so makes the check vulnerable to the problems that could arise if fsck were run on a mounted file system. All sources strongly recommend that fsck be run on unmounted file systems, or on the root file system when in single-user mode.

fsck is used to quickly check the super-blocks and the inodes for file system inconsistencies during

- the install phase,
- the bring-up phase,
- the addition of a new disk to the system,
- the problem analysis associated with a file system supported by a specific physical disk,
- preventive and predictive maintenance procedures, and
- repair procedures prior to returning a disk device to normal service.

The Install Phase

In the install phase, the operating system is loaded onto the system disk and configured for normal operation. A successful install phase yields a fully operational, configured operating system. It requires the identification of at least one operable disk (the system disk), on which the necessary number of supported, operable file systems (determined using `fsck`) can be built. This in turn requires that the host computer and hardware supporting the system disk be operable. This can often be checked at a lower level of functionality than the install phase (e.g., a PROM monitor supports communication with attached devices).

At all points in the install phase, system disk-related problems can result in failures and aborts that require user analysis to determine proper responses. Since install processes rarely attempt a detailed verification of the underlying hardware, the user must often rely on past history to select an appropriate error recovery procedure (i.e., the install is presumed to be performed only on a fully operational system).

A successful install process does not guarantee that the system disk is completely operational. The install process transfers files to the system disk and prepares it for normal operation, a procedure which requires many storage operations that are not followed by the retrieval operations that would normally detect disk-related errors. Errors encountered after a successful install may actually have originated at the time of the install.

Since `fsck` may be the only diagnostic tool used by the install process to check system disk operability, errors reported in an install should result in a more detailed test of the host computer and attached storage devices. You should not, under such circumstances, attempt to continue the install process.

A full destructive surface analysis of the media before installing an operating system on a SCSI disk or after subsequent disk-related errors have been encountered will detect most latent media-related errors that could cause errors in the install phase and in the future. These errors will also require that the user reinstall the operating system.

The following are useful guidelines for the install phase.

- If an error is reported by the system disk or any other hardware component, analyze the problem to see if a service call is necessary. (e.g., Can the error be corrected via simple user action?)

- If the install has been corrupted by the reporting of an error, try restarting the install.

- If `fsck` has reported errors, the likely suspect is the underlying storage device. The new file system, which is allegedly operable, has just been built on the storage device, and data loss or corruption by the file system is unlikely because little time has elapsed in which such errors could occur.

- If the install has not completed or initial checks have not performed successfully, take the system down to single-user mode and use `fsck` as a diagnostic probe.

- Consider any errors that occur during an install to be indicative of an abnormal condition.

The Bring-up Phase

Presuming the successful completion of an install, the system will at some time be booted and a bring-up phase is initiated. During this phase the function of fsck is again a very quick check of file system inconsistencies. If minor problems are found, fsck may be able to correct them and continue. If not, the bring-up process may require that fsck be run independently (i.e., some repair actions will be necessary).

fsck is important here because the system may have been shut down incorrectly, may have encountered a "panic" condition, or may have shut down due to errors or equipment modifications. Earlier statements regarding fsck apply here as well, but there is one notable additional factor — recorded past history in the system log.

Problems reported by fsck during a bring-up phase should prompt the user to scan the system log for device-related errors. Both soft and hard errors should be analyzed, since soft errors can evolve into hard errors.

Where difficult errors are present, especially those affecting the system disk, I suggest that you boot an operating system image over the net, boot an operating system image from a local CDROM device, or integrate into the host computer a known good disk containing an operating system. You can then use the good operating system to perform further checking and data recovery.

The Problem Analysis

fsck is not a particularly useful tool for problem determination. Errors reported by fsck require a good deal of interpretation based on intimate knowledge of the file system and the underlying storage device. Such errors should always be analyzed in conjunction with the system log, past history, experience, and a good backup and restore facility. The proper next step is rarely obvious from the query and responses provided by fsck.

The Maintenance Procedures

Preventive and predictive maintenance procedures should use fsck to probe for file system inconsistencies. Such procedures should first perform full media non-destructive testing to ensure that no blocks are accessible that could cause a future hard or soft error. Destructive media testing should be undertaken only after full data recovery has been completed.

It is possible for maintenance procedures themselves to encounter errors (even system panic conditions) that have no relation to a recorded storage device error (e.g., data corruption has occurred and the maintenance procedure is processing garbage). This should not dissuade you from developing and performing maintenance procedures, but should help you to see the importance of executing them in sufficiently secure environments (e.g., full backups have been performed).

The Repairs Procedures

fsck has a repair feature that can correct minor problems but can also, if used inappropriately, do major damage to a file system. fsck is presumed to be an expert on the file system and to have the proper repair action selected before requesting user permission to proceed. The -y option allows fsck to assume "yes" as a response to all queries about repair actions (i.e., fsck will automatically repair any system-related errors it encounters without requesting user permission).

The -y option should not be used on a file system that contains important user data because in some cases fsck's suggested repair is not appropriate. Most of these cases involve removing a file or clearing an inode. Authorizing the repairs without investigating (using the -y option) can result in data loss. The following cases have been identified empirically.

Case 1

SORRY: NO lost+found DIRECTORY or NO SPACE in lost+found DIRECTORY

Clearly, a problem with the lost+found directory requires immediate attention. You should terminate fsck until the problem is resolved.

If no lost+found directory exists, create one and then rerun fsck. If no space is left in the directory due to the number of files present, find out why so many files were placed in this directory. If no space is left in the directory due to the size of files present, determine whether the large files are valid and are not file fragments. An example would be a copy operation that could not complete successfully, with the result that only a portion of a file remains in the target directory.

Case 2

DUP TABLE OVERFLOW

This message occurs when the DUP table, which stores a list of inodes with duplicate blocks, runs out of space. Such table overflow should put the user on notice that unusual conditions have occurred and the potential for data loss is high. The recommended action is to "write down the inode numbers of inodes with duplicate blocks found after this point, and don't REMOVE any of the filenames connected to the inodes or CLEAR these inodes." [5].

An alternate suggestion, given that the overflow represents an abnormal condition, is to stop at this point and attempt to recover whatever files are accessible before proceeding. The recovery action could simply be a raw disk copy (using the dd user command).

Case 3

```
Read, Write or Seek Errors
```

These messages indicate that a hard error has occurred, and fsck is asking if it should continue in the presence of such errors. You should continue only if you are very familiar with the attached physical devices and with what fsck is attempting. A possible alternative is to perform a non-destructive surface analysis of the attached storage device.

The surface analysis should reassign a bad block if it encounters a hard error (refer to the "SCSI Disk Error Model" section). Since data may be lost in the procedure, you should record all reassigned blocks, rerun fsck, and mark as suspect all files affected by the reassignment. Upon completion, you should consider restoring files from recent backups.

Case 4

```
PARTIALLY ALLOCATED INODE I=14
CLEAR?
```

Legal inode types are given in reference [5]. A partially allocated inode is one that has a type of 0, but some information appears in the mode word. This message often indicates a block containing garbage, if this occurs frequently, the file system is likely to have widespread damage, including corrupted files.

A good practice is to record the inode numbers so that the filenames linked to the inodes can be found if necessary in phase 2. Data recovery after completion and close scrutiny of the file system during preventive and predictive maintenance procedures are recommended. If actual data corruption is found, the storage device should be re-evaluated and the file system rebuilt before returning the storage device to service.

Case 5

```
LINK COUNT TABLE OVERFLOW,
CONTINUE?
```

This message indicates that there is no more room to store inodes that have a zero link count and will recur for all subsequent inodes with zero link counts. If only one error is reported, you can allow fsck to continue; if multiple errors are reported, you should terminate fsck. Upon completion or termination, you should perform a file recovery procedure.

Case 6

```
EXCESSIVE BAD BLOCKS I=13
CONTINUE?
```

Ten bad blocks have been detected while checking this inode's blocks. Something is seriously wrong, and fsck should be terminated until the problem is resolved.

Initialization Errors

Initialization errors are worth mentioning because they can be triggered by recent problems with devices that have been performing normally over some period of time (e.g., storage devices can fail suddenly). When fsck is initiated, perhaps in response to an error message, the following error can be quite surprising.

```
Cannot stat <device name>
```

fsck cannot obtain information on the file system supported by <device name>. It is possible that the file system does not exist, cannot be opened due to permissions, or has been removed from the device tree by the device driver (i.e., the device no longer responds to commands). The appropriate response is to immediately initiate a problem determination procedure on the underlying storage device.

Repair Summary

Minor problems automatically detected and corrected by fsck rarely result in data loss or corruption. However, the potential for data loss or corruption increases up to a certainty if the user continues running fsck in the presence of clearly dangerous major errors. By placing complete faith in the ability of fsck to detect and correct errors (i.e., using the -y option), you lose control over the repair process and may remain unaware of the presence of major problems that require immediate attention.

The mfsck *Script*

When a system administrator has to check multiple file systems simultaneously, a tool for performing the checks and highlighting the problems becomes handy. The mfsck script (see the companion code disk) is a Bourne shell script that allows you to specify a large number of disks and partitions to check simultaneously. You should avoid overloading the OS by initiating too many processes when running mfsck.

`mfsck` supports a very simple interface, which is displayed if no arguments are provided.

```
mfsck <task file>
```

where

```
<task file>
```

is the name of a file containing the disks and the file systems to check.
    The syntax of the `<task file>` is

```
# comment line
<logical device> <partition> ... <partition>
```

as in

```
#
c0t5d0 0 1 6
#
```

Figure 12.1   *Sample output generated by executing `mfsck` with a single-entry `<task file>` that points to a nonexistent disk.*

```
# mfsck task.file
The Current Process ID = 949
File name extensions will contain this as identification
>Creating Log File: /usr2/local2/adm/publish/sysadm/fsck/fsck.log.949.1
Checking: /dev/rdsk/c8t0d0s3 exists
prtvtoc: /dev/rdsk/c8t0d0s3: No such file or directory
ERROR>/dev/rdsk/c8t0d0s3 is missing
> Done reading from Task File: task.file
> > > Waiting For ALL Processes to Complete < < <
All recorded background processes have completed
Scanning for partitions that were not found; unable to check
Partitions NOT found if entries follow:

Found Startup Problems With:
   /dev/rdsk/c8t0d0s3 is missing ;

>Do You Want to Remove all Log Files
>This will delete all files with log in the file name
>Proceed (Y/N) ?
y
>Removing Log Files
>Removing all Work-In-Progress Files
>Removing all Check Files
>Removing the Control File: fsck.cntl.949#
```

The following <task file> contains a single entry and points to a nonexistent disk.

```
# cat task.file
c8t0d0 3
#
```

Executing mfsck with this <task file> yields the output shown in Figure 12.1.
A single-entry <task file> that points to a valid disk would be formatted as follows.

```
# cat task.file
c1t2d0
#
```

The output from a single-entry <taskfile> is shown in Figure 12.2.

Figure 12.2   Sample output generated by executing
                 mfsck *with a simple-entry* <task file>
                 that points to a valid disk.

```
# mfsck task.file
The Current Process ID = 22769
File name extensions will contain this as identification
>Creating Log File: /usr/test/fsck/fsck.log.22769.1
Checking: /dev/rdsk/c1t2d0s7 exists
Checking: /dev/rdsk/c1t2d0s7 has mounted partitions
Executing Command:
  fsck /dev/rdsk/c1t2d0s7 >> /usr/test/fsck/fsck.log.22769.1 &
> Background Process ID 22844 Started
  Device: /dev/rdsk/c1t2d0 has started
> Done reading from Task File: task.file
> > > Waiting For ALL Processes to Complete < < <
22844 still active on c1t2d0
> > > Checking for Active Processes < < <
All recorded background processes have completed
Scanning for partitions that were not found; unable to check
Partitions NOT found if entries follow:

>Do You Want to Remove all Log Files
>This will delete all files with log in the file name
>Proceed (Y/N) ?
y
>Removing Log Files
>Removing all Work-In-Progress Files
>Removing all Check Files
>Removing the Control File: fsck.cntl.22769
#
```

mfsck checks for completion of the fsck operations, which are performed in the background. The script was designed to be broken up into smaller files for further simplification. The present form is intended to be simple and straightforward, facilitating user modifications.

Multiple <task file> specifications can be built in anticipation of future requirements. Log files generated by the script can be removed or saved at the user's option. When errors are encountered, the log files should be scanned to determine where the errors occurred.

Conclusion

fsck requires a high level of skill and experience to use effectively. fsck can be considered, in most cases, as an expert in selecting the best next step in a repair process. However, it has a very limited, and in some cases confusing, user interface. Moreover, it requires in some cases that the user record data to be used at a later stage.

fsck also has a high potential for data loss and corruption, since checking is limited to the file system. It can be used effectively as an indicator of possible current damage, but provides no assistance in the development of appropriate error recovery procedures.

Even given its limitations, fsck remains a very useful tool in the system administrator's toolbox when combined with a detailed understanding of the underlying storage devices and the file system.

References

1. "UNIX Software Operation." *UNIX System V Release 4 System Administrator's Guide*. Englewood Cliffs, N.J.: Prentice-Hall, 1990.

2. Bach, Maurice J. *The Design of the UNIX Operating System*. Englewood Cliffs, N.J.: Prentice-Hall, 1986.

3. Nemeth, Evi, Garth Snyder, and Scott Seebass. *UNIX System Administration Handbook*. Englewood Cliffs, N.J.: Prentice-Hall, 1989.

4. Fiedler, David, and Bruce H. Hunter. *UNIX System Administration*. Indianapolis, IN: Hayden Books, 1987.

5. Thomas, Rebecca, and Rik Farrow. *UNIX Administration Guide for System V*. Englewood Cliffs, N.J.: Prentice-Hall, 1989.

## Chapter 13

A Method for Verifying
System Integrity

Packey Velleca

In a development environment, several groups of people — Development, Integration, Test, and Training — may use similar platforms configured differently over the life of a product. These groups often find they need an easy way to verify a system's configuration or to discern one system from another.

System verification determines whether a machine's hardware and software are in a predefined configuration (baseline) or how far from baseline the configuration has moved. Automated configuration checks should be made

- to ensure that a group of users has consistent system resources available across a set of systems,
- to verify that a user's working environment is standard, and
- to monitor and identify system parameters that affect performance.

The verify script (see the companion code disk) is an automated, reliable tool for verifying a system configuration that is easy to use and maintain.

At a site with many different systems, an administrator is often unable to check a system configuration as soon as a user requests the check. So it is convenient to enable users to differentiate between system configurations. With verify, any user can verify a system configuration without having to learn new commands, new techniques, or obscure system calls. Placing verify in their path gives users a fast, reliable method of determining system configuration on their own.

This chapter addresses each of the reasons for automated configuration checks listed previously and contains a technical description of the verify script.

Consistent System Resources

Changes to a system configuration may not immediately ripple through all machines; this can confuse some users about the correct configuration. For example, suppose Development initially defines 60 shared memory segments as adequate for a system. Integration discovers this is not enough, so they change the kernel to support 120 shared memory segments. Now two different configurations exist for the same system.

If Development is not aware of the change, they may waste time chasing down the wrong problem. A user may suspect the kernel has not been updated, but few reliable methods exist to verify this. The kernel configuration file can be manually checked, but since users can find or make kernels on any system and copy them over, there is no guarantee that the local configuration file belongs to that kernel. Checksumming the kernel may show the two kernels as different, but it cannot tell how they differ. Changing the hostname may deliver a new checksum, but a new checksum doesn't identify a new hostname as the cause. In this case, the best way to differentiate kernels is to create a tool that reads the kernel variable directly, and incorporate it into this script. Any user can run the script to easily verify a system.

Also consider that if a set of machines is configured the same during development and integration, your organization will spend less time troubleshooting platform interface and dependency problems during the integration and delivery phases of a product. verify can help provide that consistency.

Standard Working Environment

If you use a standard user environment, you must have a way to ensure that important settings have not been changed. For example, if you require certain aliases, masks, or paths, you can use verify to easily and consistently verify that users have not modified their environment in any detrimental way.

Tuning Tool

Monitoring system parameters with `verify` is easy. For every parameter you suspect is too low or too high, place a check in the script. For example, if the kernel has been configured to support 100 processes, you can compare the current number of processes to the maximum value built into the kernel and better estimate its optimum value.

Other Methods of Verification

Generally, all verification methods have one aspect in common: they compare a current configuration to a baseline configuration. One verification method does this by calculating checksums on a set of files and comparing those sums to the baseline sums. This method can work fine, though slowly, for a small set of binary executables, such as kernels. This method is unacceptable for databases, configuration files, and network routing tables because the contents of these files are imprecise. For instance, these files often have spaces and tabs used interchangeably. You may be concerned not with the contents of an object but with its attributes, such as file permissions and file ownership.

   Another verification method has an administrator manually check each machine. This method is extremely labor intensive, prone to error, and boring. The task becomes unmanageable when a site has a moderate number of systems.

The `verify` Script

The `verify` script combines the best features of both verification methods in one automated script. It checksums the contents of a small number of files. It performs content checks on configuration files. `verify` also compares baseline values against dynamic configuration items, such as routing information, and compares file attributes. `verify` is easy to maintain and distribute. Used from a central file server, it allows one administrator to quickly, reliably, and automatically determine the configuration of a set of systems.

Technical Description

verify is invoked by a privileged user from a shell. It takes one command line argument, -v (verbose), that writes the status of all configuration items, whether in baseline or not, to standard output. Without -v, the script defaults to output of only configuration items that are out of baseline.

The most often used operation in the script is described by the following pseudo code.

```
Get the current state of a configuration item from the system.
Compare the current state to the baseline state and determine which
items are:
    within the baseline,
    extraneous to the baseline, and
    missing from the baseline.
```

This operation is used for file system mounts, partitions, network routes, and other items where resources can be added, deleted, or changed.

Another often used operation is described by the following pseudocode.

```
Check the existence of a configuration item.
```

This step verifies file existence, file permission, file checksums, application program existence, and product licenses.

verify contains all the baseline configuration data. There are no external configuration data files because in practice each system's baseline is unique enough to warrant a unique script. And as most sites run more than one system, it is much easier to maintain a single file rather than a command file and multiple data files for each system. If this is not the case at your site, then by all means set up a command file that uses configuration items in separate data files.

Figure 13.1 is a sample run of verify invoked with the -v option. Note that baseline configuration items are tagged with the prefix Baseline. Nonbaseline items are tagged ???????>. Without the -v option, only the nonbaseline items are written.

The power of this method is in its flexibility. Any verification that can be done on a system can be written into that system's script and executed many times faster and much more reliably than by hand. You can also use verify in a function that allows unattended verification of all machines in a set, with nonbaseline items automatically written to a file and mailed to interested parties.

It is also possible, though not described here, to automate insertion of baseline parameters into verify. Once a baseline is defined, another script could extract pertinent data from the baseline system and write it into verify. You might write such a script if the baseline changes often and the number of configuration items is moderate to large.

Porting `verify` to Other Operating Systems

`verify` as presented here was written for DEC Ultrix (BSD), but is easy to port to other operating systems. Each configuration item within the script has a precise data format and example. Porting is a matter of massaging data into that format using common UNIX tools like `awk(1)`, `sed(1)`, or `cut(1)`. We successfully ported the script to an SVID system in only two days, including test time.

    `verify`, as presented, checks about 100 configuration items. It runs in about 30 seconds of real time per machine. When you consider that manually performing the same number of checks with the same accuracy can take as long as 20–30 minutes per machine, preparing a verification script is well worth the effort.

Figure 13.1   A sample run of `verify` *-v.*

```
Wed Jun 29 14:12:03 EDT 1994
Configuration verification for:       riscO1
Checked against system baseline load: DEVELOPMENT LOAD CONFIGURATION A.

--- Hardware Configuration ---
Baseline amount of RAM (32)MB installed.
Baseline device (RZ56) at SCSI (0).
???????> Can't find baseline device (RX23) at SCSI (3).
Baseline device (TZK10) at SCSI (5).
???????> Device (RZxx) at SCSI (2) not in baseline.
???????> (ln1) I/F HW not installed.

--- Disk Configuration ---
???????> Partition 'a' size (33210), should be (32768).
Baseline partition 'a' mounted.
Baseline partition 'b' size (380700).
Baseline configured swap (1903)00K.
???????> Partition 'f' size (3207), should be (885706).
???????> Partition 'f' is not mounted.
???????> Mounted partition 'd' not in baseline.
???????> (9) additional NFS mounted directories.
???????> (2) additional local mounted directories, should be (0).
```

Figure 13.1 (continued)

```
--- Kernel Configuration ---
???????> (ln1) I/F SW not in kernel.
Baseline system table 'files' size (379).
Baseline system table 'gnodes' size (284).
Baseline system table 'processes' size (160).
Baseline kernel variable 'SEMMAP' size (30).
Baseline kernel variable 'SEMMNI' size (30).
Baseline kernel variable 'SEMMNS' size (180).
Baseline kernel variable 'SEMMNU' size (60).
Baseline kernel variable 'SMMNI' size (100).
Baseline kernel variable 'SMSEG' size (12).
Baseline kernel variable 'MSGMAP' size (300).
Baseline kernel variable 'MSGMNI' size (50).
Baseline kernel variable 'MSGTQL' size (200).
Baseline kernel variable 'MSGTQL' size (200).
Baseline kernel variable 'LOTSFREE' size (1953).
Baseline kernel variable 'DESFREE' size (472).
Baseline kernel variable 'MINFREE' size (244).

--- Network Routes ---
???????> Cant find baseline route [127.158 <- risc01] on (ln0).
???????> Cant find baseline route [127.157 <- risc01P] on (ln1).
???????> Route [ 163.206.27.56 <- alpha01] on (ln0) not in baseline.
???????> Route [130.240 <- alpha01] on (ln0) not in baseline.

--- Significant Running Processes ---
???????> non-baseline 'ypbind' is running.
???????> non-baseline 'sendmail' is running.
Baseline 'timed' is not running.
Baseline 'routed' is not running.
Baseline 'syslog' is running.
Baseline 'cron' is running.

Baseline 'lpd' is running.
Baseline 'elcsd' is running.
Baseline 'inetd' is running.
Baseline 'snmpd' is running.
```

Figure 13.1 (continued)

```
--- Applications Installation and Licensing ---
Baseline 'VADS' not installed.
Baseline 'SL-GMS' version (4.03).
???????> 'SL-GMS' key (75593b1) is not the baseline (123456)."

???????> 'RS/1' not Installed
???????> 'ULTRIX' license (0 user), should be (8 user).
???????> 'Emulex' not installed.

--- File Status ---
Baseline '/vmunix' file permission (755).
Baseline '/dev/mem' file permission (644).
Baseline '/dev/kmem' file permission (644).
???????> '/dev/rrz0c' file permissions should be (644).
Baseline '/dev/tty00' file permission (666).
Baseline '/usr/users' exists.
Baseline '/luser' exists.
Baseline '/bin/ksh' exists.
???????> '/etc/ttys.new' does not exist.
???????> '/usr/sys/MIPS' not stripped.
???????> '/usr/lib/DPS' not stripped.

--- User Info ---
???????> User 'test1' not found in /etc/passwd.
???????> Group 'test1' not found in /etc/group.
???????> Root umask (022), should be (002).
???????> /etc/rc.local lacks 2 active Ethernet I/Fs.

--- X11 Info ---
???????> Number of 'space*' fonts (0), should be (8).
Baseline number of '8x13' fonts (1).

--- ULTRIX Subset Configuration ---
???????> Missing subsets: SPREXE300 SPRMAN300 UWSPAT40263S421
???????> Extra subsets: UDTACCT420 UDTACCT425 UDTMH420 UDTUUCP420

--- File Checksums ---
???????> '/vmunix' checksum not matched.
???????> '/usr/bin/Xws' checksum not matched.

done.
```

## Chapter 14

Using sys1og

John Woodgate

With the merging of USL UNIX and BSD UNIX in System V Release 4, system administrators had a wide array of new commands and functions to learn. One such facility from the BSD world is sys1og, which comprises a daemon, a set of library calls, and a user command. In short, sys1og acts as a log file and records system messages. In its default configuration, sys1og provides a basic level of functionality; properly set up, it can provide virtually anything from a simple recording system to a centralised record system for distributed systems.

Although sys1og originated with BSD UNIX, sys1og is now included in SVR4 implementations. Though some manufacturers have added extra facilities, I will focus on the functions that should be common to most implementations. If you have a pre-SVR4 version of UNIX, some partial implementations available via the Internet can provide some or all of the functionality.

/usr/etc/syslogd

The deamon is the heart of the syslog facility. The daemon reads and forwards system messages to the appropriate log file, user, and remote system, depending on the message's priority and point of origin within the system. A configuration file, /etc/syslog.conf, controls the deamon, syslogd. The configuration file is read at start-up time and again whenever the daemon receives a HUP (-1) signal. In the latter case, the deamon closes all the files and devices it currently has open, rereads the configuration file, and then opens only the files and devices that are listed in the configuration file. syslogd exits when it receives a TERM signal.

Priority Facilities and Levels

syslog priorities are encoded as a facility and a level. The *facility* describes the part of the system generating the message. The *level* describes the urgency of the message and controls which users will be notified.

The facility parameter encodes a default facility to be assigned to all messages that do not have an explicit facility already encoded.

user   Messages generated by user processes. This is the default priority facility, which would be assigned to any messages not listed in this text.

kern   Messages generated by the kernel. These cannot be generated by any user process.

mail   Messages generated by the mail system.

daemon   Messages generated by system daemons, such as ftpd, routed, etc.

auth   Messages generated by the authorization system: login, su, getty, etc.

lpr   Messages generated by the line printer spooling system: lpr, lpc, lpd, etc.

news   Reserved for messages generated by the USENET network news system. This priority facility is not often implemented.

uucp   Reserved for messages generated by the UUCP system, which currently does not use the syslog mechanism.

cron   Messages generated by the cron and at facilities: crontab, at, cron, etc.

local0-7   Reserved for locally generated messages. You can assign these to your own applications.

The daemon has the ability to place a mark or time stamp into the log every interval minutes (by default, every 20 minutes). This allows you to have a time displayed on the console at the specified interval, which can be used to estimate when the machine crashed if it was running unattended. You have to balance the usefulness of the time stamp against the extra space taken up on the disk by the log files.

syslog messages consist of a single line of text, which may be prefixed with a priority code number enclosed in angle brackets (<>). The priorities are defined in the include file syslog.h and are shown in the sidebar "Priority Facilities and Levels."

Priority Facilities and Levels — continued

mark   Time-stamping messages generated internally by syslogd.

*   All the facilities except for the time stamp, or mark.

   The level is selected from an ordered list. Not all systems implement the entire list, but most members of the list will be usable on most systems. When a level is specified, all messages at that level or at a higher level will be reported.

emerg   A panic condition. This is normally broadcast to all users.

alert   A condition that should be corrected immediately, such as a corrupted database.

crit   A critical condition, such as a hard device error.

err   Other Errors.

warning   Warning messages.

notice   Conditions that are not error messages, but that may require special handling. This is the default priority level.

info   Informational messages.

debug   Messages that contain information normally of use only when debugging a program.

none   Do not send messages from this facility.

syslogd reads messages from the AF_UNIX address family socket /dev/log, from an Internet address socket specified in /etc/services, and from the special device /dev/klog for kernel messages. As it starts up, syslogd creates the file /etc/syslog.pid, which contains the Process ID (PID) of the daemon. This allows you to send signals to the daemon without having to search the process table for the PID. For example,

```
kill -HUP `cat /etc/syslog.pid`
```

will force the daemon to reread the configuration file. The following command-line options can be used to affect the actions of the daemon.

-d   Turn on debugging; typically used only if you are creating your own version of the command.

-fconfig_file   Specify an alternative configuration file to /etc/syslog.conf.

-minterval   Specify an interval, in minutes, between mark messages.

/etc/syslog.conf

/etc/syslog.conf contains the information used by syslogd to forward the system messages to the appropriate log files, systems, or users. Entries consist of two tab-separated fields in the following format.

```
selector action
```

The selector field contains a semicolon-separated list of priority specifications of the following form.

```
facility,level[;facility,level]
```

The facilities and levels are as shown in the sidebar. Note that a level entry will report all messages at that level or higher.

The action field specifies what to do with the message. action can have one of the four following values.

filename A filename beginning with a /, which indicates that messages specified by the selector field are to be written to the specified file. The file will be opened in append mode. This can also be a device file such as /dev/ttya, which might be a hard copy printer.

hostname The name of a remote host beginning with an @, which indicates that messages specified by the selector field are to be forwarded to the syslogd daemon on the named host.

username A comma-separated list of usernames, which indicates that messages specified by the selector field are to be sent to the named users if they are logged in at the time.

* An asterisk, which indicates that messages specified by the selector field are to be sent to all logged-in users.

Blank lines in the action field are ignored. Lines that begin with a # are treated as comments.

Figure 14.1 shows a common default for /etc/syslog.conf. Messages from the mail system with a level of debug or higher will be sent to the file /var/spool/mqueue/syslog. All messages from the authorization software at the level of alert or higher will be sent to the file /var/adm/badlogins. All messages at the info level or higher, except for those from the mail system, will be recorded in /var/adm/syslog. Any alert messages or higher will be displayed on the console and sent to root if root is logged-in. Any emerg messages will be sent to all logged in users.

Figure 14.1   A common default for /etc/syslog.conf.

```
mail.debug           /var/spool/mqueue/syslog
auth.alert           /var/adm/badlogins
*.info;mail.none     /var/adm/syslog
*.alert              /dev/console
*.alert              root
*.emerg              *
```

As you can see, you might want to change this configuration. For a standalone machine, a better configuration file might be as shown in Figure 14.2.

Figure 14.2   An `/etc/syslog.conf` **for a standalone machine.**

```
#
# display all important messages on the console
#
*.ERR /dev/console

#
# record all important messages (except mail) in
# /var/adm/syslog
#
*.INFO;MAIL.NONE /var/adm/syslog

#
# forward all important messages to operations staff
# (if logged in)
#
*.ERR root,operator,sysman

#
# record all bad login attempts in /var/adm/badlogins
#
AUTH.ALERT /var/adm/badlogins

#
# record all 'su' commands in the /var/adm/sulog file
#
AUTH.NOTICE /var/adm/sulog

#
# tell all users about any 'emerg' messages
#
*.EMERG *

#
# record any printer problems
#
lpr.debug /var/adm/lpd-errors
```

If you have a number of machines, one of which has been nominated as the central machine or the *home* of the operations staff, you can add the lines shown in Figure 14.3 to the configuration files of the remote machines. These lines have the effect of forwarding important messages from the remote machines to the central machine. Remember not to put this line in the central machine's syslog.conf file.

You might also want to consider whether you want to have the printer and security messages sent to the central machine, as well. This will depend on your setup, situation, and the amount of disk space you have available.

If you want hard copy output of all the messages on a suitable printer, attach the printer to a suitable printer port (remember to remove the getty process if it is a serial port), and add the line shown in Figure 14.4 to the syslog.conf file.

You could add a line to the configuration file to send suitable messages to a file for transmission via a pager to the duty support person. Another possibility is to include recording line printer usage, perhaps to allow for the charging of printer usage.

Figure 14.3   *A modification line, which will send*
**   *important messages* home, *to add to***
**   ***syslog.conf*** *on all machines except home.***

```
#
# send the important messages to the central machine
#
*.ERR @hostname
```

Figure 14.4   *A modification line, which will send all*
**   *messages to the specified printer, to add to***
**   ***syslog.conf*** *on all machines.***

```
#
# record all messages on the console log printer
#
*.INFO;MAIL.NONE /dev/console_printer
```

Where /dev/console_printer is a link to the actual device file.

The `logger` Command

The `logger` command allows you to add one-line entries to the `syslog` files from the command line. One or more message arguments can be given on the command line, in which case each line is logged immediately. You can also specify a filename, in which case each line in the file is logged. If neither is specified, `logger` reads and logs messages on a line-by-line basis from the standard input.

The following is a list of command-line options for the `logger` command.

`-t tag` Mark each line added to the log with the specified `tag`. This helps to differentiate between commands.

`-p priority` Enter the message with the specified `priority`. The message priority can be specified using the `facility.level` pair, as elsewhere. The default is `user.notice`.

`-i` Log the PID of the `logger` process with each line.

`-f filename` Use the contents of the specified file as the message to the log.

`message` Use the specified `message` as the message to the log.

Possible uses for `logger` with these options include changes to the system. For example, the following `logger` command records users added to the system.

`logger -p user.notice -t ADDUSER "User nnnnn added to system"`

The next example records when unattended backups are started.

`logger -p local0.notice -t BACKUP "Backup started"`

This example expands on the previous example by recording the contents of `backup.log` when unattended backups are started and finished.

`logger -p local0.notice -t BACKUP -f /tmp/backup.log`

The `logger` command can be used for many other purposes, including recording out-of-hours support calls, changes made to the system, visits by engineers, or anything you might also put into the written system log. In fact, if you use a hard copy printer, `syslog` can largely take the place of the system log, but with the big advantage that you can access it online if you have to dial in the middle of the night to fix a system problem.

If you are writing C utilities to perform standard system tasks, you might want to consider the syslog functions that allow you to perform the same tasks. The output message looks like a printf string, except that %m is replaced by the current error message (collected from errno). Other facilities provided with the syslog call enable you to open or close access to the syslog files or to set a mask to restrict the level of messages written to the file.

External Links

You can use syslog with a background process that will run with a tail -f on an error log file. The process could look for specific problems, perhaps a filesystem becoming full, and then take some action, such as writing a warning to all operations staff members. syslog thus can provide an element of automatic control. (Of course, if the machine that has the problems is the machine running the monitoring software, then you may not be able to detect the problems.)

Using the time stamp, you can set up a simple replacement for the ruptime command. Each host on the network could send a time stamp to the central host at a specified interval. An external shell script could then run a tail -f on a specific file, looking for messages from that particular host. If a sleep command times out before the message arrives, the system could be shown as down.

Some manufacturers, such as Sun, automatically run the configuration file through the M4 macro processor to allow you to share a common configuration file among different classes of machines. You can achieve the same effect by writing a shell script that runs the M4 processor, or a similar package, on the configuration file, redirects the output to a temporary file, and then invokes the signal to the syslog daemon using the -f option to specify the alternate file you have just created.

Administration of syslog

syslog provides administrators with a great deal of information about the system, but it also creates extra work, in that the log files themselves must be monitored for size. A possible solution is to periodically run a cron job to recycle the log files and so save on disk space. The number and size of the files depends on the settings you have used and how much information you want to have online at any one time. You should ensure that the log files are included in your backup scripts.

Conclusion

The syslog facility can be used for many tasks in addition to logging system messages. It can serve as the basis for a broad range of reporting systems, and can even provide an element of automatic control.

prq: A Print Queue Monitor and Manager

Robert Berry

BSD UNIX provides tools like lpc, lpq, and lprm to monitor and manage print queues. Each tool performs a specific task and produces a specific output. If used individually, the tools have some drawbacks. One drawback is that each command must be retyped for each print queue that the user wants to see. As a result, many users are hesitant to manage their own print jobs and prefer to ask the system administrator to do it for them.

If combined in a script, these tools become faster and easier to use. This chapter presents such a script. The script speeds monitoring and managing of the print queues and provides an easy-to-use, interactive interface to allow users the freedom to monitor and manage their own print jobs.

The script also serves as a convenient tool for system administrators, in that it lets you view and manage more than one print queue at a time. For example, you might want to see which printer is currently the least used, so that you can get a print job out as quickly as possible. Or perhaps you don't want the least-used queue, but the queue holding the fewest bytes. Although a printer may have only two jobs waiting in the queue, if those two jobs are large documents, you may want to use the printer with five small quick jobs. To get such information, you would have to use the lpq command in various forms for each printer on the network. The prq script makes this process much simpler.

The prq *Script*

prq (Listing 15.1), short for print queue, attempts to speed and simplify the process of monitoring and managing the print queue. If you set permissions so that all end users of prq can execute the script, all of your users will have an easy, interactive interface for working with their own print jobs. (You would, of course, replace the names of printers listed in the sample code with the names of the printers on your own network.)

prq uses questions with yes and no answers and menu selections to allow the user to interact with the print queues, without having to remember arguments or type multiple commands. When invoked at the prompt, prq displays all print queues on the network. It provides standard lpq information for each print queue, including the job's rank, the user's name, the job's number, the file's name, and the file's size.

After prq displays all printing queues, it asks whether you want to remove a particular print job. If you respond with an "n" or any other key, you will be returned to the shell prompt. If you respond with a "y," you will be given a menu holding more options.

The menu is divided into two regions. The first region gives the option of removing a particular print job from a particular printer, provided you are that print job's owner. Each menu number represents a particular printer on the network. The number of options is dependent on the number of printers on your own network. In the sample

---

Using lpq

lpq is a simple command with one purpose: to display the contents of a single print queue. You can display the queue contents in one of several ways, depending on the arguments used. Executed with no arguments, lpq displays all print jobs for all users currently in the queue for the default printer, which is specified in the PRINTER environment variable. Or you may specify a particular printer using the -P argument, as in the following example.

```
% lpq -Pprintername
```

If lpq is invoked in this manner, all jobs for all users currently in that printer's queue will be displayed. If you want to see only particular jobs, you may add one or more job numbers as arguments. You may also specify one or more users to see only jobs belonging to those users.

Another handy lpq option is the + argument.

```
% lpq -Pprintername + [ seconds ]
```

The + argument causes lpq to periodically redisplay the print queue contents, giving you a constant update until there are no more jobs in the queue. If a number is specified after the +, the printing queue redisplays at intervals of the specified number of seconds.

Listing 15.1   The *prq* script speeds and simplifies print queue monitoring and management.

```
############################################################
#
# This is a simple script to check the printer queue for each printer
# on the system and give the user the option to remove any print job
# that they may own. And provide the super-user with quick interface
# to move print jobs on the queue.
#
# Programmer: Robert Berry
# Date: 7/14/94
#
############################################################
#
# Variable names:
# ans.........used to accept y/n response
# prntr.......used to accept printer selection
# jobnum......used to accept job to delete
# HOME........used to see if user is super-user
#
############################################################
echo " ********** Laser 2 **********"
lpq -Plaser2
echo " "
echo " ********** Laser 3 **********"
lpq -Plaser3
echo " "
echo " ********** PaintJet **********"
lpq -Ppaintjet
echo " "
echo " ********** Plotter **********"
lpq -Php
echo " "
echo "==================================================="
echo "==================================================="
echo -n "Would you like to remove jobs? (y/n)"
read ans

########## First if statement ##########
if [ $ans = "y" ]
then
    ########## While loop ##########
    while [ $ans = "y" ]
    do echo " "
    echo " Remove jobs on..."
    echo " 1) Laser 2"
    echo " 2) Laser 3"
    echo " 3) PaintJet"
    echo " 4) Plotter"
    echo " ----------------------"
    echo " 5) List all jobs again"
    echo " 6) Rearrange print jobs"
    echo " 7) Exit"
    echo -n " Enter your choice: "
    read prntr
    clear
```

Listing 15.1 (continued)

```
############ Case statement ###########
case $prntr in
1) echo -n "Enter job number or '-' to remove all:"
   read jobnum
   lprm -Plaser2 $jobnum;;
2) echo -n "Enter job number or '-' to remove all:"
   read jobnum
   lprm -Plaser3 $jobnum;;
3) echo -n "Enter job number or '-' to remove all:"
   read jobnum
   lprm -Ppaintjet $jobnum;;
4) echo -n "Enter job number or '-' to remove all:"
   read jobnum
   lprm -Pdm $jobnum;;
5) echo " ********** Laser 2 **********"
   lpq -Plaser2
   echo " "
   echo " ********** Laser 3 **********"
   lpq -Plaser3
   echo " "
   echo " ********** PaintJet **********"
   lpq -Ppaintjet
   echo " "
   echo " ********** Plotter **********"
   lpq -Php
   echo " "
   echo "==============================="
   echo "===============================";;
############ Second menu level ###########
6) if [ $HOME = "/" ]
   then
   ans=n
   ############ While loop ###########
   while [ $ans = "n" ]
   do
        echo " "
        echo " Move jobs on..."
        echo " 1) Laser 2"
        echo " 2) Laser 3"
        echo " 3) PaintJet"
        echo " 4) Plotter"
        echo " -----------------------"
        echo " 5) List all jobs again"
        echo " 6) Back one menu"
        echo " 7) Exit"
        echo -n " Enter your choice: "
        read prntr
        clear
   ###### Second set of case options ######
   case $prntr in
   1) echo -n "Enter job(s) or user name(s): "
      read jobnum
      lpc topq laser2 $jobnum;;
   2) echo -n "Enter job(s) or user name(s): "
      read jobnum
      lpc topq laser3 $jobnum;;
   3) echo -n "Enter job(s) or user name(s): "
      read jobnum
      lpc topq paintjet $jobnum;;
   4) echo -n "Enter job(s) or user name(s): "
      read jobnum
      lpc topq hp $jobnum;;
```

script, you are given two laser printers, one PaintJet, and a plotter to choose from. Whichever print device you choose, the screen will be cleared and you will be prompted for the job number you wish to remove from the queue. You may enter a "-" to remove all print jobs belonging to you. A notification will be displayed, ensuring that your jobs were dequeued, and the menu will display once more.

The second menu region gives various unrelated options. If the screen has scrolled past the job you wanted to remove and you forgot the job number, you may reproduce the list. If you are currently superuser, you can enter a second level of menu options from which you can rearrange print jobs in a particular print queue. Finally, if you change your mind, you have the option of exiting back to the shell prompt. For exiting, the menu prompt will accept either the number of the exit selection on the menu or the lower case "x" character.

Listing 15.1 (continued)

```
        5) echo " ********** Laser 2 **********"
           lpq -Plaser2
           echo " "
           echo " ********** Laser 3 **********"
           lpq -Plaser3        echo " "
           echo " ********** PaintJet **********"
           lpq -Ppaintjet
           echo " "
           echo " ********** Plotter **********"
           lpq -Php
           echo " "
           echo "══════════════════════════════"
           echo "══════════════════════════════";;
        6) ans=y;;
        7) clear
           exit;;
        x) clear
           exit
        esac
        done
        ######## If user isn't super-user ########
    else
        echo " "
        echo "You must be Super User for this option"
    fi;;
    7) clear
       exit;;
    x) clear
    exit
    esac
    done
else
    exit
fi
#################### THE END #########################
```

If you choose the "Rearrange print jobs" option, the script will test the HOME environment variable to see if you are currently a superuser. If this variable is not set to /, which represents the root directory, then you will see a message informing you that you must be superuser to enter the menu level and the previous menu will be redisplayed.

If you are currently a superuser, a second level of menu options will be displayed. Again, this set of options is divided into two regions. The first region is a set of printer devices for which print jobs can be rearranged. Upon selecting a printing device, you will be prompted for job numbers to place at the top of the queue. You can simply type a user name and all jobs belonging to that user will be placed at the top of the queue. The system will notify you that the task was carried out and the menu selections will be redisplayed.

The second region holds the options to redisplay the print queues, return to the previous level of menu options, or exit to the shell prompt.

Using lprm

lprm has one purpose: to remove print jobs from the print queue. If lprm is invoked without any arguments, the current print job on the default printer is removed from the print queue. Of course, users can only remove jobs that belong to them. If the current job doesn't belong to the user invoking lprm, the queue remains unchanged. Users can specify a particular printer by using the -P argument.

There are three methods for removing jobs from a print queue. The first method specifies one or more job numbers, which are obtained through lpq, as arguments. This method is demonstrated in the following example.

```
% lprm -Pprintername 235 236
```

In this example, print jobs 235 and 236 will be removed from the print queue specified by printername.

The second method uses the - as an argument after the printer name. This method will dequeue all print jobs belonging to the person invoking the command. If this method is used by the superuser, all jobs will be dequeued regardless of ownership. The following is an example of this method.

```
%lprm -Pprintername -
```

The third method specifies a particular user name, and causes all print jobs belonging to the named user to be dequeued. Typically, only the superuser uses this method. It would be pointless for any other user try it, simply because their own user name would be the only legal argument available to them. The following is an example of this method.

```
%lprm -Pprintername rob
```

Conclusion

This script simplifies the system administrator's monitoring and managing of network print queues. It also provides an easy-to-use, interactive interface for users less familiar with the UNIX environment, giving them the freedom to manage their own print jobs. You can easily add other capabilities to the script.

The only drawback to prq is that if the printers on your network change or one goes down, the script must be modified in several places to represent these changes or it is rendered useless. Modifying prq isn't a particularly time-consuming task — it's just another file to maintain. The benefits should more than outweigh this inconvenience.

Using lpc

lpc controls printer operations on the network. With its various commands, lpc can start or stop a printer, enable or disable the print queues for a particular printer, rearrange print jobs within the print queue, and display the status of each printer on the network with print queue and printer daemon information.

You may use lpc either from the command line or interactively. When lpc is executed from the command line with one or more arguments, the first argument is interpreted as a command. Each argument thereafter is taken as a parameter to this command. For example

```
% lpc down laser3 Laser 3 is down for maintenance
```

In this example, down is the command that lpc will execute. The down command turns off the print queue and disables printing for a particular printer on the network — in this case, laser3. The next parameter is actually a message to be displayed if anyone inquires about laser3 in an attempt to use the printer. Notice that the message is not enclosed in quotes.

If you invoke lpc with no arguments, it runs interactively. The shell prompt will be replaced with the following lpc prompt.

```
lpc>
```

Simply type the command you wish to execute, followed by any necessary parameters. When you're ready to leave the interactive prompt, type "exit," "quit," or simply "q" to exit lpc and return to the shell prompt.

Using lpc — *continued*

The following is a list of some other useful commands recognized by lpc and a description of the task each command performs. Like the command "quit," all lpc commands can be abbreviated. If lpc is not sure which command you are trying to specify, it will display, "?Ambiguous command."

up [all | [printername...]] This command is the exact opposite of the down command. It restarts all queues or the specified queues, enables printing again, and removes the message from the printer status file.

disable [all | [printername...]] This command is similar to the down command except that it can only be used by the superuser and doesn't give the option of adding a message to the printer status file.

enable [all | [printername...]] This command reverses the disable command and is also only available to the superuser.

restart [all | [printername...]] This handy command is available to all users. If the printer daemon dies for some unknown reason, this command will try to restart it. If the printer daemon is dead when you use lpq to check on your print job, lpq will notify you that the printer daemon is not present.

topq printername [jobnumber...] [username...] This command is also handy, but is available only to the superuser. The command will take the specified print jobs, or all the print jobs belonging to the specified user, and move them to the top of the print queue ahead of all other jobs in the queue.

clean [all | [printername...]] This command removes all print jobs from all the printers or the specified printers. It is only available to the superuser.

status [all | [printername...]] This command simply displays the status of the printer daemons and queues; it is available to all users.

help [command] ... This is probably the most important command. Typed without an argument, it displays a list of all recognized lpc commands. If commands are specified, it will display a short description of the task performed by each.

## Chapter 16

Logging rm *and* kill *Requests*

Steven G. Isaacson

Sometimes users take it upon themselves to play system administrator. Usually, the assistance is welcome; when it's not, you have to play detective.

This chapter describes two logging programs that make playing detective easy. One program logs kill requests (see Figure 16.1 for a sample entry), the other logs rm requests (see Figure 16.2).

Logging kill *Requests*

We needed to log kill requests because of a problem with Informix's Standard Engine database. When a user runs a program that accesses the database, two processes are created: the original program and a daemon that handles the database access. (This is not true of Informix's OnLine engine.)

We had difficulty with a particular program locking up, and users took it upon themselves to kill their process when the program appeared to be stuck. killing your own process generally isn't a problem, but in the case of the Informix daemon it is. If you kill the Informix daemon when it's in the middle of a transaction, it's possible to corrupt the database.

The proper procedure is to `kill` only the process created from the original program. The accompanying daemon process eventually receives the signal, at which time it shuts down, does whatever cleanup work it needs to do, and then stops.

So our problem was one of education. "It's okay to kill your program," we said, "but don't kill the daemon along with it — even though you can. The daemon will die on its own when it's ready." Most of our users got the message, but a few didn't. We had to find out who kept killing the engine. We wanted to know the user ID, date and time, and information about the process being killed.

User and group ID are obtained from `/usr/bin/id`, date and time from `/bin/date`, and information about the process to be `killed` from `/bin/ps`. (You have to get information about the process before it's killed, of course.) The results are written to a log file. Finally, the real `kill` program is called to do the work (i.e., `kill` the process). Simple. The `kill` script is in Listing 16.1.

Figure 16.1   A sample `kill` log entry.

```
On September 2 root shutdown sendmail from the root directory.

Sep 2 00:07:50 PDT 1994 uid=0(root) gid=1(other) root
cwd=/
kill 19907

 F S  UID   PID PPID  C PRI NI    ADDR  SZ \
10 S root 19907    1 15  26 35 80118498 181 \
    WCHAN STIME TTY TIME COMD
    c84fdbe0 00:08:39 ? 0:02 /usr/lib/sendmail -bd -q15m
```

Figure 16.2   A sample `rm` log entry.

```
On August 31 stevei removed a file named depend.RDS,
and approximately one second later mara removed a core
file in her HOME directory.

Wed Aug 31 18:24:25 PDT 1994 uid=243(stevei) gid=154(informix) stevei
cwd=/usr/fourgen/work/accounting/ap.4gm/i_invce.cod
rm -f depend.RDS

Wed Aug 31 18:24:26 PDT 1994 uid=418(mara) gid=154(informix) mara
cwd=/usr/mara
rm -f core
```

To install the `kill` logging script, you first rename the real `/bin/kill` program to `/bin/rkill`. Then move the `kill` script to `/bin/kill`, making sure that everyone has execute permission for `kill` and write permission for the log file. The "real" `kill` program (`/bin/rkill`) is called from the new `kill` shell script. Periodic checks of the log file could then tell us who needed to be reminded about what not to `kill`.

Listing 16.1   The `kill` script is used to determine which user is `kill`ing a process.

```
:
# kill - logging script
# to install:
#     mv /bin/kill /bin/rkill
#     mv [this script] /bin/kill
#     chmod a+rx /bin/kill
#     chgrp and chown: make /bin/kill same as /bin/rkill
#     chmod a+rw /usr/spool/log/kill.log
# You may have to alter the /bin/ps flags for your system

log=/usr/spool/log/kill.log

# record who is doing what, when, and from where
echo "`date` `id` `logname`cwd=`pwd`
kill $*
" >> $log

for num in "$@"
do
    # if kill-level was specified, just continue. For example: kill -9 234

    case "$num" in
    -*) continue ;;
    esac

    # get information about the process to be killed
    /bin/ps -lfp $num >> $log 2>&1
done

# echo blank line to make reading easier
echo >> $log

# now call real kill with same arguments
exec /bin/rkill "$@"
```

Logging rm *Requests*

We developed the same logging technique for rm. In addition to the information captured in the kill script (user ID, date and time, and process information), the rm script records the current working directory. This information is needed so that files referenced relative to the current working directory can be uniquely identified.

For example, if someone uses the command rm myfile, you must know the current working directory before you can determine if /bin/myfile or /usr/sneed/myfile was removed. Of course, the current working directory is irrelevant if the file is referred to by an absolute pathname.

The rm logging script (Listing 16.2) is installed in the same way the kill logging script is installed. First the real rm program is moved to a new name (/bin/rrm) and the rm shell script is copied to /bin/rm. Now whenever someone uses the command rm filename, the request is recorded in the rm log file.

Implementation Problems to Resolve

The kill and rm scripts work well, but there are several problems to be aware of. The first problem with any logging program is the log file — it keeps growing. Each request writes multiple lines to the log file. With a frequently used command like rm, this can be a serious problem; if left unattended, the log file will eventually fill up your file system. This is a serious problem but is also easy to solve.

Listing 16.2   The rm **script is used to determine which**
user is removing a file.

```
:
# rm - logging script
# to install:
#     mv /bin/rm /bin/rrm
#     mv [this script] /bin/rm
#     chmod a+rx /bin/rm
#     chgrp and chown: make /bin/rm same as /bin/rrm
#     chmod a+rw /usr/spool/log/rm.log

# log file should be kept under maxtab control so
# it doesn't grow too large
log=/usr/spool/log/rm.log

# record who is doing what, when, and from where
echo "`date` `id` `logname`
cwd=`pwd`
rm "$@"
" >>>> $log

# now call real rm program with same arguments
exec /bin/rrm "$@"
```

What you need is a maxtab entry. Supply the filename and maximum number of lines, and a cronjob does the rest. Set the kill log file to 2,000 lines and the rm log file to 4,000 lines. This gives us a rolling history of approximately the last 285 kill requests and the last 1,000 rm requests.

The second problem is that there is no secret about what's going on. The rm and kill logging scripts are world readable — anyone can look at them to see how they work. Soon after one user was "caught" and subsequently publicly flogged (in a nice way) in e-mail, another user began using her own kill script out of her $HOME/bin directory. Her kill script was the same as the newly installed kill logging script (that is, it calls the real /bin/rkill program), but hers was different in that it didn't bother doing any of the logging.

This problem was quietly addressed by writing a C version of the scripts. The C versions work the same, but the logging feature is hidden because the contents of the resulting binary file are not as obvious as those of a shell script.

The C version of the kill program (see Listing 16.3 for kill.c). was straightforward, since the difficult part — logging information about the process to be killed — was already available (via sukill).

Listing 16.3   A C version of the kill program hides the logging feature.

```
/*
 * kill.c -- C version of kill logging script
 * Copyright 1994 by Steven G. Isaacson
 */

#include <stdio.h>
#include <ctype.h>
#include <sys/types.h>
#include <time.h>

/* log file name */
char *logname="/usr/spool/log/kill.log";

main(argc, argv)
int argc;
char *argv[];
{
    FILE *fp;
    int i, pid;
    char *cwd;
    time_t now;

/*
 * check for error opening the log file, but don't stop people from
 * working just because there is a problem with the log file.
 */
```

Listing 16.3 (continued)

```c
    if ((fp=fopen(logname, "a+")) != NULL ) {

        /* log who is doing what where */

        fprintf(fp, "\n" );
        if (time(&now) == -1)
            fprintf(fp,"time not available\n");
        else
            fprintf(fp,"%s", ctime(&now));
        fprintf(fp, "getlogin=%s uid=%d euid=%d gid=%d egid=%d cuserid=%s\n",
                getlogin(), getuid(), geteuid(), getgid(), getegid(), cuserid(NULL));
        fprintf(fp,"%s=%s ", "HOME", getenv("HOME"));
        fprintf(fp,"%s=%s\n", "NAME", getenv("NAME"));
        fprintf(fp, "cwd=%s\n", getcwd((char *)NULL, 64));

        for (i=0; i < argc; i++)
            fprintf(fp, "%s ", argv[i]);
        fprintf(fp, "\n");

        for ( i=1; i < argc; i++ ) {

            pid=atoi(argv[i]);

            /* if kill level (-9,-15, etc.) was specified, skip it */
            if ( pid < 0 )
                continue;

            plog(fp, pid);
        }
        fflush(fp);
    }

    /* now call the real kill program */
    execvp("/bin/rkill", argv);
}

/* ================================================ */
/* write pid info to log file using a pipe */

plog(fp, pid)
FILE *fp;
int pid;
{
    char cmd[50], buf[256];
    FILE *ptr;

    sprintf(cmd, "/bin/ps -lfp %d", pid);

    if ((ptr = popen(cmd, "r")) != NULL)
        while (fgets(buf, sizeof(buf), ptr) != NULL)
            (void) fprintf(fp, "%s ",buf);
    pclose(ptr);
    return;
}

/* ================================================ */
```

The rewrite of the rm logging program was also straightforward (see Listing 16.4 for rm.c). The user ID, current working directory, etc., are easily obtainable in a C program. Once that information is obtained, it's simply a matter of passing the command-line arguments on to the real rm program.

There are other problems, too. For example, with the Network File System (NFS), if you have access to a file system from any one of several machines, then you also have access to several rm and kill programs. This means that in order to log all requests, you must install the logging programs on all machines.

Also, there may be other kill or rm programs on your system. We have a program called top that dynamically displays the current processes. You can kill processes from within the top program — and bypass /bin/kill logging.

Also, a C program that calls unlink() or kill() directly is trivial to produce.

In spite of the security shortcomings, the logging programs are valuable. They are valuable because they provide previously unavailable information that can make your job easier and make playing detective as easy as checking a log file.

Listing 16.4   A C version of the rm program hides the
logging feature.

```
/*
 * rm.c -- C version of rm logging script
 * Copyright 1994 by Steven G. Isaacson
 */

#include <stdio.h>
#include <ctype.h>
#include <sys/types.h>
#include <time.h>

/* log file name */
char *logname="/usr/spool/log/rm.log";

main(argc, argv)
int argc;
char *argv[];{
```

Listing 16.4 (continued)

```
FILE *fp;
    int i;
    char *cwd;
    time_t now;

    /*
     * check for error opening the log file, but don't
     * stop people from working just because there is a
     * problem with the log file.
     */

    if ((fp=fopen(logname, "a+")) != NULL ) {

    /* log who is doing what where */

        fprintf(fp, "\n" );
        if (time(&now) == -1)
            fprintf(fp,"time not available\n");
        else
            fprintf(fp,"%s", ctime(&now));

        fprintf(fp, "getlogin=%s uid=%d euid=%d gid=%d egid=%d cuserid=%s\n",
                getlogin(), getuid(), geteuid(), getgid(), getegid(),
                cuserid(NULL));
        fprintf(fp,"%s=%s ", "HOME", getenv("HOME"));
        fprintf(fp,"%s=%s\n", "NAME", getenv("NAME"));
        fprintf(fp, "cwd=%s\n", getcwd((char *)NULL, 64));

        for (i=0; i < argc; i++)
            fprintf(fp, "%s ", argv[i]);
        fprintf(fp, "\n");

        fflush(fp);
        close(fp);
    }

    /* now call the real rm program */

    execvp("/bin/rrm", argv);
}
```

## Chapter 17

Tuning for X

David S. Linthicum

If not configured and managed correctly, X Window can be an out-of-control resource hog capable of bringing even a muscle-bound processor to its knees. To prevent this, you first need to understand the basics of the X Window system and how it uses such UNIX subsystems as memory and the CPU (see the sidebars for information on memory and CPU utilization). Then, with the basics in mind, you can go on to configuration and tuning issues.

This chapter covers some of the more important of those issues — including drivers, memory utilization, and the UNIX tunables that can be adjusted to squeeze the most performance out of your system. The chapter also discusses how to measure X Window performance using available benchmarking and system monitoring facilities, and how to use these facilities to spot and solve problems. The examples I use are from a SunSoft Interactive 386/ix 3.0 (System V) workstation running X11 and Motif. Other systems, especially those running non-System V UNIX, may yield different results.

Configuring Resources

Most X applications use resources to customize the way the X terminal and X applications look and function. This allows system administrators to control the number of processes executed by default and the amount of memory and processor time being used. For example, since it takes more memory to load a full-color background than a plain background, you can protect limited memory resources by allowing only a plain background to load.

The X system stores resource information in a series of text files called *resource files*. These files provide for system-wide, account-wide, and class-wide resource settings, allowing the system administrator to configure a hierarchy of resource defaults to control the use of memory and CPU by level. When an X application is invoked, the X system checks the X-server-wide Resource Manager for the stored resource commands. The application itself must check other configuration files located throughout the file system.

Resource settings can be Boolean or can take numeric values. Default values are set in resource files in the user's home directory and in the X resource database manager, xrdb. This utility stores resources directly in the server, thus making them available to all X clients.

Memory Utilization and X

X Window applications are rarely less than 1Mb, so the enemy of X is low memory. When UNIX runs out of memory, it begins to swap. Performance hits rock bottom and can even lead to a disaster, such as broken pipes or other system problems related to swapping portions of memory to disk. To reduce memory paging, the system must be reconfigured to provide additional memory to X applications. You can simply increase the amount of physical memory installed in the computer. If the system is at its maximum installable memory, or if you can't spend the money on more memory, the sizes of the filesystems' buffers and other kernel data structures can be reduced. Remember, though, that reducing the buffers may also reduce disk performance. Another option is to alter the paging algorithm so that the system begins paging earlier. However, this alternative is useful only when the shortage of memory is relatively small.

It's generally a good idea to install maximum RAM on the workstation on which X will be operating. Intel workstations require at least 16Mb, but 32Mb is much better, and 64Mb is best. X terminals require at least 4Mb of memory to process a reasonable number of X or Motif applications at a respectable speed.

The only sure way to increase performance and cut memory consumption is to monitor the number of X applications that are executed by the users and determine whether all the applications are necessary. Users may not need xclock, xeyes, or xload.

The X Window system makes heavy use of buffers, generally opting for smaller (usually 128 bytes or less) rather than larger buffers. Most systems with X installed need to increase the value of NBLKn, as noted in this chapter's main text.

Even individual X applications store default resource files within the file system, usually /usr/lib/X11/app- defaults. Such files configure the actions and the presentation of a single program. Figure 17.1, for example, contains the default settings for the X application xload.

The primary resource files (.Xdefaults or .Xresources), which are stored in the home directory of the users, determine the defaults for the client applications. These defaults can be set system-wide by the system administrator (Figure 17.2). Custom resources can even be set by the CPU if a network is employed. Command-line options take precedence over defaults set in the resource files, so users can override the defaults, if needed.

Figure 17.1   A sample X application resource file with the default settings for xload.

```
XLoad.input:      false
XLoad*Label*Justify:      left
XLoad*JumpScroll:      1
XLoad*internalBorderWidth:      0
XLoad*showGrip:      FALSE
```

Running the Buffer Cache Subsystem

Although disk I/O is not a primary concern with X Window performance, it does affect the performance of some X applications and is certainly a factor if the system is paging. When an I/O device request is made to a disk drive, the buffer cache system provides intermediate storage for information moving back and forth from the tracks of the disk. The buffer cache subsystem improves performance, which allows the I/O to make sizable ordered transfers, thereby minimizing seek time on the physical disk drive. It also allows programs to read and write from cache memory, whenever possible, instead of going to disk.

The type of buffer cache subsystem differs among UNIX systems, but the basic concept is similar. The buffering cache subsystem is handled by the kernel, which allocates a portion of memory for buffer cache space. This portion of memory is configurable (see the NBUF parameter). The kernel then writes to memory as if writing to a file. At some point, the modified information is written to disk. The interval at which the information is written from memory to disk is also configurable (see NAUTOUP).

The size of the buffer cache is configurable in most UNIX operating systems. This is the major tuning parameter NBUF, and is the cause or cure for most system and disk I/O performance problems. A system with a lot of memory may have a large buffer cache system because the buffer cache may be a greater memory consumer than the kernel itself.

So what is optimal buffer cache size for X Window? You must compromise. The more memory you allocate to the buffer cache, the less you have for user programs and processes, and vice-versa. When buffer cache memory is reduced to make room for more or larger processes, disk I/O performance suffers.

Figure 17.2   A sample primary resource file with default settings for client applications.

```
xbiff*onceOnly:        true
! xbiff*update:        5
#if PLANES>1
#endif
#if PLANES>4
xbiff*foreground:      blue
#endif

#if PLANES>4
xcalc*Foreground:      black
xcalc*Background:      white
xcalc*DispBack:        blue
xcalc*DispFore:        white
xcalc*FKeyBack:        skyblue
xcalc*NKeyBack:        black
xcalc*OKeyBack:        red
xcalc*FKeyFore:        black
xcalc*NKeyFore:        white
xcalc*OKeyFore:        white
#endif
#if WIDTH>1024
xcalc*KeyFont:         10x20
xcalc*DisplayFont:     *courier*bold*18*
xcalc*FlagFont:        10x20
#endif

! xclock*analog:       false
! xclock*chime:        true
! xclock*update:       1
#if PLANES>1
xclock*hands:          LightGray
#endif
#if PLANES>4
xclock*hands: blue
xclock*highlight:      black
#endif

#if PLANES>4
! xpcterm*foreground:  blue
#endif

xpcterm*alwaysHighlight: false
xpcterm*borderWidth:   0
xpcterm*jumpScroll:    false
xpcterm*marginBell:    false
xpcterm*saveLines:     512
xpcterm*visualBell:    false

Mwm*clientAutoPlace:   false
Mwm*positionIsFrame:   false

Mwm*buttonBindings:    DefaultButtonBindings
```

Reconfiguring and Rebuilding the UNIX Kernel

The kernel is the "traffic cop" of the UNIX operating system. It controls the memory, schedules processes, and manages I/O and every other task associated with an operating system. The kernel is always present in physical memory (never paged) and can be quite large, especially on systems where it is clogged with several device drivers.

Your primary goal regarding overall X system performance should be to minimize the memory requirement of the kernel. You can accomplish this by setting parameters in the kernel's configuration files (Figure 17.3) and relinking or building a new kernel, which takes effect at the next boot.

Figure 17.3   A sample UNIX System V *stune* **file sets parameters to minimize kernel memory requirement.**

```
*ident "@(#)stune    2.5 - 89/10/11"
NBUF          1000
NINODE        600
NS5INODE      600
NFILE         600
NPROC         120
NREGION       500
NCLIST        260
MAXUP         60
NHBUF         256
NAUTOUP       20
SHLBMAX       8
NSTREAM       128
NQUEUE        512
NBLK4096      4
NBLK2048      32
NBLK1024      32
NBLK512       32
NBLK256       64
NBLK128       128
NBLK64        256
NBLK16        256
NBLK4         128
NOFILES       64
NUMSP         50
NUMTIM        32
NUMTRW        32
```

The process of configuring the kernel varies from one UNIX version to the other, but most versions provide interactive programs that will configure the kernel for you. On SCO ODT v2.0, this is the tunesh utility. On SunSoft 386/ix systems, administrators can use the kconfig utility. Other UNIX systems may have their own version of this facility. It's generally safer to go through these kernel configuration utilities rather than edit the tunable files directly. If you do edit a file directly, be sure to make backups so that you can restore the system if you get yourself into too much trouble.

Tunable Parameters

This section examines some of the more important tunable parameters and discusses their significance for tuning X.

NBUF   sets the number of buffer headers allocated at one time. When this number is reduced, the system is forced to allocate buffers more often, which can have a negative effect on system performance. When NBUF is increased, the system can allocate buffers less often, but the additional buffers take up valuable memory. You can find the optimal NBUF setting by monitoring system performance.

NPROC   sets the size of the process table — that is, the maximum number of simultaneous processes that the system can run. This parameter is particularly significant for X systems, because a typical X workstation runs many processes simultaneously. If NPROC is set too low, users may receive a "cannot fork: too many processes" message when the specified number of processes is exceeded.

NREGION   sets the number of program regions that are allowed to be active at any given time. There are three regions in a UNIX process: text, data, and the program stack. As a rule of thumb, this parameter should be set to at least three times the size of NPROC.

MAXUP   sets the maximum number of processes that a single user can have active at one time. This must always be less than the number set for NPROC, but should be set relatively high for X, since an X workstation typically runs many processes. Generally speaking, users should be able to run at least 90 percent of the NPROC number. If the number of processes is exceeded, the user receives a "too many processes" message.

NHBUF   sets the number of "hash buckets" to allocate for the buffer cache system. Increasing this value makes the cache searches more efficient. As a rule, it is usually one quarter of the number set by the NBUF parameter and must be a power of 2.

NAUTOUP sets the number of seconds between buffer flushes to disk. If it is set too high, the system reliability may be sacrificed, but X performance is slightly increased. If this parameter is set too low, system performance is affected negatively.

NSTREAM sets the maximum number of streams that can be opened at any given time. This parameter is very important to the X Window system because X uses the STREAMS facility. The more X activity on your CPU, the higher this parameter should be set. Generally speaking, systems running X should set this value over 100.

NQUEUE sets the maximum number of STREAMS queues that the system will support. This value should be set at four times the value set in NSTREAM.

NBLKn sets the number of data blocks and data buffers of size n. The STREAMS facility of UNIX uses these parameters to allocate message blocks and buffers within the system. The number of message blocks of size n is about 1.25 times the number of data blocks of size n. As with the other parameters that affect STREAMS, these are very important to the performance of the X Window system.

CPU Tuning Considerations

If you support a great many X Terminals, you should consider increasing the size of the process table (NPROC and MAXUP for System V or maxusers and MAXUPRC for BSD). This is particularly important if there are several users operating X Window at the same time via X terminals and other remote display devices.

Two idiosyncrasies make X Window problematic. The first is that X requires processes of its very own. The second is that users tend to open lots of windows and run lots of X and Motif applications. Each window requires at least two processes — in some cases, more than two. These processes consist of a terminal emulator, a shell, and the actual X or Motif application.

The obvious answer — to increase the size of the process table — entails problems of its own. If the process table is too large, it will require too much memory and force the system to begin swapping. Swapping slows X Window (and everything else) to a crawl. If the process table is too small, not enough space is allocated to handle the extensive process load of systems running X Window (see the sidebar "CPU Utilization and X" for more information).

CPU Utilization and X

In the past, UNIX users typically worked on standard async terminals or CRTs that ran and processed I/O for only one application at a time. Today, X Window and Motif users can run several applications, either X Window and non-X Window, at a time. Multiple applications execute within several windows on a large graphical terminal provided through X Window and Motif. These terminals replace the older drab character-based display with a new GUI that users love.

The increase in the process load generated by X systems brings CPU utilization up to a maximum. Figure 17.4, for example, shows a process status listing (ps -eaf) of the programs operating on only one computer running only one X server. Notice the number of X and Motif management daemons running, as well as several X applications and common UNIX processes like cron and lpsched. This load is relatively light compared to that generated by X systems processing database operations or data acquisition tasks, which are pet applications for X Window system developers.

This increased work load puts system administrators in a dilemma, given that a single X terminal can absorb more CPU cycles than 10 or more older character-based terminals. Along with the configuration and performance monitoring measures discussed in this chapter (and apart from expensive ideas like new processors), there are a number of little things can you do to increase the speed of X Window.

First, your system may be able to do without certain processes, including: accounting system daemons, mail system daemons, network daemons, printer control daemons, and security daemons. Security daemons (such as the ones that come with "Secure UNIX") are significant CPU and I/O users; they can usually be disabled or even removed, though not if you're working for an organization in which security is a high priority.

Second, you can train users to run large, CPU-intensive tasks (such as DBMS operations) at night when the CPU has more idle time or to run the tasks at a lower priority. While users may be more difficult to manage than the system itself, you can show them how to use some of UNIX's delay execution and prioritization facilities.

Sharing the Load

Another strategy is to use the X Window system's ability to distribute the processing load over several CPUs. This allows the most burdened system to move processes to other CPUs connected via a network (loosely coupled processors). Using the "remote control" facilities provided by UNIX, like rsh, rlogin, or telnet, users can change the execution location of X or Motif applications.

The key is to determine which programs should run where. With a little trial and error, you can balance the process load among the connected CPUs and then train users to execute X applications on remote CPUs. Executed properly, load sharing can be a major benefit to overall system and X performance. It can also be an administrator's nightmare if activity on all processors is not constantly monitored.

Benchmarking X

Benchmarking allows you to determine whether your new configuration has hurt or helped overall system and X Window performance. The measure in a benchmark test is the length of time taken to execute a set of X Window operations.

UNIX provides several tools you can use to perform a benchmark, and other benchmarking programs are available from various sources. Some of these are specifically designed for X; others, for UNIX as a whole. The following are benchmarking tools that you may find helpful.

x11perf   This X terminal benchmark can measure 276 different types of X requests. It requires X Window. I have found it to be the best available for measuring X performance. The x11perf system is available on UUNET.

xbench   This X Window-oriented benchmarking utility measures some commonly used X functions and started the ratings know as Xstones. The xbench system requires X Window. A shortcoming of the xbench system is that is does not take into account different screen sizes or resolutions. Also, if fonts are in use, it does not factor

---

Figure 17.4   A sample process status listing of the programs operating on one computer running one X server.

```
     UID PID PPID C   STIME    TTY TIME COMMAND
    root   0   0 0   Dec 27      ? 0:00 sched
    root   1   0 0   Dec 27      ? 0:02 /etc/init
    root   2   0 0   Dec 27      ? 0:00 vhand
    root   3   0 0   Dec 27      ? 0:05 bdflush
    root  86   1 0 00:12:40    vt01 0:00 /etc/getty /dev/vt01 vt01
    root  87   1 0 00:12:40    vt02 0:00 /etc/getty /dev/vt02 vt02
    root  88   1 0 00:12:40 console 0:00 /etc/xgetty -display :0 console console
    root  73   1 0 00:12:36      ? 0:00 /etc/cron
    root  77   1 0 00:12:37      ? 0:01 /usr/lib/lpsched
    root  89  88 0 00:13:12 console 0:02 xdm -nodaemon -server :0 localTransient /usr/bin/X11/X :0
    root  90  89 6 00:13:14 console 1:20 /usr/bin/X11/Xvga :0 -auth /usr/lib/X11/xdm/auth-server
    root  91  89 0 00:13:16 console 0:00 xdm -nodaemon -server :0 localTransient /usr/bin/X11/X :0
    root 105  91 0 00:14:07 console 0:00 /bin/sh //.xsession
    root 154 105 1 00:14:11 console 0:11 xpcterm -ls -iconic -fn ega -fb ega -name xpcterm -geometry 80x25+0+20
    root 155 105 0 00:14:11 console 0:00 xclock -iconic -geometry 100x100-0-0 -analog
    root 156 105 0 00:14:11 console 0:04 mwm
    root 158 154 0 00:14:18    ttyp0 0:01 -sh
    root 238 236 0 00:28:31    ttyp1 0:00 sh
    root 222   1 0 00:27:31 console 0:01 xclock
    root 224   1 0 00:27:36 console 0:01 xbiff
    root 230   1 0 00:28:07 console 0:02 puzzle
    root 236   1 0 00:28:29 console 0:00 xpcterm -name VGA -fn vga -fb vga
    root 241 240 0 00:28:43    ttyp2 0:00 sh
    root 240   1 0 00:28:39 console 0:00 xpcterm -name EGA -fn ega -fb ega
    root 335 158 0 00:50:02    ttyp0 0:01 xload
    root 339 158 5 00:50:38    ttyp0 0:00 ps -eaf
```

them into the benchmark. These omissions mean that an xbench test may not truly represent the actual performance of the X terminal. However, xbench may be a good tool for comparing two or more X terminals. Figure 17.5 shows a sample xbench results file. The xbench system is available on UUNET.

Figure 17.5   A sample xbench results file.

```
GENERAL INFORMATION

server: Interactive 386ix X11
client: Dell
communication: 10Mb
notes: Test for Sys Admin Magazine


SERVER INFORMATION

Servervendor : INTERACTIVE X11 - INTERACTIVE Systems Corp.
XSERVER version : 11.2000
Revision : 0
Defaultdepth rootwindow : 4
Server Byte-Order : LSBFirst
Server BitmapBitOrder : LSBFirst
DisplayWidth : 640
DisplayHeight : 480


XBENCH INFORMATION
VERSION: 1 TIMEGOAL = 10 sec; NRUNS = 3

============ line10 ============
LINES

216576 vectors of len. 10 in 10 secs
rate = 21657.60 vectors/sec
============ line100 ============
LINES

82944 vectors of len. 100 in 10 secs
rate = 8294.40 vectors/sec
============ line400 ============
LINES

28416 vectors of len. 400 in 10 secs
rate = 2841.60 vectors/sec
============ dline10 ============
DASHED LINES

114432 dashed vectors of len. 10 in 10 secs
rate = 11443.20 vectors/sec
============ dline100 ============
DASHED LINES

30720 dashed vectors of len. 100 in 10 secs
rate = 3072.00 vectors/sec
```

Figure 17.5 (continued)

```
============ dline400 ============
DASHED LINES

10752 dashed vectors of len. 400 in 12 secs
rate = 896.00 vectors/sec

============ wline10 ============
WIDE LINES

36864 wide vectors (linewidth=5) of len. 10 in 10 secs
rate = 3686.40 vectors/sec

============ wline100 ============
WIDE LINES

11520 wide vectors (linewidth=5) of len. 100 in 12 secs
rate = 960.00 vectors/sec
============ wline400 ============
WIDE LINES

4608 wide vectors (linewidth=5) of len. 400 in 16 secs
rate = 288.00 vectors/sec
============ rects10 ============
RECTANGLES

81408 rectangles with 10 pixel sides in 10 secs
rate = 8140.80 rectangles/sec (325632 Pixels/sec)
============ rects100 ============
RECTANGLES

32768 rectangles with 100 pixel sides in 10 secs
rate = 3276.80 rectangles/sec (1310720 Pixels/sec)
============ rects400 ============
RECTANGLES

11520 rectangles with 400 pixel sides in 11 secs
rate = 1047.27 rectangles/sec (1675636 Pixels/sec)
============ fillrects10 ============
FILLED RECTANGLES

226048 rectangles with 10 pixel sides in 10 secs
rate = 22604.80 rectangles/sec (2260480 Pixels/sec)
============ fillrects100 ============
FILLED RECTANGLES

16128 rectangles with 100 pixel sides in 10 secs
rate = 1612.80 rectangles/sec (16128000 Pixels/sec)
============ fillrects400 ============
FILLED RECTANGLES

2304 rectangles with 400 pixel sides in 19 secs
rate = 121.26 rectangles/sec (19402105 Pixels/sec)
============ tiledrects10 ============
TILE-FILLED RECTANGLES

54528 rectangles with 10 pixel sides in 10 secs
rate = 5452.80 rectangles/sec (545280 Pixels/sec)
```

Figure 17.5 (continued)

```
========= tiledrects100 =========
TILE-FILLED RECTANGLES

4352 rectangles with 100 pixel sides in 14 secs
rate = 310.86 rectangles/sec (3108571 Pixels/sec)
========= tiledrects400 =========
TILE-FILLED RECTANGLES

1280 rectangles with 400 pixel sides in 38 secs
rate = 33.68 rectangles/sec (5389473 Pixels/sec)
========= stippledrects10 =========
STIPPLE-FILLED RECTANGLES

47104 rectangles with 10 pixel sides in 10 secs
rate = 4710.40 rectangles/sec (471040 Pixels/sec)

========= stippledrects100 =========
STIPPLE-FILLED RECTANGLES

3584 rectangles with 100 pixel sides in 13 secs
rate = 275.69 rectangles/sec (2756923 Pixels/sec)
========= stippledrects400 =========
STIPPLE-FILLED RECTANGLES

1280 rectangles with 400 pixel sides in 52 secs
rate = 24.62 rectangles/sec (3938461 Pixels/sec)
========= invrects10 =========
INVERTED RECTANGLES

177806 rectangles with 10 pixel sides in 10 secs
rate = 17780.60 rectangles/sec (1778060 Pixels/sec)
========= invrects100 =========
INVERTED RECTANGLES

8171 rectangles with 100 pixel sides in 12 secs
rate = 680.92 rectangles/sec (6809166 Pixels/sec)
========= invrects400 =========
INVERTED RECTANGLES

1506 rectangles with 400 pixel sides in 34 secs
rate = 44.29 rectangles/sec (7087058 Pixels/sec)
========= arcs10 =========
ARCS

33916 arcs with 10 pixel diameter in 10 secs
rate = 3391.60 arcs/sec
========= arcs100 =========
ARCS

12666 arcs with 100 pixel diameter in 10 secs
rate = 1266.60 arcs/sec
========= arcs400 =========
ARCS

4336 arcs with 400 pixel diameter in 11 secs
rate = 394.18 arcs/sec
```

xload xload provides the user with a graphic display of certain system performance statistics. The xload program requires X Window. Although nice to look at and neat to use, xload does not provide enough information to make it a very useful X benchmarking tool. This program comes with most X systems.

Figure 17.5 (continued)

```
========= filledarcs10 =========
FILLED ARCS

26522 filled arcs with 10 pixel diameter in 10 secs
rate = 2652.20 filled arcs/sec
========= filledarcs100 =========
FILLED ARCS

7396 filled arcs with 100 pixel diameter in 10 secs
rate = 739.60 filled arcs/sec
========= filledarcs400 =========
FILLED ARCS

2042 filled arcs with 400 pixel diameter in 14 secs
rate = 145.86 filled arcs/sec
========= filledpoly100 =========
FILLED POLYGONS

3762 filled polygons with 5 points (size 100) in 10 secs
rate = 376.20 filled polygons/sec

========= screencopy10 =========
COPYAREA (SCREEN->SCREEN)

12996 copies with 10 pixel sides in 10 secs
rate = 1299.60 copies/sec (129960 Pixels/sec)
========= screencopy100 =========
COPYAREA (SCREEN->SCREEN)

1608 copies with 100 pixel sides in 13 secs
rate = 123.69 copies/sec (1236923 Pixels/sec)
========= screencopy400 =========
COPYAREA (SCREEN->SCREEN)

516 copies with 400 pixel sides in 49 secs
rate = 10.53 copies/sec (1684897 Pixels/sec)
========= scroll =========
SCROLL

804 scrolls (area: 640 x 400) in 16 secs
rate = 26.80 scrolls/sec (6860800 Pixels/sec)
========= bitmapcopy10 =========
COPYPLANE (BITMAP->SCREEN)

13569 copies with 10 pixel sides in 10 secs
rate = 1356.90 copies/sec (135690 Pixels/sec)
```

sar   Because of its versatility, sar is one of the most popular benchmarking utilities. sar provides information pertaining to CPU and memory usage, including idle time. This utility is available only on System V UNIX. Figure 17.6 presents three sar reports. The last of these was run while X Window was running on a 386 with just 3Mb — it shows a very slow, sick system screaming for additional memory.

sar can also be used to produce system performance reports. The following are reports available with sar, most of which are helpful when testing a system running X.

- Buffer Cache Usage and Hit Rate
- Paging Activity
- Kernel Memory Allocation Activity
- Average Queue Length
- Unused Memory Pages and Disk Blocks
- CPU Utilization
- Status of System Tables
- Swapping and Paging Activity
- Network Operations
- Terminal Activity
- Network Subsystem

Figure 17.5 (continued)

```
========== bitmapcopy100 ==========
COPYPLANE (BITMAP->SCREEN)

1985 copies with 100 pixel sides in 12 secs
rate = 165.42 copies/sec (1654166 Pixels/sec)
========== bitmapcopy400 ==========
COPYPLANE (BITMAP->SCREEN)

577 copies with 400 pixel sides in 28 secs
rate = 20.61 copies/sec (3297142 Pixels/sec)
========== imagestring:fixed ==========
DRAW IMAGE STRING - font="fixed" (height = 13)

318570 chars in 10 secs
rate = 31857.00 chars/sec
========== complex1 ==========
WINDOW CREATE/DRAW/DESTROY

339 runs 10 secs
rate = 33.90 runs/sec
```

X is often used over an Ethernet network that connects the X Server (such as an X terminal or X workstation) to the client. Generally speaking, the Ethernet network provides a large enough bandwidth that performance of an X terminal will not be hindered. Problems that do occur can usually be easily diagnosed with the standard network diagnostic facilities. The network should not be the primary focus when tuning the system for maximum X performance, but there are a few things to consider.

Figure 17.6   *Three sample* sar *reports provide information on CPU and memory usage; the last report shows a very sick system.*

```
sar -r 5 30

homework homework 3.2 2 i386     12/29/92

00:52:02  freemem   freeswp
00:52:07      43     18896
00:52:12      41     18896
00:52:17      37     18896
00:52:22      31     18896
00:52:27      44     18880
00:52:32      59     18880
00:52:37      58     18880
00:52:42      59     18880
00:52:47      54     18880
00:52:52      55     18880
00:52:57      57     18880
00:53:02      57     18880
00:53:07      57     18880
00:53:12      57     18880
00:53:17      57     18880
00:53:22      57     18880
00:53:27      57     18880
00:53:32      57     18880
00:53:37      57     18880
00:53:42      57     18880
00:53:47      57     18880
00:53:52      57     18880
00:53:57      57     18880
00:54:02      57     18880
00:54:07      57     18880
00:54:12      57     18880
00:54:17      57     18880
00:54:22      57     18880
00:54:27      57     18880
00:54:32      57     18880

Average       54     18882
```

First, the network must be capable of transferring data across networks without errors.

Second, the network must have sufficient bandwidth to support the traffic on the network. If the bandwidth is too short, X terminal information takes too long to move from client to server and back again. Each system must have the capacity to handle the network processing load assigned to that particular node. One slow system can cause the entire network's performance to suffer, thus hindering the performance of X Window.

Figure 17.6 (continued)

```
sar -b 5 30

homework homework 3.2 2 i386    12/29/92

00:52:11 bread/s lread/s %rcache bwrit/s lwrit/s %wcache pread/s pwrit/s
00:52:16       3       8      60       0       1     100       0       0
00:52:21       0       2     100       0       1     100       0       0
00:52:26       5      12      56       0       1      71       0       0
00:52:31       0       2     100       0       1      75       0       0
00:52:36       0       0     100       1       1      33       0       0
00:52:41       2      13      84       0       1     100       0       0
00:52:46       1      12      88       1       1      57       0       0
00:52:51       0       2     100       0       1      80       0       0
00:52:56       0       0     100       0       0     100       0       0
00:53:01       0       2     100       1       1      43       0       0
00:53:06       0       0     100       0       1      50       0       0
00:53:11       0       2     100       0       1      75       0       0
00:53:16       0       0     100       0       1      67       0       0
00:53:21       0       2     100       0       1     100       0       0
00:53:26       0       0     100       0       1      67       0       0
00:53:31       0       2     100       0       1      75       0       0
00:53:36       0       0     100       0       0     100       0       0
00:53:41       0       2     100       0       1      60       0       0
00:53:46       0       0     100       0       0     100       0       0
00:53:51       0       2     100       0       1      75       0       0
00:53:56       0       0     100       0       0     100       0       0
00:54:01       0       2     100       0       1      75       0       0
00:54:06       0       0     100       0       1      67       0       0
00:54:11       0       2     100       0       1     100       0       0
00:54:16       0       0     100       0       1      67       0       0
00:54:21       0       2     100       0       1     100       0       0
00:54:26       0       0     100       0       0     100       0       0
00:54:31       0       2     100       0       1      71       0       0
00:54:36       0       1     100       0       1      86       0       0
00:54:41       0       2      90       0       0     100       0       0

Average        0       3      84       0       1      76       0       0
```

Figure 17.6 (continued)

```
sar -uby 30 10

junk junk 3.2 2 i386    11/02/91
```

	%usr	%sys	%wio	%idle	bread/s	lread/s	%rcache	bwrit/s	lwrit/s	%wcache	pread/s	pwrit/s	rawch/s	canch/s	outch/s	rcvin/s	xmtin/s	mdmin/s
00:04:35	1	7	49	43	16	1	-1282	0	0	75	0	0	0	0	1	10	0	0
00:05:05	2	9	25	65	10	3	-210	0	1	62	0	0	0	2	4	0	0	0
00:05:35	0	4	18	78	5	1	-375	0	0	50	0	0	0	0	1	0	0	0
00:06:05	1	5	33	61	10	0	-29900	1	0	50	0	0	0	0	0	10	0	0
00:06:35	0	2	8	90	2	1	-72	0	2	62	0	0	0	0	0	0	0	0
00:07:05	0	0	0	100	0	0	100	0	0	40	0	0	0	0	0	0	0	0
00:07:35	1	5	23	70	8	1	-23900	0	0	50	0	0	0	0	0	36	0	0
00:08:06	1	6	31	61	11	1	-984	0	0	60	0	0	0	0	36	13	0	0
00:08:38	1	6	40	52	10	0	-31900	0	0	33	0	0	0	0	0	35	0	0
00:09:10	2	10	55	33	26	3	-754	0	0	25	0	0	0	0	1	5	0	0
Average	1	5	28	65	10	1	-799	0	0	57	0	0	0	0	4	11	0	0

Device Driver Considerations

The most important I/O device for X Window is the graphics controller — or graphics adapter, if a workstation is employed — and graphics device drivers are critical to UNIX system tuning. Poorly written or improperly configured drivers can significantly diminish X terminal application response time. Writing device drivers to optimize I/O is most likely the UNIX or device vendor's job, and is thus out of your control. But a super-fast graphics controller or adapter is useless if the driver in use is not optimized correctly. It may bring the performance of the X terminal down to a crawl.

Conclusion

You can make your UNIX system a better X Window workhorse by using tuning tools (such as the benchmarking facilities described here) and by gaining a knowledge of UNIX subsystems that affect X performance. You'll find that in the world of X, things are going to get much worse in terms of processor and memory loads required. This will be your challenge for the '90s.

References

Hare, Chris. "Getting the Info — u386mon." *Sys Admin*. September/October 1992.

Johnson, Eric F, and Kevin Reichard. *Using X, Troubleshooting the X Window System, Motif & Open Look*. MIS:Press, 1992.

Laukides, Mike. *System Performance Tuning*. Sebastopol, CA: O'Reilly & Associates, 1990.

Linthicum, David S. "UNIX Facilities for Database Tuning." *Database Programming and Design*. January 1992.

Quercia, Valerie & Tim O'Reilly. *X Window System User's Guide*. Sebastopol, CA: O'Reilly & Associates, 1990.

Taht, Michael. "Configuring for X Terminals." *SCO Magazine*. October 1992.

Chapter 18

Standard UNIX Network Diagnostic Tools

Emmett Dulaney

Once the software has been installed, the appropriate cards added, and the cabling completed, it's time to test the network to see if all components are communicating as they should. A variety of diagnostic tools can be purchased from third parties, but the UNIX operating system contains many that do a remarkably competent job, without requiring the outlay of additional capital.

The UNIX network diagnostic utilities are included with almost every vendor's UNIX networking package. They are useful not only on a first install, but anytime an administrator needs to check the status of the connections. There are seven such utilities, or tools: `ping`, `netstat`, `ifconfig`, `rwho`, `ruptime`, `rlogin`, and `remsh`. The last four work only when two or more UNIX stations are involved, and not with connected processors running another operating system.

ping

Submarines use sonar waves to test the water and see if any other objects, including other submarines, are out there. This process is known as *pinging*, and the creators of the ping utility thought the analogy close enough to borrow its name.

Typically, /usr/etc or /var/etc contains ping, whose purpose in life is to test network applications and connections. ping reads addresses and entries from the /etc/hosts file and is able to communicate with host machines listed there. The first entry in this file is always

```
127.0.0.1 me loopback localhost
```

This provides an internal address to the network card. You can test the status of that card by using ping me. This creates a loop wherein a signal is sent through the internal hardware to verify that all is working properly.

Two versions of ping are presently in use: the first continues to send signals until interrupted; the second performs a quick operation and reports the outcome. The following is a sample session with the first version.

```
# /usr/etc/ping me

PING me: 56 data bytes
64 bytes from 127.0.0.1: icmp_seq=0. time=2 60th of sec
64 bytes from 127.0.0.1: icmp_seq=1. time=1 60th of sec
64 bytes from 127.0.0.1: icmp_seq=2. time=1 60th of sec
64 bytes from 127.0.0.1: icmp_seq=3. time=2 60th of sec
64 bytes from 127.0.0.1: icmp_seq=4. time=1 60th of sec
64 bytes from 127.0.0.1: icmp_seq=5. time=1 60th of sec
64 bytes from 127.0.0.1: icmp_seq=6. time=1 60th of sec
64 bytes from 127.0.0.1: icmp_seq=7. time=1 60th of sec
64 bytes from 127.0.0.1: icmp_seq=8. time=1 60th of sec
64 bytes from 127.0.0.1: icmp_seq=9. time=1 60th of sec
64 bytes from 127.0.0.1: icmp_seq=10. time=1 60th of sec
(<Ctrl><D> pressed by user):

----me PING Statistics----
11 packets transmitted, 11 packets received, 0% packet loss
round-trip (60th of sec) min/avg/max = 1/1/2
#
```

The following is a sample session for the second version.

```
# /usr/etc/ping me
PING me: is alive
```

In both instances, all is as it should be — the packets were sent and received, with zero packet loss. To test another machine on the network, specify its name in place of me.

```
# /usr/etc/ping QUEEN
PING QUEEN: 56 data bytes
64 bytes from 197.9.200.17: icmp_seq=0. time=2 60th of sec
64 bytes from 197.9.200.17: icmp_seq=1. time=1 60th of sec
64 bytes from 197.9.200.17: icmp_seq=2. time=2 60th of sec
64 bytes from 197.9.200.17: icmp_seq=3. time=1 60th of sec
(<Ctrl><D> pressed by user):

----SUN7 PING Statistics----
4 packets transmitted, 4 packets received, 0% packet loss
round-trip (60th of sec) min/avg/max = 1/1/2
#
```

In this example, known host QUEEN is able to be reached and no errors occurred during the packet testing. Errors that can occur include the inability to send packets, due to the machine being down, or an unknown host on the network, as shown in the following example.

```
# /usr/etc/ping SUN7
PING SUN7: 56 data bytes
(<Ctrl><D> pressed by user after several seconds):

----SUN7 PING Statistics----
11 packets transmitted, 0 packets received, 100% packet loss
#
```

In this instance, the machine is down, so nothing is received or echoed back. With the second ping version, the result would indicate that the machine is not alive. If you are using the first version of ping, which continues testing until interrupted, you can specify the number of bytes to be sent in each packet and the number of packets to be sent, causing ping to automatically time out at the desired count.

```
# /usr/etc/ping me 64 4
PING me: 64 data bytes
72 bytes from 127.0.0.1: icmp_seq=0. time=1 60th of sec
72 bytes from 127.0.0.1: icmp_seq=1. time=1 60th of sec
72 bytes from 127.0.0.1: icmp_seq=2. time=1 60th of sec
72 bytes from 127.0.0.1: icmp_seq=3. time=1 60th of sec

----me PING Statistics----
4 packets transmitted, 4 packets received, 0% packet loss
round-trip (60th of sec) min/avg/max = 1/1/2
#
```

Apart from providing information about whether or not the other host can be communicated with, ping reports two other items. icmp_seq is the sequence number in which the packets are arriving at the host; if they are not in numeric order, then packets are being scrambled and there could be a hardware conflict. time is the amount of time in milliseconds that it is taking for a round trip of the packet, from send to receive.

netstat

ping is useful for checking the status of one host. netstat gives you information on how the whole network is interacting with this host. netstat can be called with the following options to provide more detailed information.

-A   adds the associated protocol control block to the display.

-a   shows all network interfaces.

-i   displays configured network interfaces.

-n   shows the output in numeric form.

-r   gives a routing table display, where applicable.

-s   displays statistics.

netstat is a very powerful diagnostic tool, as Figures 18.1 through 18.5 show. Figure 18.1 presents a standard invocation of netstat, while Figure 18.2 changes the display from alphanumeric representations of the hosts to straight numeric. Figure 18.3 lists the routing tables. In this instance, no router is used; thus the only entry other than me is for the host itself. Also note the interface of en0, symbolizing an ethernet connection.

Figure 18.4 shows all the networked interfaces. The processes that have been highlighted are network daemons that are running. Notice the states that processes are in when netstat -a is invoked. ESTABLISHED means a connection is presently in progress. LISTEN means the host is waiting for a connection request. TIME_WAIT means the host is waiting for sufficient time to pass to ensure the remote has received the acknowledgment to close its connection.

Figure 18.1   A standard invocation of netstat.

```
# netstat
Active Internet connections
Proto  Recv-Q  Send-Q  Local Address    Foreign Address    (state)
tcp       0      105    QUEEN.rlogin     KINGS.1023         ESTABLISHED
tcp       0        0    QUEEN.rlogin     SUN8.1018          ESTABLISHED
tcp       0        0    QUEEN.rlogin     SUN5.1022          ESTABLISHED
tcp       0        0    QUEEN.rlogin     SUN1.1023 E        STABLISHED
udp       0        0    QUEEN.1027       HONOR.*
#
```

Figure 18.2   *An invocation of* netstat -n *changes the display from alphanumeric to straight numeric representation of the host.*

```
# netstat -n
Active Internet connections
Proto   Recv-Q   Send-Q   Local Address      Foreign Address    (state)
tcp        0       105     197.9.200.3.513    197.9.200.7.1023   ESTABLISHED
tcp        0        0      197.9.200.3.513    197.9.200.13.1018  ESTABLISHED
tcp        0        0      197.9.200.3.513    197.9.200.15.1022  ESTABLISHED
tcp        0        0      197.9.200.3.513    197.9.200.11.1023  ESTABLISHED
udp        0        0      197.9.200.3.1027   197.9.200.1.*
#
```

Figure 18.3   *An invocation of* netstat -r *lists the routing tables.*

```
# netstat -r
Routing tables
Destination   Gateway   Flags   Refcnt   Use      Interface
proto         QUEEN     U       0        853870   en0
me            me        UH      0        0        lo0
#
```

Figure 18.4   *An invocation of* netstat -a *shows all the networked interfaces.*

```
# netstat -a
Active Internet connections (including servers)
Proto   Recv-Q   Send-Q   Local Address   Foreign Address   (state)
tcp        0       125     QUEEN.rlogin    KINGS.1023        ESTABLISHED
tcp        0        0      QUEEN.rlogin    SUN8.1018         ESTABLISHED
tcp        0        0      QUEEN.rlogin    SUN5.1022         ESTABLISHED
tcp        0        0      QUEEN.rlogin    SUN1.1023         ESTABLISHED
tcp        0        0      *.telnet        *.*               LISTEN
tcp        0        0      *.exec          *.*               LISTEN
tcp        0        0      *.remsh         *.*               LISTEN
tcp        0        0      *.rlogin        *.*               LISTEN
tcp        0        0      *.finger        *.*               LISTEN
tcp        0        0      *.ftp           *.*               LISTEN
tcp        0        0      *.smtp          *.*               LISTEN
udp        0        0      QUEEN.1027      HONOR.*
udp        0        0      *.host_tab      *.*
udp        0        0      *.tftp          *.*
udp        0        0      *.who           197.9.200.255.*
#
```

Other possible states, many of which sound very similar to each other, are listed in the following text.

LASTACK The host has sent and received a request to close the connection and is waiting for acknowledgment from the remote.

CLOSING The connection is closing.

SYNSENT The machine is waiting for an open connection request from the remote.

SYNRECEIVED The open connection request has been sent and received and the host is now waiting for a request acknowledgment.

CLOSEWAIT The machine is waiting for a close connection request from the local host after receiving such a request from the remote.

FINWAIT1 The local host has requested a close connection and is now waiting for the same from the remote.

FINWAIT2 The local host is waiting for a close connection request from the remote.

Figure 18.5 is probably the most useful netstat invocation of all. netstat -s shows the statistics for network transactions that have occurred on this host. The statistical categories are described in the following paragraphs.

Figure 18.5   An invocation of netstat -s **shows the statistics for network transactions on a host.**

```
# netstat -s
ip:
        0 bad header checksums
        0 with size smaller than minimum
        0 with data size << data length
        0 with header length << data size
        0 with data length << header length
icmp:
        0 calls to icmp_error
        0 errors not generated 'cuz old message too short
        0 errors not generated 'cuz old message was icmp
        Output histogram:
                echo reply: 7
                echo: 11
        0 messages with bad code fields
        0 messages << minimum length
        0 bad checksums
        0 messages with bad length
        7 message responses generated
        Input histogram:
                echo reply: 7
                echo: 7
```

ip   deals with incoming packets. Numbers greater than 0 can indicate problems with the internal boards or with the cabling leading to the host.

icmp   pertains to the Internet Control Message Protocol, which sends error or control messages from one host to another. In this example, no errors have occurred.

tcp   contains important information, including acks   for   unsent   data, out-of-order packets, packets discarded for any reason, and the number of packets

---

Figure 18.5 (continued)

```
tcp:
        516142 packets sent
                377071 data packets (37185001 bytes)
                22 data packets (8342 bytes) retransmitted
                23235 ack-only packets (25069 delayed)
                0 URG only packets
                0 window probe packets
                8 window update packets
                160 control packets
        627955 packets received
                375408 acks (for 37184345 bytes)
                115508 duplicate acks
                0 acks for unsent data
        207487 packets (252481 bytes) received in-sequence
                1 completely duplicate packet (0 bytes)
                3 packets with some dup. data (11 bytes duped)
                0 out-of-order packets (0 bytes)
                0 packets (0 bytes) of data after window
                0 window probes
                33 window update packets
                0 packets received after close
                0 discarded for bad checksums
                0 discarded for bad header offset fields
                0 discarded because packet too short
        5 connection requests
        161 connection accepts
        166 connections established (including accepts)
        173 connections closed (including 2 drops)
        0 embryonic connections dropped
        374779 segments updated rtt (of 374794 attempts)
        23 retransmit timeouts
                1 connection dropped by rexmit timeout
        0 persist timeouts
        115481 keepalive timeouts
                115478 keepalive probes sent

                3 connections dropped by keepalive
udp:
        0 bad header checksums
        0 incomplete headers
        0 bad data length fields
        0 packets dropped due to stream Q full
        0 packets dropped due to endpoint not idle
#
```

received after close. Packets received after close are lost for good — they should never occur, but often do in the real world. packets sent represents the total number of packets TCP has sent to the network board, while packets received is the number sent from the board to TCP. connection requests is the number of times this host has accessed another, while connection accepts is the number of times other hosts have accessed this one. connections closed is an unpredictable number and so not useful as a reference. The one thing to note is that the number should always exceed the number of connections established.

ifconfig

ifconfig, which usually resides in the /usr/etc or /var/etc subdirectories, shows the value of the network interface, and can also be used to set it. To see the value, you must specify the network card. In the example in Figure 18.3, an ethernet card is shown by netstat as en0, as specified in the following example.

```
# ifconfig en0
en0: flags=3<UP,BROADCAST>
inet 197.9.200.7 netmask ffffff00 broadcast 197.9.200.255
#
```

This machine is configured as 197.009.200.007 and the broadcast address is the reserved 255 ID.

ifconfig can be used to change values, as well. For example, to change from a class C network to A, use the following command.

```
# ifconfig en0 128.9.200.7 netmask 255.255.255.0 broadcast
128.9.200.255
```

rwho

The rwho utility, much like the who utility but on a larger scale, shows who is logged onto each host machine attached to the network. This can be crucial in verifying that users on other hosts are able to access a machine. Figure 18.6 shows a typical output from the utility.

By default, the only users shown are those who have not been idle for an hour or longer. Idle time is depicted in minutes at the rightmost column of the display. Constant activity is represented by no entry in this column, as shown in the second line for the user quick.

Users who have been idle an hour or more are not shown. Using the -a option, however, causes all users to be shown, regardless of idle time, as shown in Figure 18.7.

Figure 18.6 **A sample output from** rwho **shows users logged in who have been active within the last hour.**

```
# rwho
daily       HONOR:ttyv00b    Aug 29 20:24 :48
quick       KINGS:ttyv00a    Aug 29 21:12
root        QUEEN:ttya       Aug 29 17:49 :36
sunadmin    HONOR:ttyv008    Aug 29 13:17 :39
sunadmin    HONOR:ttyv009    Aug 29 13:53
sunadmin    HONOR:ttyv00a    Aug 29 16:04 :21
sunadmin    NIGHT:ttyv008    Aug 29 12:54 :30
sunadmin    KINGS:ttyv008    Aug 29 13:36 :21
sunadmin    KINGS:ttyv009    Aug 29 14:17 :03
sunadmin    NOBLE:ttyv009    Aug 29 16:45
sunadmin    NOBLE:ttyv00b    Aug 29 13:33 :45
sunadmin    JOKER:ttyv008    Aug 29 16:45
sunadmin    JOKER:ttyv009    Aug 29 20:22 :36
sunadmin    JOKER:ttyv00b    Aug 29 13:34
#
```

Figure 18.7 **A sample output from** rwho -a **shows all users logged in, no matter how long they have been idle.**

```
# rwho -a
monitor     HONOR:ttyb       Aug 30 01:52 8:01
monitor     NIGHT:ttyb       Aug 30 07:25 2:27
monitor     KINGS:ttyb       Aug 30 01:52 8:00
monitor     NOBLE:ttyb       Aug 30 01:54 7:57
monitor     JOKER:ttyb       Aug 30 07:25 2:27
monitor     QUEEN:ttyb       Aug 30 01:14 8:35
quick       KINGS:ttyv00a    Aug 30 09:30 :21
sunadmin    HONOR:ttyv008    Aug 30 01:32 :12
sunadmin    HONOR:ttyv009    Aug 30 09:07
sunadmin    NIGHT:ttyv008    Aug 30 08:09 :24
sunadmin    NIGHT:ttyv00a    Aug 30 07:43 :39
sunadmin    NIGHT:ttyv00b    Aug 30 08:01 1:39
sunadmin    KINGS:ttyv008    Aug 30 01:32 :22
sunadmin    KINGS:ttyv009    Aug 30 08:23 :18
sunadmin    KINGS:ttyv00b    Aug 30 09:31 :06
sunadmin    NOBLE:ttyv008    Aug 30 01:25 :45
sunadmin    NOBLE:ttyv009    Aug 30 08:52 :21
sunadmin    JOKER:ttyv008    Aug 30 01:15 :09
sunadmin    JOKER:ttyv009    Aug 30 02:47 :24
sunadmin    JOKER:ttyv00a    Aug 30 08:50 :09
#
```

ruptime

Just as rwho is a who process for each machine on the network, ruptime is an uptime process for each machine on the network. Figure 18.8 shows a sample output from this command.

Each machine's host name is given, as well as the amount of time the host has been on the network in terms of days and hours. KINGS, for example, has been on the network 20 days, 11 hours, and 29 minutes. Following that is the number of users and the load. Loads are averages in three columns — the last minute, the last five minutes, and the last fifteen minutes.

Both ruptime and rwho obtain their information from the rwhod daemon process running on every host machine:

```
# ps -ef | grep rwho
root 264 1 0 Aug 9 ? 21:57 /usr/etc/rwhod
#
```

This daemon updates files every three minutes that are traditionally kept in the /usr/spool/rwho subdirectory. Thus it is possible for a user to be logged on for two minutes and not show up in an rwho listing if the files have not updated yet.

It is the responsibility of the rwhod daemon process to produce a list of who is on the current machine, broadcast that to all other machines, and listen for other rwhod's broadcasts of their status to this host. This information is kept in data files within the subdirectory — one for each host. You can check the last update time by listing these files. You can use the od utility (octal dump) to view the contents.

Figure 18.8 A sample output from ruptime ***shows the uptime, number of users, and load for each host on the network.***

```
# ruptime
HONOR    up 2+09:49,     4 users,    load 1.07, 1.13, 1.15
NIGHT    up 10+13:43,    1 user,     load 0.18, 0.18, 0.15
KINGS    up 20+11:29,    2 users,    load 1.00, 1.09, 1.14
NOBLE    up 20+11:28,    2 users,    load 0.03, 0.13, 0.14
JOKER    up 10+13:43,    3 users,    load 0.03, 0.12, 0.14
QUEEN    up 20+11:28,    1 user,     load 1.00, 1.00, 1.00
#
```

rlogin

Once you've confirmed that a host machine is up and talking to the network (as verified with ruptime), the next step is to test access to the machine. To login on a remote machine as the same user you are on the current machine, use the rlogin utility with a parameter of the remote host name. This establishes a connection as though your terminal were directly connected to the remote host.

The rlogin process first attempts to log you in without a password by checking for entries in the /etc/hosts.equiv file. If it cannot find the file or an entry for you in the file, it next checks the /etc/passwd file to find your $HOME directory, which searches for a .rhosts file that will allow you to login without verification. If it cannot find that, it prompts you for a password.

If you enter the password correctly, you are allowed into the system. If you enter the password incorrectly, you must give the login and password combination again, but the connection stays live.

Once connected and successfully logged in, you can perform any UNIX command as if you were sitting at a terminal connected to that host. When you are finished with the session, type exit to close the connection and return to your own machine.

To connect to the remote machine as another user (e.g., you are user karen_d on this machine, but are user karen on the other machine), follow the normal command with -l and the name of the user you will be on the other machine, as in the following example.

```
$ rlogin KINGS -l karen
```

When a remote login has been established, the following text will appear in the process table as the rlogind daemon.

```
# ps -ef | grep rlogind
root 5924 259 0 19:39:28 ttyv00a 0:00 rlogind 197.9.200.12
#
```

The user name is not given (though it will appear in who listings); instead, the address of the remote host is shown — in this case 197.9.200.12.

Toggling Back and Forth

When remotely logged into a host, you can jump back and forth between the remote host and the one at which you are truly sitting. To return to your host, type ~z. To return to the remote host, type exit on your machine. Figure 18.9 shows a representation of this.

The tilde is interpreted as the default escape character. If this is inconvenient, you can redefine the escape character by using the -e option. For example, to change it to the dollar sign, use the following syntax.

```
rlogin KINGS -e$ -l karen
```

Figure 18.9   An example of toggling between a local and remote host in an rlogin session.

```
# uname -n
QUEEN
# rlogin KINGS -l karen
You have mail.

$ uname -n
KINGS
$

$~z
# uname -n
QUEEN
#
# exit

$ uname -n
KINGS
$
```

remsh

One of the most useful methods of testing the status of a host in relation to the network is to remotely run a job on that host. TCP/IP has a utility that allows you to do this without logging in to the remote machine. The name of the utility is dependent upon the vendor who supplied the version, but it will usually be rsh or remsh — both indicating that you are remotely running a shell process. In this text, the name remsh is used.

For remsh to be successful, the local and remote host must have proper permissions into each other. /etc/hosts.equiv and .rhosts files must allow one machine to access another without password verification. Figure 18.10 demonstrates using the df utility to test the permissions.

If one user does not have permission to run the process remotely, the -1 option can be used, as with rlogin, to specify another user. If no command is given following the host name remsh KINGS, an rlogin session is initiated.

Quotation marks become all important with remsh commands. When run from QUEEN,

```
remsh KINGS cat this >> that
```

appends the contents of the KINGS:this file to the QUEEN:that file. However,

```
remsh KINGS "cat this >> that"
```

appends the contents of the KINGS:this file to the KINGS:that file. You will always get what you ask for, so be careful to specify exactly what you want.

Figure 18.10   An example of testing *remsh* **permissions with** df.

```
QUEEN> df -t
/        (/dev/dsk/38s1 ):      246688 blocks     30275 i-nodes
total: 571496 physical (71437 4096-byte logical) blocks 35712
QUEEN>

QUEEN> remsh KINGS df -t
/        (/dev/dsk/38s1 ):      162968 blocks     30855 i-nodes
total: 571496 physical (71437 4096-byte logical) blocks 35712
QUEEN>
```

Summary

These seven utilities, standard with UNIX networking packages, allow you to verify that all hosts are communicating correctly. They can not only tell you the status of each machine, but also give you the ability to access it, tell who is logged on, and perform remote shell operations.

Chapter 19

Monitoring and Optimizing NFS Performance

Robert Berry

The Network File System (NFS) is an essential part of your LAN communications, and its transparency to the network users is directly proportional to its response time. Finding that optimum performance can be difficult, and therefore, performance tracking and optimization of NFS can be a challenging task for systems administrators. The UNIX environment provides tools that enable you to gather the statistics needed to pinpoint areas in which to improve network response time. As a first step, you must familiarize yourself with the network resources and the users of those resources. Then compile the statistics on the current configuration, and determine if the statistics provide you with good news or bad news. Finally, if you determine that the news is bad, you must identify the bottlenecks, based on the statistical results.

Familiarize Yourself with Your Network

You may believe you already know your network inside and out. But take a moment and think. Are you familiar with the type of work conducted by each client on the network? Do you know the types of Remote Procedure Call (RPC) requests that are typically generated by this work? Do you know which servers provide most of the resources for each client? Do you know the network's busiest time? Its lag times? Essentially, you need to know who does what, where, and when on the network.

Information of this sort helps you to model your networking environment. If you understand the nature of the network's workload, you should be able to develop an extremely accurate representation of your system when you try to create a set of benchmarks.

Gather Stats on Your Current Network Configuration

The UNIX environment supplies you with numerous tools for gathering network statistics. Some of the more useful tools are netstat, nfsstat, vmstat, iostat, uptime, and spray. The following sections show an example of each (except for vmstat and iostat) and explain their usefulness for collecting information. vmstat and iostat were explained thoroughly in Chapter 6.

netstat

The command-line syntax is

```
netstat [-n] -i
```

Figure 19.1 demonstrates a sample output.

Figure 19.1   A sample output from `netstat [-n] -i`.

Name	Mtu	Net/Dest	Address	Ipkts	Ierrs	Opkts	Oerrs	Collis	Queue
le0	1500	sun-ether	Worf	281537	0	508676	0	3766	0
lo0	1536	loopback	localhost	7327	0	7327	0	0	0

The netstat utility gives you information on the reliability of your local network interface. The first column of the output is the device name of your network interface. The second column, Mtu, represents maximum transmission unit. The third column, Net/Dest, is the actual network to which your interface is connected; this will be the actual numbered address if the -n option is used. The fourth column, Address, displays the local host's name or, again, the actual IP address if the -n is used. The remaining columns display the number of input and output packets, as well as the number of errors that occurred with each. The Collis column displays the number of times a collision occurred each time the host transmitted.

The input and output error columns are of most concern here. A high number of input errors could result from electrical problems, from corrupt packets being received from another host with a damaged network interface, from damaged cables, or from a device driver that has an improper buffer size. A high number in the output error column may indicate a problem with your own network interface.

This analysis assumes that your network as been up and running for some time. However, a high number of errors could show up in either category if your system has just recovered from a network-wide power outage — particularly if you have many diskless clients. The key word here is high: both input and output errors should be as close to zero as possible. Still, there will usually be some errors present, especially if you have recently disconnected and reconnected cables or if your network has periods of intense traffic.

The number in the collision column will likely not be zero, but should be a low number relative to the number in the output packet column. You can calculate the percentage of collisions observed by a particular host by dividing the number in the collision column by the number in the output packet column and multiplying the quotient by one hundred. Hal Stern, in *Managing NFS and NIS*, suggests that a collision rate of over 5 percent indicates a congested network in need of reorganizing.

A collision rate can also be obtained for the entire network. To calculate this you would add all hosts' output packet columns and all hosts' collision columns, divide the latter by the former, and multiply by one hundred, as above. This method is more appropriate than taking the sum of all the collision rates for each individual host and dividing by the number of hosts, because by this method the busier hosts will weigh more heavily on the average than the less busy hosts. Again according to Hal Stern, if the rate is greater than 10 percent, your network is ripe for partitioning.

One caveat is in order here. If you notice a host with significantly more collisions than a similar host with similar network usage, this may be an indication of electrical problems rather than network congestion.

nfsstat

nfsstat displays statistical information concerning the status of your NFS and RPCs for both the server and client aspect of your system. Each field in the output is a window into the heart of your network operations.

The command-line syntax has three useful forms.

```
nfsstat -s
```

```
nfsstat -c
```

```
nfsstat
```

The first form will display server side statistics only (Figure 19.2); the second will display client side statistics only (Figure 19.3); and the third will display both server and client side statistics, respectively. The server display indicates how successfully your server is receiving packets from each client. The fields in the display are listed in the following text.

calls   indicates the number of RPC calls received.

badcalls   indicates the number of calls rejected by the RPC layer. Such a rejection would be generated by an authentication failure. It also includes the combined totals of the badlen and xdrcall fields.

Figure 19.2   *A sample output from* nfsstat -s.

```
Server rpc:
calls       badcalls     nullrecv     badlen     xdrcall
1613        0            0            0          0

Server nfs:
calls       badcalls
1613        0
null        getattr      setattr      root       lookup     readlink     read
0 0%        43 2%        0 0%         0 0%       25 1%      0 0%         80 4%
wrcache     write        create       remove     rename     link         symlink
0 0%        1465 91%     0 0%         0 0%       0 0%       0 0%         0 0%
mkdir       rmdir        readdir      fsstat
0 0%        0 0%         0 0%         0 0%
```

nullrecv indicates the number of times an nfsd daemon was scheduled to run but did not receive a packet from the NFS service socket queue.

badlen indicates that the server received RPC calls that were too short in length.

xdrcall indicates that RPC calls were received that could not decode the XDR headers.

The client display indicates how successful your client is in communicating with all the NFS servers. The fields in this display are listed in the following text.

calls indicates the total number of calls made to the NFS servers.

badcalls indicates the number of RPC calls that returned an error either by time-outs or because of an interruption of the RPC call itself.

retrans indicates the number of times a call had to be retransmitted because there was no response from the server.

badxid indicates the number of times a reply from a server was received that didn't correspond to any outstanding call. When a request is generated, it is given an XID. At any one time, there are several calls requesting services on any number of servers. Occasionally, a response is received with an XID that has already been serviced. At this time badxid is incremented. I will discuss the significance of this field later.

timeout indicates the actual number of calls that timed out waiting for a server's response.

Figure 19.3   A sample output from nfsstat -c

```
Client rpc:
calls     badcalls   retrans    badxid    timeout   wait        newcred    timers
1600      0          0          0         0         0           0          499

Client nfs:
calls     badcalls   nclget     nclsleep
1600      0          1600       0
null      getattr    setattr    root      lookup    readlink    read
0 0%      35 2%      0 0%       0 0%      23 1%     0 0%        74 4%
wrcache   write      create     remove    rename    link        symlink
0 0%      1465 91%   1 0%       2 0%      0 0%      0 0%        0 0%
mkdir     rmdir      readdir    fsstat
0 0%      0 0%       0 0%       0 0%
```

`wait` indicates the number of times a call had to wait because a client handle was either busy or unavailable.

The remaining fields of the client RPC section are not relevant to the current topic, and are omitted from this text.

uptime

uptime is a simple tool that allows you to get the current time, the amount of time the system has been up, the number of users on the system, and the three load averages (Figure 19.4). The three load averages are a rough measure of CPU usage over 1-, 5-, and 15-minute intervals.

What's considered high for these three categories depends on the number of CPUs on your system and whether or not your tasks are CPU-intensive. AEleen Frisch, in *Essential System Administration*, notes that any value under 3 would not be critical.

spray

The command-line syntax is:

```
spray hostname [-c count] [-l length] [-d delay]
```

spray reports the number of packets sent to a particular host, the time needed to send those packets, the number of packets received by the host, and the number and percent of packets that were dropped by the host (Figure 19.5).

Figure 19.4   A sample output from uptime.

```
2:31pm up 3 days, 20:28, 1 user, load average: 0.32, 0.74, 0.89
```

Figure 19.5   A sample output from spray.

```
sending 1162 packets of lnth 86 to Bones ...
        in 0.4 seconds elapsed time,
        308 packets (26.51%) dropped
Sent:   3160 packets/sec, 265.4K bytes/sec
Rcvd:   2322 packets/sec, 195.1K bytes/sec
```

spray is a useful but somewhat limited tool. The output gives the number of packets that didn't make the distance, but it doesn't indicate at what point in the network the packets were lost. Another limitation is that in the real world, packet sizes can vary and usually occur in random bursts. But by default, spray sends 1162 packets of 86 bytes in length. With the -c and -l options, you can minimize this limitation by varying the number and size of packets. With the -d option, you can even simulate some delay between packets.

Running spray from each of your machines will give you a good estimate of a server's performance capabilities and of the speed of a particular machine's network interface. You may find that a server that receives a large portion of the network traffic has a slow network interface; you might then decide to move the file systems to a faster machine or provide it with a faster network interface.

Obtaining NFS Benchmarks

You can use the UNIX tools described previously to measure your network's performance under normal conditions. This will give you a set of benchmarks by which to judge your system. This will be handy the next time a user comes up and complains about the network being sluggish. Simply run the test again and compare it with past results.

The key here is knowing what "normal" is on your network. This is the point where being completely familiar with the network workload is important. The benchmarks will serve no purpose if they do not accurately represent the type and proper proportions of RPC requests, commonly generated on the network.

To produce benchmarks for your system, you may purchase any one of many NFS benchmark traffic generators or you may build your own using UNIX utilities. I chose the latter in this case.

Certain UNIX commands can generate the same RPC requests that are normally generated by the work conducted on your network. Generating a NFS RPC mixture in this fashion can be far more flexible than using a ready-made package, which is incapable of changing to fit changing workloads. With a script, as the nature of the workload changes on your network, you can reflect the changes in the script.

NFS Traffic Generation Script

The first step in creating your own NFS traffic generation script is to know which RPC requests are generated by the work conducted on your network. To get a listing of the NFS RPC percentages generated by your network, run the nfsstat utility on each of your servers. This information will help you build a script that comes as close as possible to an accurate representation of your network usage.

Next, you will need to know what UNIX utilities generate what RPC requests. Table 19.1 shows some basic utilities and the NFS RPC requests they generate. Use a combination of these in your script to generate the NFS traffic for your benchmarks, paying close attention to the NFS RPC percentages reported for your network.

Listing 19.1 provides an example of an NFS traffic-generating script. This example is simple, but keep in mind that an NFS traffic generation script can be whatever you want it to be, as long as it closely represents your network workload. For instance, in this scenario, the network is a UNIX network on which large CAD and raster files traverse back and forth across network lines. Under heavy network usage, RPC request percentages on a particular client will be approximately 50 percent reads and 40 percent writes, with the remainder divided among various other RPC requests, such as getattr and lookup.

The sample script starts with an uptime report to give you an indication of your CPU usage. This is not essential; I added it to give an overall picture of the network. The script next runs the nfsstat utility and displays the current RPC requests percentages for the client before reinitializing all the percentages back to zero with nfsstat -z. You must become superuser before running this script because the nfsstat utility requires you to be superuser in order to use the -z parameter.

The meat of the script is the series of cp commands. To generate the 50 percent reads and 40 percent writes, the script copies a large file in an NFS directory to a subdirectory, copies it from the NFS directory to a local client directory, and then copies it to a second local client directory. You may have to experiment to achieve the desired RPC percentages. For example, when this script was being built, it turned out that the client was able to cache fairly large files. With the file located in the cache, four or no disk reads were being requested. To get around this, the file had to be made much larger — in this case, it was 12Mb.

Table 19.1 Some basic UNIX utilities and the NFS RPC requests they generate.	
Command	**NFS RPC Request**
Find	lookup, readdir, getattr
cp	read, write, setattr
ls	lookup, getattr, readdir, readlink
ln	symlink
mv	rename
(From "Managing NFS and NIS")	

Listing 19.1 *RPC_gen — a simple example of an NFS traffic-generating script.*

```
###############################################
#
# Title       : RPC_gen
# Programmer  : Robert Berry
# Date        : 8/23/94
# Description : This is a NFS traffic
#     generation script. It will attempt to
#     generate RPC requests that reflect the
#     type of RPC requests that are generated
#     by the normal network work-load.
#
###############################################
# When running this script you must be super user
# and should set permissions accordingly.
###############################################
# Display NFS client information before you
# reinitialize the settings.
###############################################
echo "_____"
echo "These are the stats for the client before "
echo "the system is reinitialized."
echo "_____"
echo
echo -n "UPTIME REPORT"
uptime
echo
nfstat -cn
echo
###############################################
# The first copy is simply to get the file where
# I want it.
###############################################
echo "Performing setup....please wait."
cp bigfile /remote_fs/bigfile1
```

Finally, the script performs some cleanup and generates another uptime report along with the final nfsstat client report to check the RPC request percentages produced. The spray utility is added for good measure. The script runs spray on each server to give you some idea of the server's current packet handling capabilities.

Remember that your script can be any sequence of UNIX utilities, as long as they reflect the RPC requests generated by your network's workload. I used the cp utility because it generates read and write RPC requests (Table 19.1). You will need to experiment with combinations of utilities to meet your own requirements. It is also a good idea to run your script at various times over several days to see if it will produce close to the same results each time.

Possible NFS Performance Bottlenecks

When examining possible performance bottlenecks on your network, keep in mind that there are two sides to the network: the server side and the client side. You must determine whether the server hardware and software is inadequate for the client's jobs or the client's jobs too numerous and difficult for the server hardware and software.

Server

On the server side, a number of key hardware components can cause bottlenecks and should be watched closely. I mentioned earlier the network interface itself, but some others you should consider are the CPU, memory, and the hard disk.

Regarding the CPU, the concern is not so much the speed of the CPU — although faster is better — but how quickly jobs are scheduled for CPU usage. A potential bottleneck is an increased latency in scheduling NFS daemons. nfsd daemons have kernel process priority and, under normal conditions, are run by the CPU immediately upon an NFS request. But if the server has a number of I/O interrupts or other kernel priority calls running, NFS requests can build while nfsd daemons are waiting for CPU time. A solution might be to limit local access to a server to reduce the number of I/O and kernel priority system calls. iostat and vmstat provide useful information on CPU job loading.

The main concern regarding memory as a bottleneck is to ensure that the server has enough to handle all its processes. This will reduce page swapping, which can interfere with NFS services. With hard disks, as with CPUs, the bottleneck is caused not so much by the speed of the drive (although, once again, the faster the better), but the overloading of NFS disk access requests. If you have a disk that receives more than its share of NFS requests, you might want to consider spreading the heavily used filesystems over several disks.

Listing 19.1 (continued)

```
#############################################
# Set all RPC percentages to 0%
#############################################
echo "Reinitializing nfsstat percentages."
nfsstat -z > nul
echo "Running test..."
#############################################
# These three cp commands will generate approx
# 50% reads and 40% writes.
#############################################
cp /remote_fs/bigfile1 /remote_fs/subdir/bigfile2
cp /remote_fs/subdir/bigfile2 /localdir/bigfile3
cp /remote_fs/subdir/bigfile2 /localdir/bigfile4
rm /remote_fs/bigfile1
rm /remote_fs/subdir/bigfile2
rm /localdir/bigfile3
rm /localdir/bigfile4
echo "_____"
echo "This is the RPC percentage results after"
echo "the artificial traffic generation."
echo "_____"
echo
echo -n "NEW UPTIME REPORT"
uptime
echo
nfsstat -cn
echo
echo "_____"
echo " SPRAY STATS ON ALL SERVERS"
echo "_____"
echo
for a in Server1 Server2 Server3 Server4
do
    echo -n "============="
    echo -n $a
    echo "============="
    spray $a
done
echo
echo "****************END OF TEST**************"
```

Client

In some instances you might discover that the server isn't the bottleneck of the network. In fact, it might turn out that there is no bottleneck at all — only a client that wants too much in too little time. If this is the case, then some constraints must be placed on that client.

A client sends an NFS request to a particular server. If it doesn't receive a reply within the allotted time period, the request will timeout and be retransmitted. The client does not respect the fact that you've tuned the server to the best of its hardware capabilities. The client doesn't care if the request is still queued on the server and will be served eventually. All the client knows is that it didn't receive a reply in the allotted time, so it sends the request again. The server will then respond even more slowly as NFS requests build.

You may see an indication of this problem with the nfsstat utility. If you run nfsstat -rc and notice a large number in the badxid field and an even larger number in the timeout field, then it is likely that your client is demanding too much from your server. A simple correction for this problem is to increase the timeout parameter in the mount utility.

Conclusion

Monitoring and optimizing NFS performance is a challenging process. UNIX provides you with useful tools to perform this task. Each of the tools covered here provides extensive capabilities, of which only a small sample were touched upon in this chapter. I suggest that you experiment with these tools and develop your own cause-and-effect analysis of NFS performance.

Bibliography

Frisch, AEleen. *Essential System Administration*. Sebastapol, CA: O'Reilly & Associates, Inc., 1991.

Peek, Jerry., Tim O'Reilly, and Mike Loukides. *UNIX Power Tools*. Sebastopol, CA: O'Reilly & Associates/Bantam Books, 1993.

Stern, Hal. *Managing NFS and NIS*. Sebastopol, CA: O'Reilly & Associates, Inc., 1992.

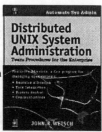